LIES IN A MIRROR
An Essay on Evil and Deceit

ABOUT THE AUTHOR

Peter Charleton is a barrister. He graduated in law from Trinity College Dublin in 1980 where he later lectured in criminal law. His previous books are: *Controlled Drugs and the Criminal Law* (Dublin, 1986); *Irish Criminal Law, Cases and Materials* (Dublin, 1991); *Offences Against the Person* (Dublin, 1991); and *Criminal Law* (Dublin, 1999, with P.A. McDermott and M. Bolger).

Lies in a Mirror
An Essay on Evil and Deceit

PETER CHARLETON

BLACKHALL
PUBLISHING

This book was typeset by SUSAN WAINE for

Blackhall Publishing
33 Carysfort Avenue
Blackrock
Co. Dublin
Ireland

info@blackhallpublishing.com
www.blackhallpublishing.com

ISBN 10: 1 84218 101 7/ISBN 13: 978 1 84218 101 0 Paperback
ISBN 10: 1 84218 102 5/ISBN 10: 978 1 84218 102 7 Hardback

A catalogue record for this book is available from the British Library.

Printed by
Athenaeum Press Ltd.

Contents

Le

Fiona Ní Dhálaigh

Preface

THIS BOOK IS ABOUT the transformative power of hatred. It is impossible to ever find the answer to where hatred comes from. It may be just about possible to describe some of the circumstances that activate human violence. This was not ever something that I wanted to think about, much less write about. The patterns of evil that I observed over twenty-five years of practice as a lawyer ultimately became so burdensome that I had to try to make some sense of what confronted me from week to week. Fundamental to why people hate, it seemed to me, was a perversion of the truth. This was the human resource of deceit taken to its ultimate grade whereby people lived out, and killed for, an upside-down version of myth.

As a child I had loved folk tales, whether Rapunzel or Fionn MacCumhaill. These stories seemed to represent the truth, telling those who encountered them what to watch out for in life: how people tended to be like a limited number or characters and how events repaid selflessness and kindness. That is not what I saw when hatred led to violence. Instead, myths emerged which told nothing of the truth. These myths seemed to be the dynamic drive behind destruction: the myth of being chosen for a glorious mission, the myth that other people had no rights, the myth of self-aggrandisement, the myth of the cunning enemy, the myth of the victim who is himself the cause of all the trouble, the myth of the respectable man who is a secret paedophile. They went on and on.

The difference between the myths recorded by our ancestors as fairy stories and those lapping below the surface in our criminal courts, was that there was no truth in the myths that generated violence. It was lies that seemed to prize open the worst aspects of human conduct. I began to believe that there was evil within all of us, and that deceit was the spell that unleashed its power. Hate is not static. It causes results: destruction of the victim is only the most obvious. The less obvious is the result to the perpetrator. How were they affected when they used lies and, even worse, when they began to live out their own lies? It might be easy to think that they were diminished. After all, there are few complete and heroic individuals sitting in the dock of the criminal courts anywhere. A more rigorous examination of the fundamental questions as to the suspected link between lies and destruction was called for. This is my attempt.

Perhaps people will be puzzled by my reticence in describing details of the cases of those with whom I have dealt and whose experiences are published here, at least in part. Nothing I have written repeats any legal confidence. All of the facts recounted are those that anyone could have heard or observed in open court. Many of the cases went unreported and unremarked anywhere. Even so, the use of initials, wrong initials at that, and the reference to facts in a slightly disguised way reflects my firm belief that after these things are public property, they relapse back into the private sphere. People are entitled to be left alone, even apart from considerations of professional ethics.

My thanks are due to my wife Fiona and to my children Clara, Anna-Rose and Matthew and my family and my friends. Many of them offered encouragement or read passages from what follows and offered invaluable suggestions. They cannot be responsible for the result. I owe a debt of gratitude to, among others, Michael Collins, Paul Anthony McDermott, Vladimir Baranov, Lisa Baranova, Harry Kennedy, Shane Dwyer, Mary Redmond, Patrick Marrinan, Éilis Daly, Fou Ts'ong, Wai Tim, Martha O'Neill, Thomas O'Connell, the late Charlotte O'Connell von der Schulenberg, Conor Daly, Ciarán Branigan, the late Ciarán Clarke, Amabel Clarke, Andrea Martin, the late Eamon Leahy, Zhao Fung, Kathleen Leader, Shane Murphy, Paul M. MacDermott, Anthony Barr, Georgina, Isabel and

Colette Charleton and the Daly, FitzGibbon, O'Neill and Charleton families. My thanks are also due to Ruth Garvey, my editor, and to Kathleen Myers and to Sharon Kearney for their help with the manuscript. I would like to thank my publishers for taking a risk with this book and I gratefully acknowledge permission to quote material in any circumstances beyond the "scholars exception" in the Copyright Convention.

PETER CHARLETON
Lá Fhéile Pádraig 2006

CHAPTER I

The Dynamic of Evil

THERE IS A LIE behind every crime. In order to cheat people of their money, fraudsters first dispossess them of their prudence by lying to them. When someone goes out to rape or kill another person, they will ensure that their victim is disarmed into a false sense of security by pretending, up to the critical moment, that they mean no harm.

In twenty-five years of practice in the criminal courts, it has become evident that deceit is the primary instrument for doing evil. What is not so immediately obvious is that underneath the actions that we can see, the pattern of lies that trap the targets of crime into violence and theft, the perpetrators, as well as deceiving their victims, are also lying to themselves. The most successful fraudsters believe their own lies; that is why they are convincing. Murderers often kill to defend a gigantic self-image that the victim has done no more than question. People defend the vilest of actions on the basis that they, and not the person who has been destroyed by them, are the true victim. And in Ireland, as is common with other parts of the globe, the idea that the righting of historic injustices will usher in a new dawn of unity and happiness, has justified limitless cruelty.

People who perpetrate evil live in a myth. Not one that tells the truth, as do the folk tales that over countless generations were that method of transmitting wisdom to the young but, rather, a myth that bases their lives on deceit. It is this that evokes the dynamic of evil.

It is not respectable to say that you are living in a place that is haunted. Even less, I suspect, to admit that someone, or some event, is haunting you. Yet, it happens. When our ancestors set down their folk tales, a dominant theme was the notion that a person could be dead but still remain a present influence. Sometimes the deceased would reach out to a person needing help; thus repaying some previous kindness. Other times, they were the opposite; interfering with peoples' lives and turning them to misery.[1] Nowadays, instead of saying that someone is haunted, we might say that someone is obsessed. This means that no distraction can blot out a dominant idea. There is only one remedy: to find out why the thought of a person almost never leaves you. By asking, and finding out, what the image of a person in your mind is trying to say makes it possible to lay the ghost to rest.

In 1983, I defended a man, whom I will call MD, on a series of charges of abusing adolescents. Shortly after the case concluded he died. In no sense did he ever appear to me, or talk to me, but in some way the nature of what he was stayed with me demanding that I should try to work out the puzzle of what he did and what he was.[2] MD worked as a teacher in a large secondary school in Dublin. He was highly respected and much enjoyed that status. His gift as a teacher appeared to be the ability to take an interest in weaker pupils and to bring them up a level academically. Sometimes, it seems, the results were good but, even if they were not, the parents appreciated the time and effort that he gave. Schools sometimes organise educational

---

1 Examples of both are found in any collection of folk tales. For example see S. Ó Catháin (ed.), *Síscéalta Ó Thír Chonaill* (Dublin, 1977) numbers 19 and 114.

2 Lawyers work under a duty of confidence. Although this does not extend to facts that are publicly stated in court, I have changed all relevant dates, names and places that might be used for identification. Some of the facts have also been altered so that the essence of a situation might be approached from descriptions that allow the preservation of the privacy, that time has restored to them, of those involved. No confidence by a client is repeated here.

trips. At the present time, when everyone is ultra-suspicious of claims of sexual abuse, a school will ensure that a number of teachers travel together and that they should never be alone with the pupils in any intimate setting. Back then, parents and teaching staff were much more innocent. When MD organised a teach-in weekend at a hotel and suggested to some parents that their boys take part, four of them agreed. The fee was reasonable, consisting of little more that the cost of off-season accommodation. Looking back at the eventual victims of that "scholarly weekend", it is apparent that both of them had the signs of vulnerability that paedophiles prey on. In consequence perhaps, they had fallen behind in their schoolwork in the transition to senior level. They were also highly sensitive. But, instead of their feelings helping them to sniff out trouble, they were completely confused, not least as to their emerging sexuality. The other boys on that weekend were similar but not as open to suggestion since, from what I could gather later, one had a couple of close friends and the other had an outlet in playing in a youth orchestra. These two were not touched. What they all had in common was that MD had previously closely, but casually, questioned them as to their sexual preferences. The two that were vulnerable enough, to later respond to his blandishments, ended up in his shower and in his bed.

There is enough pornography in this world and I do not intend to add to it. It suffices to mention that a video camera, then a rare enough object, was used in these sessions. A chambermaid, doing her rounds early, became suspicious of the two empty beds and alarmed by what she found in the other room. The police were called and MD was arrested. Confronted by statements from the two boys, he denied everything over several hours of questioning. Under relentless pressure, he "admitted" that two of the boys had come to his room "out of homesickness" and that he had allowed them to stay in his bed "under a separate cover". This is what "any normal parent" would have done, he told his interrogators. The allegations of touching were fantasies, though it was possible that he might have "brushed against" one of the boys "accidentally". None of this is a crime. However, the video was kept as an exhibit, something about which I, as defence counsel, knew nothing. At that time, in cases tried before a judge, as distinct from a jury, no statements of witnesses were given in advance to the defence and no exhibits were listed. The prosecution were entitled to spring these as surprises during the hearing of the case. The recording became central to the prosecution's case.

Having read his defence instructions, I met MD, a proudly erect man, in a small solicitor's office. As the defence was accidental touching, a statement had been prepared to add to what he had already told the police. Since a lawyer's job is to advise what might, and what might not, be regarded as reasonable in terms of raising a doubt, we seemed to have a defence. When it came to the hearing, a different picture, this time literally, emerged. The boys gave evidence. The cross examination of them was effective enough. The accused's word, as a man of standing, might still be accepted in contradiction. Then the prosecution produced a television and played the video. It was horrible. In terms of the picture, and even more from the accompanying sound track of MD "encouraging" the boys, any chance of a defence was out of the question. As we looked at and listened to the television, MD visibly diminished. His demeanour became withdrawn. Physically, he shrank away and his colour faded. No one had asked him a single question. He realised that there was no answer to the charges. Worse, his secret life had been revealed. Simply, he had been confronted with himself. The case was at an end. Early on in his prison sentence, imposed on a change of plea to guilty, MD suffered apparent heart failure and died. He had been in robust health and, as they say, a "pillar of the community" up to the point when his own behaviour had changed the public nature of the face that he showed to the world.

No one but his victims is aware of the extent to which MD blighted their lives. It may be that there were more than the two whom I formally encountered across a courtroom during the hearing of his case on the one particular crime for which he had been caught. What is certain is that his actions were evil. Equally certainly, his life was a lie. Although his paedophile obsession dominated his thoughts, he played the role of someone dedicated to upholding the highest Christian norms. It would seem that he believed the lie about himself because otherwise, when it collapsed, he might have found the strength to pursue what remained of his life. But, what was left of it after the fundamental charade of his existence had been exposed?

This book is about patterns. If you look at peoples' lives you will find patterns everywhere: rituals for birth, marriage and death are obvious examples, but there are many others.[3] Where a trait of human behaviour can be identified, then it may be possible to predict the dynamic that stands behind a pattern of human action. This does not so much refer to the particular circumstances that make an action likely, as asking what aspect of human make-up drives us into acting constructively or destructively. In this work, evil is the focus of our attention. In particular, the link between deceit and evildoing that keeps recurring as an unexplained pattern in the worst crimes in history. If lies are the driving force of crime, then the question of how human nature makes deceit the doorway on to our most repulsive side needs to be explored. Could it really be the case that merely by lying we risk leaving ourselves open to committing all manner of hatred and violence?

In 1971, the historian Gitta Sereny was given the opportunity to engage in a series of lengthy interviews with Franz Stangl, the former commandant of the Nazi extermination camp at Treblinka. Over three months they discussed the nature of the process that had lead to the murder of about 900,000 people and the issue of his guilt. There was no practical reason for Herr Stangl to be coy or evasive. He had already been sentenced to life imprisonment for his co-responsibility in mass murder. Yet, he found it impossible to accept that he was

---

3   D.E. Browne, *Human Universals* (New York, 1991).

morally culpable for even a single death. This, despite being the chief executive over a machine that every day had dispatched life after life, as in a slaughterhouse. The nature of his evasions and justifications surface elsewhere in this book, as examples of how deceit can colour actions and allow people to live with evil. Remembering my experience with MD, however, what struck me most was the end of the historian's relationship with Herr Stangl. Right up to their last interview, he had always denied any personal wrong. Even then, he reverted to the defence which he had employed at his trial: that his conscience was clear because he had never himself "intentionally hurt any-one".

After he had repeated this yet again, Sereny decided not to challenge it. The conversation stopped and there was silence. His interviewer gave him no help by way of a prompt or a question and a long pause resulted. Then he said: "But, I was there. So, yes, in reality I share the guilt…" In her book *Into That Darkness*, Sereny describes how his body and his face sagged.[4] He explained that rather than bear the guilt of still living, he ought to have had the courage to die. Whether by rebellion back then, when he claimed to have been under Nazi coercion, or, whilst later in prison, by suicide, he left unstated. The next day he died of heart failure. The author gave this as her reaction to the reason why death had coincided with his shaking off the lie in which he had lived: "I think he died because he had finally, however briefly, faced himself and told the truth".[5]

At the end of the Second World War, the Swiss psychologist Carl Jung wrote an article for a magazine entitled *After the Catastrophe* in which he analysed how and why the world had been drawn into the vicious explosion of evil of which Treblinka had been a part. He wrote that evil drew us to itself because it is part of our nature. Violence is a dominant force of modern entertainment dressed up in cinema plots and news

---

4   G. Sereny, *Into that Darkness: From Mercy Killing to Mass Murder* (London, 1974) p. 364.
5   Ibid., p. 366.

reports. No one could countenance destruction unless deep inside us there were strong needs to destroy. The "right" circumstances can unleash this inner drive. Similarly, it seems obvious that people would not be drawn to pornography but for their inherent sexual drive. Violence destroys us, Jung thought, because in responding to the wrong done to us we use the same destructive forces in punishing our enemy. This seems right. We do not walk away: we strike back. We do not apologise: we blame the enemy. We never accept our own wrong: we draw others into a group based on a shared dynamic of hatred. No matter how we disguise our motives, we pleasure in the suffering of others and this makes us as bad, or worse, than those we hate. Retribution, as the international enforcement of self-defence and justice, Jung thought, was merely an excuse to hide our evil nature from ourselves. In reality, both sides in a conflict could not escape becoming participants in the process of sating the human urge to destroy. Once launched, the process of destruction fed on itself drawing people into an unconscious process of revenge and limitless hatred. It was then almost automatic. If there was to be any solution to the causes of cycles of hate and violence, he considered that it had to come with each individual analysing their own, and not their enemy's, conscience and asking how they had contributed to demeaning and perverting life. Anyone who arrived at a state of realising their own guilt, he thought, would be enriched with honour and spiritual dignity.[6]

In theory, this may be true. But the reality is that people who are made to admit repulsive crimes to themselves, never mind to other people, are crushed in the process. Solzhenitsyn demanded in *The Gulag Archipelago* that all those who had taken part in torturing and killing the millions of innocent people who were subjected to attrition camps in the time of Lenin and Stalin should be forced to publicly confess: "Yes, I was a murderer and

---

6   C.G. Jung, *Collected Works* (London, 1994, reprint) volume 10 paragraph 416. Hereafter this series is referred to as C.W. 10.416.

an executioner". With a wild spark of idealism, the Russian author proclaims that when an accused person confesses his guilt during a legal process, that this is "the ultimate height that a criminal trial can attain".[7]

Both are wrong. Guilt does not enrich people. In general, it destroys them. Criminals live out a lie. When that lie dissolves then, in the worst cases, they are left with nothing. They cannot accept their culpability because it takes strength to admit your own wrong. Do lies diminish the human personality? The case of MD was typical of the many dozens of sexual abuse cases that I dealt with. Someone faced with allegations of incest within the family, or of savage violence towards the inmates of an institution, or of rape, never spontaneously came forward and said: "Yes, I was utterly evil". Instead, in order to avoid shame, a damages claim or a criminal conviction they used the tools of which years of practice had made them the masters. They lied. They continued to live out their own myth of service to others through hard work and dedication. When found out, the best advice a friend, as opposed to a lawyer, could give would surely be that the person should accept that they had done wrong and devote their energies to rebuilding their lives. However, this almost never happened. They did not have the strength.

Virtually everybody lies. A study carried out by Professor Bella de Paulo at the University of Virginia required participants to keep a diary recording the lies they told in everyday social interactions, of at least ten minutes, over a given week. In about one-quarter of exchanges during any day, the participants reported that they lied. Over the course of the week, lies were told to one-third of those with whom they interacted. Discomfort in conscience was awakened only when lying to those to whom they felt emotionally close. Less than one-fifth of the lies were detected. Multiple reasons are advanced as to why people lie: to create a positive social impression, to avoid

---

7   A. Solzhenitsyn, *The Gulag Archipelago* (London, 1974) p. 176.

detection in discreditable conduct, to help a friend, to convince a prospective employer that one has the relevant skills or simply to cause mischief.[8] People who resort to lies gain obvious advantages. They may be more likely to land the desirable job, or the permit to develop a business or to capture the spouse of high social status. It is not to be inevitably predicted that they will be the ones to murder, rape and plunder. You could argue that liars merely gain a competitive edge. No doubt they do, just as bullies and cheats do in sport as well as in life. But most people control their lying, only resorting to deceit for limited advantage and with at least some awareness of the limits to which they will go.

What distinguishes the deceit of those who become immersed in evil, and therefore its instrument, is that the lie becomes fundamental to their being. Small deceits move us in that direction. They open up the possibility of evil. But it is only when we live out a lie, so that it defines us, that we risk being submerged in evil. Writing perhaps from the perspective of his background in physics, Solzhenitsyn suggests that evil has a threshold magnitude; people move in and out of wrongdoing and are not necessarily lost thereby to constructive behaviour. He thought that there was a point where wrongdoing gave way to evildoing: when this threshold was crossed, a person left their humanity behind. [9] The Soviet political prison camp system thrived on enforced confessions obtained by torture. These torturers he describes as "a space totally infected with putrefaction".[10] One wonders what would have been left of them had they been stripped of their power and had suddenly obtained a clear-sighted view of themselves. Would they have been so totally repulsed by their crimes that their strength to live would have been sapped?

---

8   The relevant studies are cited in A. Vrijj, *Detecting Lies and Deceit: The Psychology of Lying and the Implications for Professional Practice* (Chester, 2000) pp. 1–17.
9   Solzhenitsyn, p. 175.
10 Solzhenitsyn, p. 144.

Murder breaks people. It wrecks the victim's family and demeans that of the killer.[11] In general, people who have killed are utterly changed by what they have done. Often, in the aftermath of a murder, the killer simply cannot understand what he or she has done. They believe that something inside themselves drove them on. One might wonder if the idea that outbursts of evil are spontaneous and almost unwilled might be correct.

Ireland is a small country, yet almost every year cases occur where violence suddenly overwhelms an apparently innocent situation. Alcohol, the depressant drug of our time, combined with sexual attraction and a lonely place where no one might possibly come to help the victim, provide the setting for a recurrence of murders. KE was a typical case. He was from a broken home that had witnessed violence. After a day of binge drinking, he met a girl at a nightclub. They left the company of others late at night and ended up in a deserted house. In terms of facts, we only know for certain that she ended up strangled and that he rushed home and put his clothes in the washing machine. In court, he later testified that he really did not know what had happened and could only remember what he said was some taunt by the girl. This may only have been a joking remark but, whatever it was, it evoked rage. KE could not explain what had happened to him. He was crushed by what he had done; by what he could not explain. JL was accused of a murder that seemed to have occurred in a more calculating fashion. His long-term girlfriend had broken up with him and returned to her mother's home, making it clear that the relationship was at an end. Shortly before the killing he was seen outside the victim's home taking out a flick-knife and apparently talking to it. He then knocked on the door. When his ex-girlfriend's mother answered it, his ostensibly manic state changed to reason: he needed to see the girl in order to discuss outstanding rent on their flat and how to dispose of certain domestic items. The lies breached the barrier. He was allowed in. Within minutes the girl

---

11 Bernie Hanley, personal communication.

was dead. His answer to the charge was that he had brought the knife so that he could make a demonstration before her of his intention to kill himself. When she was unimpressed he claimed, like KE, that he had been so overcome by something inside his mind that his body had acted without his will in killing the victim. Lawyers call this defence automatism.

SO'R was another case that echoed this claim. A young man had received upsetting news and went out drinking. After becoming increasingly disorientated, he remembered that an old friend of his, who might offer him a sympathetic hearing, lived on the outskirts of Limerick city in an area with which he was unfamiliar. In the small hours of the morning he tried to hitch a lift. He was picked up by SO'R, an older man who later claimed that he thought that the victim shared his homosexual orientation. They stopped in a side street. SO'R claimed that after some willing fondling that the young man had rebuffed him. SO'R then knocked him unconscious. It later proved impossible to say just how bad that particular assault was because he then drove the unconscious man out into the countryside and beat him to death with a car jack. According to the killer, the young man had recovered some consciousness and had insulted him. In response, SO'R, as he testified, "completely lost control". Again, like the others he claimed that he could not account for his violence. There are many similar cases, of which these are just instances.

These claims seem unlikely. In most legal jurisdictions a murder is defined as an intentional homicide. At the time of the last case, a colleague of mine was researching the manner in which juries reach their verdicts and the reasoning which they employ in the process.[12] She had spoken to some of the jury members in these cases. They told her that the idea that a sane

---

12 The idea was to attempt to determine the extent to which juries followed the legal direction of trial judges. The research was not finished because the Court of Criminal Appeal, in another case, proclaimed that it was undesirable to break the secrecy of the jury room.

person could kill apparently intentionally, but without the mind directing their body, was something which they accepted. In some situations they thought that the mind could overcome a person's will and make him or her into an unwitting killer. In SO'R's case they might have accepted it as a defence if the victim had been killed during the first attack and not been coldly, as they put it, driven away and then murdered. In JL, the jury regarded it as possible that his real intention was to commit suicide but that the lies, which he told to gain entry to the house, showed how he continued to calculate his moves shrewdly notwithstanding his emotional turmoil.

Rejection and disappointment are so much a part of life that no one can expect to avoid them. The ordinary hurts of life do not necessarily turn people into killers. These cases had more than an ordinary disappointment to them. There were common features to their lives with those of many cases of savage violence; of people living out a fantasy existence at the expense of the suffering of others. In these cases, hidden from view, the killers had inflated their self-regard so that they became volatile to any challenge. They had no real support in terms of family and nor did they have any real friends. Their relationship to the victim, as affirming their false selves, was everything. They had no culture: no sense of inner education that might link them into the continuity of generations that have survived the ups and downs of life but who have found a response from somewhere deep inside themselves in art, literature or music. Whether in folk tales or symphonies, the fundamental answer to the problems of life does not seem to be accessible through deceit. Truthfullness does not characterise the approach of the violent people whom I have encountered. Instead, the necessity to be affirmed in the false way in which they saw themselves became the core of their being. In the words of one psychologist, their egos "hung from a balloon".[13] They responded with rage when it was shattered.

---

13 A. Miller, *The Drama of Being a Child: The Search for the True Self* (London, 1995, revised edition) pp. 31–78.

This pattern is not confined to amorous disappointments. Gangland killings are usually not so much about broken drug deals and lost money, as the challenge to the authority of the boss-figure. His ego is so enormous that no one will cross him without being crushed.[14] Like nations on the verge of aggressive warfare, those who order others to murder for them are twisted up in notions of their own prestige and how their authority might be diminished unless they strike down their enemies. They want control, because being in control allows a person to think what they choose about themselves without challenge. In many murders, of which JL is but an example, any breach of a dominating relationship challenges the core self-deceit of the abuser. Any fundamental loss of control risks the total deflation of people who have constructed their lives in that way.

When you stop lying in those circumstances what are you left with? Without his public image of righteousness MD, the "respectable" schoolteacher, had nothing. Similarly, when a dominating partner is told that the abusive relationship is over, his house of cards collapses. Where you live out fundamental lies to support your own grandiose notions you are left empty when they are gone. Men with power and weapons look formidable. That is why they acquire them. When they have been taken away only banality will be left. Hannah Arendt made a similar observation while watching Adolf Eichmann being tried on charges of mass murder. During the Holocaust, he was masterly: a close confidant of the all-knowing leader and a person tasked with the improvement of the human race, no less. Contesting the charge, years later, he was living out all that he had left of the lie about himself: he was following orders. To her, he looked more like a clown than a monster.[15]

Instead of being crushed by a clear view of yourself you can, however, always choose denial. KE, who murdered the girl whom he met at the disco, was deflated because he recognised

14 Michael Finn, personal communication.
15 H. Arendt, *Eichmann in Jerusalem: A Report on the Banality of Evil* (London, 1963) p. 54.

the wrong that he had done. Others cling to a version of events that maintains, so far as possible, something of their false selves. There are many ways of doing this. Blaming the victim is one way. MD was the one who induced the two boys to come into his hotel bedroom. That was not his case, however. As I remembered it, at that time it seemed an insignificant detail that he had claimed that they, in the middle of the night, had knocked on his door out of loneliness. In truth, the facts were the opposite of what he claimed.

That is also a pattern; inversion of an evil intention. You accuse those you hate of every despicable action you are planning yourself. You attribute hateful motives to others that, in truth, describe your own state of mind. When you hear people complaining about other people, if you listen carefully, you will find that they are talking about themselves.[16] In the aftermath of a particularly upsetting case, a colleague once said that to me. Two people, PJ and RM, had a business relationship. It became so intense that they shared regular meals in each other's homes, as if they were all part of the same family. Then the business began to go down and relationships soured. The man who eventually died, RM, attempted to get out of the mess. Naturally, he proposed to take some of the business clients with him. He wrote a letter suggesting a share-out. This was treated as an affront. Unless he left with nothing, his friend was just not going to be happy. One day, they were both in the home of RM to discuss the matter when the telephone rang and a client, who was particularly coveted by PJ, rang and spoke at length to RM. This left his partner incensed. From outside, his secretary heard him yelling while RM responded forcefully. She went in and saw PJ hit his friend several blows with an office implement as he tried to push him away. In the process of killing RM, PJ broke a finger. During the later court case, the precise nature of the cause of death became important. Why is irrelevant here. When a person is examined after a homicide, photographs of the

---

16 Blaise O'Carroll, personal communication.

injuries are taken at the direction of the forensic pathologist. These are of both external injuries and the internal signs on dissection. In the absence of the jury, these were being discussed with the judge and were visible in court while the accused was testifying. On PJ being asked a series of questions on the defence which he had mounted that the dead man had provoked him, he suddenly lifted his hand, showing a slightly damaged finger, and said: "Look at what that man did to me". It was eerie. A man was dead and he had killed him. He never thought to contrast his trifling injury with the brain swelling his attack had inflicted on the deceased. Not even in sight of photographs showing the blood clotted inside of his former friend's skull.

As we shall see, inverting evil and blaming it on your enemy is a form of human conduct that runs through the history of aggressive war and genocide. RM, an honest enough man, was called every name under the sun in the evidence of his former partner and accused of every form of discreditable conduct. The dead man was a monster and the accused was his victim. That can indeed happen. But it didn't happen here.

It is pretty easy in practice to make such a lie float. After all, in a tense emotional situation any person will surely do something discreditable eventually, big, small or medium. That can be latched on to and twisted into the criminal-as-victim defence. Overarching greed seemed fundamental to the attitude of PJ. He wanted literally everything. Apart from that, there was again a breakdown in control and a direct challenge to his view of himself as indispensable: the partner who attracted and serviced the best clients.

When people hate other people, then everything that the hated person does becomes a manifestation of their loathsomeness. If they answer a provocation, they are aggressive. If they assert their rights in any way, such as by insisting on a fair sharing of resources, then they are grasping and greedy. If they are polite, they are cold. If they make a mistake, they are calculating. In one case, two families who lived close to each other had been on very bad terms for years. The cause does not matter and, in any case, it was not over very much. When the patriarch of one family ended up in hospital, the son of the other paid his family a brief visit at home in order to enquire after his health; probably he was thinking "let bygones be bygones". To them this was a shocking insult. The sick man's son, MG, hired a killer who murdered him.

What people think about others bears no resemblance to reality once hatred intrudes. The very nature of the person changes: just as in a folk tale a witch, a metaphor for hatred, may transform a character into a rat or a toad. So will a goblin, a metaphor for black mischief, rejoice and laugh at another's misfortune. Because it is a joke to them, they are delighted to stir up trouble, assisting the process of hatred. I resort to mythology because nothing said in hatred relates to reality. What is equally unreal is the view that the aggressor has of themselves. They are seeking only fairness or respect; they feel victimised by what the person they hated has done. That is what they obsess about and it does not matter about the cost to others. This fits in with the phenomenon that the deflation of grandiose self-regard is a dangerous medicine. It goes wider than homicide because the pattern, at least potentially, describes one of the aspects of how people think in mass murder. In the conduct of genocide, as we shall see, that mythological separation of the two sides into the loathsome and the God-endowed is central to the thinking that enables mass killing. Millions of people in history have behaved as if they believe that they, and the ideological movements that they served, were the summit of perfection – with terrible consequences. If deceit is a core aspect of the conduct of mass murder then we need to know what it is about lies that apparently opens a gateway to destruction.

All of the cases to which I have referred have been about individuals who killed other individuals. People are at their most dangerous when they combine. If you take the worst mass murderer in human history that acted alone, you may be looking at a person who dispatched a number of dozen victims. As part of a group, that number multiplies exponentially. About a million Armenians were killed by the genocide staged in Turkey during the First World War. Around six million Jews were systematically murdered under the Nazis about one-quarter of a century later. Some millions of Slav "sub-humans" were also killed, as were homosexuals and Roma people, among others. In Hitler's war of aggression against Russia perhaps twenty-five million died. All through this, Stalin was sending millions of innocent people to prison labour camps, where the conditions killed most of the inmates over time, or he had them executed outright. People of my generation could not understand this. It looked to be something in the past. When we thought that perhaps genocide needed special conditions to occur, including the cloak of a major conflict, the Rwandan majority dispatched about a million members of the Tutsi minority over a few months in 1994. At its height, the genocide accounted for ten thousand victims a day. All of this took a major degree of cold-blooded planning. Imagine them there, these planners at their desks, or wherever, what must they have been thinking? What feelings were inside them?

Those who organise others to do their killing for them may find the process so repulsive that they are personally unable to dispatch a single victim. Even the sight of a person being killed may sicken them. I think that any experienced criminal lawyer would be familiar with this pattern. You can mastermind a murder down to the last detail, even following how it is progressing by telephone, but turn up in court and be unable to look at the police photographs showing the results of your handiwork. I have seen this. Here is the paradox. One may think that "putting yourself offside", as the underworld lingo expresses it, is just a sensible strategy. Certainly, you can avoid conviction much more easily if you use another person to do your murdering for you. But that is not all that there is to it. The worst murderers may never get their hands bloody. Franz Stangl claimed that he never violently touched a single person in Treblinka; or in the Hartheim euthanasia institution in Berlin

where he was previously the overseer of the murder of hundreds of handicapped children and adults. In some way, his
physical distance from death dealing enabled him to administer
it. He managed to become a mass killer while apparently
remaining a timid man when it came to cruelty. People use
weapons that kill others from afar and, in so doing, empower
their ability to destroy when they would otherwise shrink away.
Using a hired killer and sending in long-range bombers to
destroy a city are but examples of this.

This, however, cannot be the only self-delusion that facili-
tates evil. While some remain at a distance, others wallow in the
process of slaughter. On an individual level, every criminal justice system has to deal with individuals who torture and kill
repeatedly because they derive vile pleasure from the suffering
they inflict. For them, the closer they get the better.[17] In the
group conflicts of aggressive war and mass murder, the human
race seems to arrange itself into specialised functions: killers and
organisers.

Having a number of people working together to commit a
crime allows for this kind of specialisation. You can have those
who will use their hands to "do the job" and others who will
assist them. The support group can operate scanners to listen in
to police communications, guard a premises from the street
while a robbery takes place inside and later dispose of the proceeds; or the weapons used in a murder.

The central mystery here is a paradox. How can it be that
some people find it easier to kill by hiring others to do it, while
there are others that revel in death? For me, a series of cases
focused that question, but did not resolve it. Every country, but
perhaps Ireland in particular, needs to protect elderly farmers
living alone in rural areas. They are vulnerable to attacks by
"knockers"; criminals who pretend to be door-to-door sales-
men but who have robbery in mind. Several of these cases have
resulted in murder. Why did many of these cases descend into a

---

17 B. Masters, *Killing for Company: The Case of Dennis Nilsen* (London,
1985).

spiral of violence, and how did that happen? Then there was the problem of division: there were those inveigling their way in, usually women, and those who rushed in after them and put the women on watch outside the door. So many times, in later statements to the police, those on the outside claimed to be unaware of the intention of the other gang members. Killing happens both at a distance and through immersion in the business of slaughter. Perhaps this is beyond any explanation? Part of the problem must have something to do with the nature of the dynamics within the gang.

Maybe, in a given situation, you might begin to predict how a person might act. Once he or she draws a number of other people into the enterprise, prediction becomes impossible because it depends on how they share their ideas. Or their lies. It becomes impossible because each supports the other in whatever shared aspect of hate only they know. Is this why criminal gangs are formed?

Groups act differently to individuals. If their comrades in crime support them, people are less open to being devastated by a guilty realisation of their own conduct. Good police practice indicates that, where gang members are arrested, they should be held and interrogated in isolation from one another. Within the group it is easier to maintain a self-supporting fiction. Each can tell the other that the person killed was "asking for it" because they were "warned", about poking in their nose where it wasn't wanted, if an outsider, or because they were a "traitor", if an insider. They can each tell the others that they are the victims. Indeed, all over Europe, in typical cases of rural gang robbery the perpetrators can often come from marginalised groups who have real complaints to make about their exclusion from society. Whether marginalised or not, playing at being a victim is a feature of many of the personalities that I have seen drawn to violence.

There are any number of excuses for evil, depending on the circumstances. For gangsters, breaking ranks is the ultimate offence. There is a logical reason for this. Criminal conspiracies can only function in secrecy and silence. There is also a less apparent dynamic; the need to shut out the truth. When the Nazis embarked on the Holocaust of the Jewish people they lied to the victims, to the outside world and to themselves. First they buried the murdered. In eventually using ovens to cremate the corpses, they were following a plan that no trace of what they had done was ever to remain. They even went to the extreme lengths of exhuming the earlier pits full of decomposing bodies and burning them. No one was ever to know. Not even history. Could it be that even they might have cared not to be despised for atrocious crimes? No light was ever to enter the darkness of their consciousness. After all, what might it show?

It seems that when you retreat from reality you have two basic choices. You can either be like MD, a man with a repulsive secret who displays himself as a dedicated selfless educator. Or, you can bring in others to the circle. This seems ridiculous. One person's condemnation must surely be as good as another's. But it isn't. Those who are chosen for a group of paedophiles, or drug importers or murderers, are selected to think as the others think and to act as the others act. No one of them is likely ever to suddenly stand up and yell: "This is wrong". Each one reinforces the other in the lies that they tell. They are each a false mirror to the other. As for outsiders: they are people who are not "us" and who do not matter. In short, gangs have little, or no, reflective capacity. They are deliberately put together that way.

A confederation of lies achieves its own form of perfection when the circle of intention becomes so closed that no one outside the group counts. It is only those who are of us, or perhaps like us, that mater. We see this pattern in the execution of mass murder. It needs several bloody hands, and many administrators, to achieve deaths in multitude. Provided the black circle is never broken, the killings will go on uninterrupted. All of the many victims may be crying out for mercy but their distress does not appeal to anything in the killers. Anything good that is. But, as we shall see, there is an exception. In a few rare cases, killers who have been shamed in the act of murder by one of their own, or by a sudden assertion of the dignity of the intended victim, may suddenly back off. How can it be that the circle of darkness may be broken: usually, only for an instant? We know this can happen because a very few have escaped in this way. Ranks quickly close again against the truth. Discipline demands that the lies are reinstated in a community of delusion and the killings continue.

Ideology is the most important way of keeping a circle closed towards an evil purpose. Basically, it turns everything that we might expect of human nature on its head. An ideological homicide is not the same as an ordinary murder. The participants themselves proclaim this. They demand to be called different names. Not the accused, when on trial, or the prisoner, when convicted. It is not usually anything personal that motivates them against their victims. They do not hate them because of a greedy self-delusion over a business relationship, or because they have disturbed the peace and prosperity of a drug-importing enterprise. Nor is it because a grandiose self-regard has been shattered by rejection, or any other "normal" reason. In all probability they never even met the people whom they want to kill. They hate them in the abstract.

One can examine this hatred and find an apparent reason. After all, ideological campaigns of aggressive war and mass murder are distinguished by tidal waves of lying excuses. Appropriate lies hiding atrocities, or emphasising the necessity of the operation, can be told to neutralise the squeamish outsiders: to cook public opinion. If you want examples, the rest of this book is full of them. Other kinds of murderers keep quiet about why they want to dispatch someone and how much, and why, they hate them. Ideologists want everyone to know that there is a good reason why they need to kill, or dispossess, or enslave, people whom they know only as an abstraction: in fact, as a myth. They want people on their side; supporting the cause. They would like to divide half of the globe to their side and wreck the other half of it. In fact, just as the enfacement of communism and democracy once divided the world behind an iron curtain, now those who proclaim they are for or against terror have replaced these doctrines with the age-old test as to who is for us and who is against us.

In this country we have seen terror. On 11 September 2001, my family was gathered in Belfast to bury one of its last senior members. As the funeral lunch took place, one of my cousins went from table to table telling people about the attacks in New York and Washington that had killed thousands of people by explosion and fire. We were all sitting in the dining room of the La Mon country house and restaurant. On the evening of 17 February 1978, two firebombs, hooked on to the security bars of the hotel's downstairs windows, had been detonated. Sheets of ignited petrol had exploded through the room where we heard of the news from America. Twelve people died and twenty-three others were hideously maimed. One lady survived through having the presence of mind to go through the fire that engulfed her and walk towards an exit. She recited the Lord's Prayer as she went. According to the self-styled "Irish Republican Army", the hotel was a "legitimate target". They blamed the civic authorities that a warning by telephone had not arrived in time.[18] In another part of the Belfast of that time, a gang of Unionist murderers were planning how they might waylay Nationalists so as to enjoy torturing them with knives before murdering them by slitting their throats. Who did they

---

18 The facts are taken from J. Bardon, *A History of Ulster* (Belfast, 1992) and from the two Radio Telefís Éireann documentaries on the subject. References to historical works are to the facts stated therein. For observations on the ideological conflict in Ireland, I have drawn on the following works by Martin Dillon, *Political Murder in Northern Ireland* (London, 1973); *The Shankill Butchers: A Case Study of Mass Murder* (London, 1989); *The Dirty War* (London, 1990); *Killer in Clowntown* (London, 1992); and *Stone Cold: The True Story of Michael Stone* (London, 1992). The rebellion of 1916 which founded the State was proceeded by a public proclamation from the Provisional Government of the Irish Republic that prayed to God that the cause of Irish freedom would never be dishonoured "by cowardice, inhumanity or rapine".

blame for this? Their victims, of course.

The pattern that "others are to blame" is already familiar. Evil being described as good is the essence of ideology.[19] That too is a pattern. Osama Bin Laden who, whether he was or not, chose to regard himself as the spiritual author of the 2001 outrages, described them as the "blessed operations". [20] In Ireland we were already familiar with multiple murders being described as such things as "a boost to the entire Republican community". What about this as a morale booster? Chaining a man into the driving seat of his own lorry, packing it with explosives and suggesting that he seek help at a British Army checkpoint. In the result, those who tried to assist died too. What was "legitimate" as a "target" for "military operations" expanded over time from soldiers, police and prison officers to catering suppliers and building contractors.

A recitation of outrages loses focus. It becomes an evil in itself: something that people enjoy dabbling in. They take pleasure in the belief that evil is over there in that other group, in that other person, not in all of us. The point is that they would be unable to take pleasure in the notion of the evil in another person were evil not already there, in themselves, and in a way that allows it to be enjoyed.

It is popular to believe that criminals are different: that they are freaks of nature apart from the human race on whom, like Dr Frankenstein's monster, some random stroke of fate has inflicted a "criminal brain". None of the people mentioned in this chapter were ever examined and diagnosed with a major, or any, psychiatric illness. None of the mass murderers were either, except for Stalin and, even in his case, only speculatively and from a very safe distance.

Crime is the preserve of the sane. Killing is perfectly normal.[21] The fact that it is evil is neither here nor there. Evil is part of all of us. In societies with very high levels of violent crime,

19 Solzhenitsyn, pp. 172–5.
20 BBC news broadcast of 18 April 2002, 22.00.
21 Dr Art O'Connor, personal communication.

such as the United States of America, many people feel that they are surrounded by hostility. To some sections of the law-abiding population it is as if there is a war on their own doorstep: "The criminals are attacking us; it is up to us to fight back", is the attitude that I encountered over there. So they execute them. Even a dozen years after the crime, killers are themselves killed: redemption does not exist; what you have done marks you for life. Certainly, murdering someone changes the killer. Apart from clear-eyed ideologues, that is. But the fact that murder weighs people down and, in my observation, alters them not only mentally but also physically, is a sign that an innate human sense of responsibility remains in some kind of working order. Killing murderers adds to the burden of violence that the human race already bears.

We derive enormous satisfaction from the guiltiness of others. We choose not to believe this. Films become a big box-office success by saying that evil exists outside of us, usually in a mythic form. Here it is in the shape of some cannibalistic murderer who is so cunning and dangerous that pump-action shotguns have to be kept trained on his uncaged presence at all times. You know the theme. It gives us this cosy feeling that evil is over there; in that other person. Never in ourselves. Like hatred, it is always someone else who is scheming, uncompromising and deceitful. Calling the other person despicable shows our own failure of awareness.

Solzhenitsyn believed that no matter what happened, an inner nucleus of human good had to remain even in those who devoted themselves to torture and murder. The Big House was a prison in Leningrad run by Stalin's secret police. To it, many thousands of innocent prisoners were brought. There they were tortured and made to confess to non-existent conspiracies to overthrow the Soviet state and to kill its leader: officially "the wisest man on earth". The jailers, male and female, saw and participated in some horrific things. They were known, naturally enough, for their icy reserve towards the prisoners, shunning any human expression. During one bombing raid by the Nazis, the high-explosive shells fell and detonated right beside the Big House as if the very next one was going to land on NP, a prisoner, and her jailer as they walked down a corridor to an interrogation. Terrified, the guard threw her arms around the prisoner, desperate for a human embrace in the moment of death. When the bombing stopped, the coldness came back and the prisoner was marched on to her destiny.[22] It always involved some form of torture.

One wonders what would have happened if the bombs had struck and groups of prisoners and torturers had found themselves entombed together. For their last hours what would they have done? That might depend on how deep a diminishment of humanity had been inflicted. Of course, depending on their status, they could hope, or despair, that rescue would return them to their allotted roles. Then they could behave as before under the guiding hand of the great leader who had so wisely arranged all of this for them. Was this behaviour towards NP unusual? Perhaps, even in the moment of death, hatred and deceit might prevail. Maybe the people working in the Big House were also prisoners. After all, they could not break out of their role. Some of them basked in the process of torturing the captives inside the jail, while outside a different role was expected: that of committed party member and moral guardian of Soviet ideology.

When you think of it, there is very little good that could be said of the functionaries of the Big House, or Treblinka, or any other place where degradation is accomplished. In fact, if you met them, face-to-face, very little could be said of these people at all. Reading Sereny's account of her conversations with Franz Stangl, and her later book about meeting Albert Speer, is like meeting a horrible person; it adds nothing to your vitality. [23] The Stangl book comes alive when his surviving victims are allowed to speak. They have nothing to hide. Unlike him, their

---

22 Solzhenitsyn, p. 172.
23 G. Sereny, *Albert Speer: His Battle with the Truth* (London, 1995).

personalities do not seem to be constrained by iron walls of self-regard, justification and evasion.

The rest of this work focuses more on the experiences of the victims of aggression than on their tormentors, who can tell us little. Evil diminishes people. Each successive lie kills off some part of whatever it is that makes up a person. Perhaps, like the terrified guard, something of what they could have been is left somewhere, but in residue. If it is, it is often powerless. When decency goes, something else takes over. Those working in criminal gangs share similarities with the functionaries of Treblinka, and the other places of mass murder and torture. Both are constrained by the structures of evil. In turn these set up patterns within which the degradation of life became a day's work. It has to be the case that there was more involved in this process than cutting people off from their "growth", as current psychology texts put it. As we shall see, certain situations set off eruptions of the most savage violence. The victims of this, as far as possible, strove to maintain some sense of dignity. Prisoners in attrition camps were under far worse pressure than any of their captors and they had almost no power. What they had was used in prolonging at least their own life. Those in control of rituals of humiliation tend to have their own vulnerability. Something is triggered off in them, which can make them wantonly savage against those in their control. The notion of "being overcome", familiar to a criminal practitioner, asserts itself in the pages written by, or on behalf of, those who have received the inhuman fury in human nature.

But what is it that takes people over: if this is true? Surely it is possible to describe it? What struck me about those killers who claimed to have been overwhelmed by a violent impulse is that they put themselves in a situation which energised the negative part of them. In the cases of KE, JL and SO'R their personalities were already so fragile that they found it hard to resist whatever emotions erupted because of rejection. If you met them in an ordinary situation, they might appear quite normal. But in circumstances of rejection, the fragility of their self-regard both caused an eruption and made it difficult for them to resist it. You could say that they were diminished. But anyone can be diminished. Loss causes panic. The thought of loss also panics people. If a person, or a society, lives on the edge of panic, it is open to emotion. Conscious controls are lessened by strong emotion. You would not say that PJ, who killed his business partner, was a diminished character. Yet he was. His diminishment consisted of the enormity of his self-regard. MD, the abusive schoolteacher, shared that hidden flaw until he was found out. All of these characters had unusual views of themselves. You could say that they were living out a myth.

Does that make you less of a man or woman? And then there are the mythic qualities to what people believe in the wider context of group violence: their mission; the chosen nature of their group; the future of radiant promise; the despicable nature of those who oppose them. Is myth still a living dynamic in peoples' lives? It seems ridiculous. But unreality does not just drop from the sky. People invent it for their own purposes, just as they lie for their own purposes. Lies mixed with the potential we all seem to have for mythic thinking appears to dominate in the worst cases of mass aggression. Is it really the case that violence erupts most easily when deceit draws us into living out a myth based on lies?

CHAPTER 2

Myths and Theories

E VIL IS A REAL FORCE with real energy. It is not just the absence of good. The absence of truth from the human personality, however, helps it to flourish. Lies are the means whereby a real connection with the world is stripped away to be replaced by dangerous nonsense.

It is certainly evil to pretend that an innocent person has committed a crime. Of all the ways in which an offence can be proved, the confession of a suspect is both the most certain proof, if it is true, and the most dangerous to justice, because it can be falsified. Just when DNA profiling was emerging as a new way of linking a suspect to the scene of a crime, I prosecuted a man on a charge of rape. He had been exercising in an almost deserted city park early in the morning at the same time as an elderly woman had been walking her dog. She was overpowered and raped. RP, the suspect, was arrested essentially because he was the only person known to be near the victim at the time when she was attacked. He confessed. The text of his admission was not very detailed but, after all, what detail was required? He had seen the woman, brought her down, dragged her into a secluded spot and sexually assaulted her. The statement added how he had returned home, washed and later heard the news of the attack on the radio. Apart from what he said, there was nothing independent to connect him to the crime: no transfer of hair or fibres, no footprint of his shoes at the scene but there was a semen sample. At the time of the investigation there was no means of testing it against his blood. By the time of the trial, eighteen months later, DNA comparison was in its early infancy. The defence asked the prosecution to consent to an adjournment and requested a test. It emerged that the suspect had been accused in the wrong and that his confession was false because the sample could not have come from him.

You would be completely naïve, no matter what country you live in, if you thought that the police are never tempted into falsifying evidence. One common motive is disgust at not being able to secure sufficient proof against a savage recidivist who has terrorised a community. RP was not such a person. He was a gentle young man with a mild mental illness who was doing his best to live a reasonably independent life in a flat near the park. One of his problems was that he was prone to suggestion. This quality put him within the profile of the kind of vulnerable individuals who are either easily overborne by repeated questioning or who can believe what people tell them about themselves.[1] Others who falsely confess tend to fit other identifiable profiles, such as attention seekers.[2] While this is both nasty and unfortunate, it is still understandable. Evil, if you like, is still within understandable limits. Understandable, because the police believe in the guilt of a suspect whom they confront with the details of a crime. Limited, because they are not so much attempting to exploit a personality flaw in the prisoner as mistakenly seeing it as the key to why he committed the crime. None of that makes it right.

In all the cases of mass murder by ideological groups, of which I am aware, confessions of a different kind feature somewhere in the story. They are incomprehensible. The questioners, for which read "the torturers", do not believe in any real sense

---

1 G. Gudjonsson, *The Psychology of Interrogations and Confessions: A Handbook* (Chichester, 2003) pp. 215–43, pp. 458–512; for another instance see A. Miller, *Timebends: A Life* (London, 1988) pp. 554-9, which discusses the case of US v Peter Reilly.

2 Gudjonsson, pp. 541–72.

in the guilt of the suspects. They are right because the suspects are completely innocent. But, for some bizarre reason, guilt is projected on to them and it must be confirmed. The interrogators are certain, on ideological grounds, of some sense of inner guilt. The Big House is as good a place to start as any. If you were to believe Solzhentisyn, and I do, none of the political arrestees brought there during the Terror were guilty of anything.[3] At most, their innate sense of liberty had made them enter a debate on the nature of Soviet society. This, after all, was the very "thought crime" for which the Russian writer had himself been arrested in February 1945. In any moderately free society, people will have opinions on its leadership. Of these, a small number will want to make a name for themselves by challenging accepted orthodoxies; claiming that society is badly run and that they might do better. In no normal sense could you call such people "plotters to overthrow the State". That was the basis for the condemnation of millions under Lenin and Stalin. Most of those imprisoned in gulags were innocent, even of bad thoughts. Some, as we shall later see, merely knew someone whom the authorities wanted to destroy. Those who were arrested certainly had their guilt suggested to them, as is normal in any system of police questioning, and more. Perhaps a society can go mad. Perhaps, when that happens, the rulers believe that they are under siege from enemies within the realm linked to invaders outside it. Can we explain how the fantasies of a leader can cause a series of societies to respond by confirming non-existent plots through forcing confessions out of prisoners?

Soviet society was born through terror. Any challenge to it was ruthlessly put down. It is possible that, over time, societies can calm down even from the highest pitch of rage so that people begin again to ask what is right and what is wrong. Torture, as a means of extracting "admissions of guilt", then becomes less acceptable since it merely confirms the prejudices of the questioner. That kind of development was not welcomed in Russia.

---

3   A. Applebaum, *Gulag: A History of the Soviet Camps* (London, 2004) p. 127.

The principle was: "The best evidence, no matter what the circumstances, is the confession of the defendants".[4] In January 1939, the traditional methodologies of the Big House, and its sister houses, were reaffirmed. Stalin ordered the NKVD, his secret police throughout the Soviet empire, and his Communist Party functionaries, that heretics against the ideology of which he was the chief priest were to be rooted out by the traditional methods. Kruschev, in his secret speech to the twentieth Communist Party Congress, explained that, prior to this directive, the leaders of local party organisations had begun to rein in the NKVD by questioning confessions extracted through physical pressure. The truth was intruding onto the territory conquered by deception. That territory was to be re-occupied through torture. This is how Stalin justified its use:

> *It is known that all Bourgeois intelligence services use methods of physical influence against representatives of the socialist proletariat and that they use them in their most scandalous forms. The question arises as to why the socialist intelligence service should be more humanitarian against the mad agents of the Bourgeoisie, against the deadly enemies of the working class and the Kolkhoz workers. The Central Committee of the All-Union Communist Party considers that physical pressure should still be used obligatorily as an exception applicable to known and obstinate enemies of the people, as a method both justifiable and appropriate.*[5]

The trials conducted under Stalin were rituals scripted to reveal a threat to the hegemony of Bolshevik rule. It is probable that he watched from a secret gallery in the courtroom as some of his enemies were being crushed.[6] All of this assumed definite, but not unique or unprecedented, tinges of madness. In 1937, in order to

---

4   A. Solzhenitsyn, *The Gulag Archipelago* (London, 1974) p. 377, quoting Protsess Promparti (Moscow, 1931).
5   Khrushchev – secret speech to the Twentieth Party Congress, 24, 25 February 1956, text taken from the *New York Times* 5 June, 1956 and quoted in F. Chalk and F. Jonassohn, *The History and Sociology of Genocide: Analyses and Case Studies* (Yale, 1990) p. 303.
6   Solzhenitsyn, p. 411.

prove the existence of "a centre" of "anti-Soviet rightists, Trotskyite double-dealers and Japanese-German diversionists and spies", as they were floridly described, one of Stalin's henchmen, Leonid Zakovasky, had party members arrested and terribly tortured. One prisoner, a man called Roszenblum, was tasked with proving, by his confession, the presence of a "terrorist centre" in Leningrad:

> *Zakovasky told me the NKVD would prepare the case of this centre, remarking that the trial would be in public ... "the case of the Leningrad Centre has to be solidly built, and for this reason witnesses are needed ... you, yourself will not need to invent anything. The NKVD will prepare for you a ready outline for every branch of the centre; you will have to study it carefully and to remember well all the questions and answers which the court might ask ... your future will depend on how the trial goes and on results. If you begin to lie and testify falsely, blame yourself. If you manage to endure it, you will save your head and we will feed and clothe you at the Government's cost until your death".*[7]

Stalin was not alone in the reasoning that he employed to justify the torture of the innocent. It is unlikely that he studied Papal documents. In 1252, the Papal bull Ad Exterpanda confirmed the justification for the long-standing practice of torturing confessions out of prisoners suspected of the Cathar or Waldensian heresies:

> *The podesta or ruler is hereby ordered to force all captured heretics to confess and accuse their accomplices by torture which will not imperil life or limb, just as thieves and robbers are forced to accuse their accomplices and confess their crimes, for these heretics are true thieves, murderers of souls and robbers of the sacraments of God.*[8]

The same fundamentalist notions run through both the Papal and Communist statements; the over-ruling supremacy of a dogma that justifies striking savagely against its opponents. At all costs, what the ideology supported was to be protected.

---

7 Khrushchev in Chalk and Jonassohn, p. 302. For further examples see Solzhenitsyn, pp. 371–431; Applebaum, pp. 127–47.

8 Quoted in M. Ruthven, *Torture: The Grand Conspiracy* (London, 1978) pp. 90–7 and in turn quoted in Chalk and Jonassohn, p. 131.

Opposition to it characterises its enemies as evil. After all, how does anyone deal with evil? The nature of this kind of fantasy of evil against people demands that they be crushed violently.

As one looks at this, one begins to wonder whether enclosed dogmatic societies produce similar fantasies against their enemies. Myths have been the backdrop for savage violence from the second to the twentieth centuries. If you look at their nature then, like folk tales from different eras and countries, there seems to be a shared underlying pattern.

In the second century, Christians were persecuted by the Roman Empire. Those who were murdered were ordinary people. Those who destroyed them ascribed to them repellent rituals that broke the Christian communities away from the natural protection of human sympathy. They were described as worshipping animal idols; encouraging unbridled sexual licence during religious services; adoring of the genitals of the presiding priest; and ritually killing children. It was reported that the drinking of the sacrificed child's blood enforced vows of secrecy.[9] The historian Norman Cohn traces the fantasies about the early Christians to parallel allegations that were later laid against medieval heretics that led to the first burnings for witchcraft in 1022. These later "apostates" were supposed to have celebrated a blasphemous form of the Mass. The "heavenly food" of the heretic communicants became, in the chronicles of their persecutors, the bodies of sacrificed children which they ate. Prayer meetings became opportunities for unbridled lust: conditions that allowed, it was believed, for the manifestation of the devil in person.[10] Two centuries later, the Holy Inquisition, under the leadership of Conrad of Marburg, pursued "heretics in league with Satan" who again

---

9   N. Cohn, *Europe's Inner Demons: The Demonization of Christians in Medieval Europe* (London, 1993) chapter 1, quoting Minicus Felix – Octavius, chapters IX and X.

10 For a modern manifestation of what in depth psychology could be explained as the externalising of an internal image through the pursuit of ritual see J. Cornwell, *Powers of Darkness, Powers of Light* (London, 1991) pp. 350–70.

appeared to his faithful when summoned by similar obscene rituals.[11] Numerous heretics were burnt, aided by the greedy denunciations of those who wished to inherit their property and by the forced confession of the accused themselves. Conrad of Marburg was murdered in 1233. Cohn argues that the support of Pope Gregory IX for these actions, up to that point, was due to "demonological fantasies about heretics ... implanted in his mind" by Conrad. The satanic menace was unreal, he writes, and the "creation of a single obsessed mind".[12] If that is so, how could such an idea be implanted in a mind? Did the denunciations really follow a script and, if so, who invented it? How could others believe in it and follow through on a "legal process" based on it?

In the two centuries after the death of Conrad of Marburg, Christian sects continued to be persecuted for their doctrinal unorthodoxy. The "heresy" of these groups was again manifested, people chose to believe, in orgies and devil worshipping.[13] The accusation of child murder and ritual consumption appear once more in the trial of the Fratacelli sect in 1466. In the course of their sexually obscene rituals, a child was said to be passed among the faithful, killed and then burnt. Bread made from its body was then eaten as a blasphemous communion. This fifteenth century fantasy of the burning of children to make bread, Cohn traces back to a twelfth century manuscript. He argues that interrogation by torture confirmed a fantastic literary tradition preserved in monastic chronicles, and thus kept alive. He notes that a close parallel exists between documents which describe the choosing of the leader of a heretical sect in Italy in the fifteenth century, and that of a sect in Armenia seven centuries earlier.[14] The man

---

11 Cohn, chapters 3 and 4.
12 Cohn, pp. 48–50.
13 For further examples see the material quoted in Chalk and Jonassohn, pp. 114–72.
14 This accusation was first laid against the Jews in the fourteenth century and became a typical element in the fifteenth: See J. Trachtenberg, *The Devil and the Jews: The Medieval Conception of the Jew and Its Relation to Modern Anti-Semitism* (Philadelphia, 1983), p. 134.

in whose hands the sacrificed child had expired was declared to be "the supreme pontiff" in the Italian tradition and "the head of the sect" in the earlier Armenian ritual. This, according to Cohn, is to be explained by the possible translation into Latin of the earlier Armenian manuscript.[15] He writes that there was a widespread belief, at the time of the great heretical enquiries, that children were devoured in the ritual meetings of apostates. He speculates that because some accused women in witchcraft trials had a belief that they could fly at night or that they had sexual intercourse with visitors, which are very common forms of dreams and fantasies, that some degree of voluntary confession by the accused confirmed at least some elements of the classic demonising allegations.[16]

Incorrigibility of disposition to evil is the essence of a demonising fantasy. In order to further the currency of such an idea, is there a resort by deliberate design to literary traditions embodied in ancient manuscripts? In other words, where similar evil things are thought about an enemy in different places and eras, are these due to people using the same script? Throughout the centuries of the operation of the Inquisition, and the hunt for witches in Europe, the notion that the target group took, killed and ate children, the blood libel, remained the ultimate sign of dedication to evil.[17] When accusations of sorcery require evidence, as in any other legal case, the legal codes in medieval Europe generally protected the accused from fantastic allegations simply because proof was absent. The Inquisition, however, was not to be stopped. It resorted to incrimination through confession by torture. As a sign of penitence, the "confessing" accused were required to provide details of the sect of heretics to which they belonged together with full lists of the names of their associates. The Jewish defendants

---

15 Cohn, pp. 72–5.

16 Cohn, pp. 205–10.

17 For example see Cohn, pp. 1, 65, 68, 71, 92, 72, 145, 161, 205, 35, 38 and 203. For an example from Africa see Cohn, pp. 176–180 quoting J.R. Crawford, *Witchcraft and Sorcery in Rhodesia* (London, 1967).

Hugh of Lincoln in 1255 and Simon of Trent in 1474, for example, both had been tortured by methods no one could withstand into admitting ritual murders.[18] In this way, the fantasies of the interrogators were confirmed. They regarded themselves as being bound to stamp out evil plots against the peace of God on earth.[19] Which came first, the evil thoughts or the evil people?

In the nineteenth and twentieth centuries, the allegation of child murder was also levelled against Christian missionaries in China and Christian medical personnel in Moslem countries.[20] In those instances, the explanation of cultural transmission is doubtful. Aspects of these medieval allegations resurfaced again in the Europe of the mid-twentieth century. The Nazis accused the Jews of stealing, killing and ritually eating children. The Nazis researched the blood libel against the Jews and decided to revive it to furnish material for their plan of extermination. We know that they were using scripts borrowed from ancient times. Any vile lie was convenient. It is obvious that they, in describing other people as evil, were describing themselves. Perhaps, therefore, like evil people throughout history they might have similar fantasies? Reading through accounts of life in Ukraine under Nazi occupation, I was struck by how the Metropolitan of Lviv, Andrei Shepetytsky, used a similar idea of the stealing and murder of children in his denunciation of those who were killing the Jews. He was hiding Jews in monasteries under his control and the Chief Rabbi in his house.[21] It follows that he was a good man and not a bad one. In his pastoral letter "Thou Shalt Not Kill" he denounced those who were murdering the Jews as a danger to all of their neighbours: as "children might disappear", he

---

18 Trachtenberg, pp. 132, 136–7.
19 Cohn, chapter 3 and see p. 4.
20 Trachtenberg, p. 245.
21 For an account see P. Magocsi (ed.), *Morality and Reality: The Life and Times of Andrei Sheptyts'ki* (Edmonton, 1989), pp. 125–62. The account of the Rabbi is in A. Kahane, *Lvov Ghetto Diary* (Massachusetts, 1990).

wrote.[22] He properly despised those killers. In feeling this, he came up with the same thought about those intent on murdering the Jewish people as the Nazis and their followers themselves abused to "justify" inhuman slaughter.

Under Philip IV in the fourteenth century, the Knights Templar were forced by torture to publicly condemn themselves as sodomisers, deniers-of-Christ, idol-worshippers, child-murderers and cannibals.[23] How can such fantastic self-deceit be explained? Was it that the torturers racking the body of their enemies could only have their minds satisfied by the confirmation of devilish plotting by widespread groups?

Totalitarian forms of inquisition exist now as they did before. Frank Chalk and Kurt Jonassohn of the Montreal Institute for Genocide Studies, describe the elements of a totalitarian inquisition as including: denunciations taking no account of family or kinship; the extraction of confessions under torture; the naming of fellow participants in imaginary plots as being essential to a proper confession; and the impossibility of the retraction of any admission of guilt. They argue that these characteristics were

---

22 Kahane, pp. 158–62. Here is the quote: "The curse of the shedding of innocent blood stirs to life the demons of greed in his soul, who from now on goad him to seek gratification of his desires in the suffering and torment of his fellow man. The sight of blood arouses in him the lust associated with cruelty, which can be satisfied only through the agonies of the victim and his death. Bloodthirstiness can be transformed into lust which will derive pleasure from tormenting the victim and his death. A murderer who attains this level of bloodthirstiness and who takes sadistic pleasure from torments, torture, and death, unquestionably becomes a danger to his fellow man. For him, crime becomes a necessity. Without crime he suffers and undergoes unceasing torments, just as a man deprived of food and drink suffers hunger and thirst. Those forced to live in close proximity to such a person must be constantly on guard. Children might disappear and crimes might be committed and often it proves impossible to uncover the perpetrators".

23 M. Barber, *The Trial of the Templars* (London, 2003) pp. 113–40, 225–58.

invented by the Inquisition[24], in the Middle Ages, and were later sharpened during the hunt for witches. Their claim is that because of the success of methods applied by the Inquisition, they have been "copied by totalitarian regimes ever since".[25] Yet, confession under torture is a universal feature of totalitarian systems. It is not dependent on cultural transmission. The Armenian genocide, as we shall see, featured this kind of crazed confession. Here, for the moment, is an example. A German eyewitness recorded this instance of an interrogation by soldiers in the town of Moush:

> One old priest was tortured so cruelly to extract a confession that, believing that the torture would cease and that he would be left alone if he did it, he cried out in his desperation: "We are revolutionists". He expected his tortures to cease but on the contrary the soldiers cried: "What more do we seek? We have it here from his own lips". And instead of picking their victims as they did before, the official had all the Armenians tortured without sparing a soul.[26]

Even apart from confessions, every mass murder proceeds on the basis that the victims are demonic. It really does not matter if the subjects of aggression agree or not because they are going to die anyway. No evidence suggests that the instigators and shapers of the Armenian genocide, of War Communism and the Soviet Terror, based their methods on a close, or any, reading of the chronicles of medieval man. The Nazis had scholars at their disposal but, even then, we must ask how did they involve themselves in such crazy nonsense?

The Inquisitors proffered mercy on proof of genuineness. This was accepted only where the prisoner, suspect is too strong a word, produced a chronicle of dates and places of forbidden rites and the names of those present at them. The methods ordi-

---

24 Chalk and Jonassohn, p. 152.
25 Chalk and Jonassohn, p. 114.
26 Viscount Bryce, *The Treatment of the Armenians in the Ottoman Empire 1915–1916* (London, 1916) chapter 23.

narily allowed, which supposedly did not imperil the life or limb of the captives, included prolonged solitary confinement in unhealthy conditions, starvation, the use of prisoners posing as confidants in heresy and the deliberate delay of proceedings to keep alive a state of unbearable panic at not knowing one's fate. Solzhenitsyn comments: "a rack or hot coals are not really necessary to drive the average human being out of his mind".[27] All the gentler methods of the Inquisition find a precise parallel in the interrogation techniques of the Soviet secret police.[28] The result was the same in each case: surrender to the fantasy of the interrogator by a litany of abasement in imaginary plots and far-flung webs of intrigue against the will of the people as expressed through Stalin. Is there a difference between that and a plot against the will of God as expressed through his ministers on earth?

Both the Inquisition and Stalin's terror share but one fundamental characteristic. It is the core idea from which all other ideas are derived. It is conclusively presumed that enemies-of-the-people and heretics-allied-to-Satan exist. Both are the same. This idea, often confirmed by torture-induced confessions, drives destruction. The idea is false. It is hard to see it as a culturally transmitted idea. Instead, could it be a reflection of an unconscious form of idea?

Instruments and methods of torture are often taken up only to confirm that which is already known.[29] There is no evidence that dissident Christian groups in the early middle ages ate chil-

---

27 A. Solzhenitsyn, p. 103, and see 111. Barber makes a similar comment at pp. 64–5, quoting W. Sargant, *Battle for the Mind: A Physiology of Conversion and Brain-Washing* (London, 1957) p. 181.
28 For a list of methods see Solzhenitsyn, pp. 103–17.
29 Solzhenitsyn, p. 733 quoting Protsess Prompartii, pp. 452. For forced confessions in Armenia see, for example, H. Riggs, *Days of Tragedy in Armenia: Personal Experiences in Harpoot, 1915–1917* (Ann Arbor, Michigan, 1977), pp. 46, 48. For forced confessions during the Cultural Revolution see P. Short, *Mao: A Life* (London, 1999) pp. 572, 578, 595.

dren as part of their rituals. Nor is there any evidence that early Christians, or that Jews in any era, ever engaged in the ritual murder of children.[30] Insofar as apparent confessions to these crimes exist, they are fabrications. What do they tell us? Since what these "confessions" relate is unreal, they cannot reflect anything other than a surrender by the prisoner to his interrogators. The fact that such confessions were made, whether to wrecking schemes, to plots against the authorities, to plans to take over and dominate society, to foul rituals or to unbelief, speaks only to what the interrogators needed to believe about their victims. All of the interrogators were servants to some kind of movement to purify their communities. Is it to some ability to believe in the demonic opposite to the great crusade for good that the torturers have succumbed?

As early as 1927, Stalin had been secretly diagnosed as a typical case of severe paranoia. In order to make such a diagnosis fit with classic psychiatric theory, it has been suggested that psychotic episodes, where the mind becomes dominated by a delusional system immune to any argument referable to reality, happened to him for substantial periods.[31] In psychosis, people can believe almost anything; "the police want to kill me" or "the electricity system is primed to explode". No demonstration of fact or reason will move them. Despite such psychotic episodes, if they occurred, the orders of Stalin, apparently an insane person, continued to be carried out. These orders required the machinery of the Soviet Union to dedicate itself to uncovering myth-based plots. Stalin's adages were tasked with finding and destroying a class of people, be they "wreckers" in the guise of engineers or "traitors in the Red Army", whose existence could only be proven through fantasies being beamed on to innocent victims. Many of them were chosen for no better reason than that Stalin hated them. Apart from people whom Stalin knew and wanted to destroy, anyone who said anything that suggested

---

30 See Trachtenberg, pp. 124–39.
31 The relevant arguments are set out in A. Bullock, *Hitler and Stalin: Parallel Lives* (London, 1993) p. 383.

that he was anything less than the greatest man on earth was liable to be reported and imprisoned, at least. This accounted for millions. His followers were able to believe that it was right for them to listen out for any noise of heresy and to crush any non-conformists without mercy.

The pattern underlying the exercise suggests a parallel with earlier organised descents into fantasy-possession. If it can be argued that Pope Gregory IX suffered from similar delusions, as did his predecessors, successors and all of their functionaries who drove on the Inquisition, it remains to be explained how the insane fantasies of a leader figure do not serve to topple him from power but can, instead, enjoin a slavish pursuit of his will. If some aspect of the unconscious mind is at work in these phenomena, then a mental pattern ought to be capable of being found. An outline should be discernable despite the passage of generations and the expression of ideas being different through varied cultures.

How can this happen? The answer of the psychoanalyst Erich Fromm is attractively simple. The leaders of these societies were malignant sadists and necrophiles: they loved cruelty and death. In societies created under them, functionaries rose to positions of power because people who were destructive were needed to carry out the work of destruction. What is the basis of this theory?

In his 1915 essay "Instincts and their Vicissitudes", Freud had described a form of hatred that involved the oral phase of "incorporating or devouring" something so as to abolish the "object's separate existence". This was the first phase of a child's development. When the anal phase supplanted it, an "urge for mastery" took over which was indifferent to any "injury or annihilation" of the object. If the personality progressed into the next phase, the genital, then love might supplant hatred in productiveness. While not abandoning these observations, by 1930 Freud had organised his thoughts on human nature into dualistic terms. There was an erotic instinct, which sought to combine "more and more living substances into greater entities" and a death instinct that sought to "dissolve those units and bring them back to their primeval inorganic state". [32] When Fromm came to publish *The Anatomy of Human Destructiveness* in 1974, he based his view of the dynamic of violence on Freud's anal-personality theory. His clinical experience had led him to conclude that sadism is rooted in a passion for "unlimited, god-like control over men and things".[33] Necrophilia was not limited to interest, sexual of otherwise, in death and corpses but was a passion to tear living structures apart.[34] Both sadism and necrophilia were, for him, expressions of the death instinct and both, in turn, were rooted in the anal character. With a colleague, Fromm developed a questionnaire that helped to devise what percentage of the population was predominantly necrophilous. Their results indicated 10 to 15 per cent. Such people had "anti-life" tendencies.[35] Their extreme personality dynamic and large numbers made them very dangerous to the community at large. On the surface they would very likely appear normal. They might have lifeless characters, believe in the supremacy of rules, live in a joyless atmosphere, wear dark clothes and have a sniffing expression. On the other hand, Freud's principle of compensation might account for them having opposite traits to those expected. For Fromm, the modern technology-oriented world is an expression of the dominance of these people: as they love death, they have substituted lifeless artefacts for living creatures.

Fromm does not explain where hate comes from. As to how the dominance of a necrophilous personality trait may come about in any individual, Fromm says very little. If there are death instincts at work, there must be some way of indicating how the life instinct becomes subservient. For Fromm, these

---

32 New Introductory Lectures on Psychoanalysis (1933) and Civilisation and Its Discontents (1930) both quoted in E. Fromm, *The Anatomy of Human Destructiveness* (London, 1974, reprinted 1982) pp. 581–631.

33 Fromm, pp. 226, 384.

34 Fromm, p. 437.

35 Fromm, pp. 430, 434, 454.

traits simply exist because people have not developed into creative beings. He explains, however, that the pursuit of genuine work can enhance the life-instinct aspect of the personality. Even this, however, can be misunderstood. A person who works hard may be a narcissist. This personality trait is related to aggression. A narcissist feels as real only himself, his feelings, his family (as property) and everything pertaining to him. Other persons and things not part of his world are intellectually recognised but are experienced without emotional weight or colour.[36] When any of his plans are opposed, or there is any perceived insult to his conviction of his own superiority, the narcissist is likely to react with intense rage. He attacks in order to defend himself, as he has defined himself. This kind of personality is driven to seek attention, almost forced to achieve notoriety, because recognition is what is craved above all else.

Fromm does not say how ideology drives people. Groups can react with aggression but this, for him, is merely an extension of group narcissism. The talentless person can attach himself to a movement that proclaims its own greatness, thereby quashing individual doubts in a collective self-regard. Any attack on the group is responded to in the same way as a slight on the individual narcissist; with extreme aggression. This is why, according to Fromm, an opposing group is seen as devilish, cruel and treacherous.[37]

Actually, it does not fully explain this. The theories of narcissism, cruelty as control and necrophilia do not account for the way hate changes facts. Nor does it explain how people can believe fantastically untrue things about others. None of the murderers I encountered displayed, as far as I could tell, any evidence of obsession with machines or anal-hoarding personality traits. This is not to denigrate Fromm's achievement in a book from which one learns something new on every page. Rather, it seems to me that he supplies a theory that emphasises the

---

36 Fromm, pp. 271–7.
37 Fromm, p. 276.

flawed nature of the human personality: its dual nature rooted in good and evil. I suspect that any person who studies accounts of group aggression and genocide would come to the same conclusion. The late Iris Chang, for instance, who explored the violent abuses of the Chinese by the Japanese during the Nanking massacres, said that such instances were not isolated aberrations but an indication of the universal condition of human nature.[38] When I forced myself, during my time with people who have been instruments of evil in the world, to ask whether I could do similar things, no definite answer came, just a fear of what was inside me. Fundamentally, I could not feel I was different to them. The most puzzling aspects of those cases were how hatred inverted the thinking of the attacker, distorting facts in his favour, and how explosions of violent rage could erupt that were out of all proportion to any insult apparently offered.

Sigmund Freud and Carl Jung were once friends but they ended up agreeing on very little. Even where they might seem to agree as to a theory, different terms are used. The concept of a death instinct has no place in Jung's scheme of understanding the mind. The shadow has. It can be seen as corresponding with the death instinct, but only somewhat. Freudians would explain that a lot of mental illness comes about through repression. Leaving aside sexual repression for the moment, experiences that a person was unable to cope with in the past tend to be buried in a subconscious area of the mind. From there they harry the subject, causing unwanted symptoms until they are recovered and dealt with consciously. With this Jung agrees, but only to a degree. You can refuse to acknowledge something about yourself and repress it. Your hidden guilt-laden personality will, nonetheless, annoy you with outbursts of your hidden traits that will be the devil for you to control.[39] Then, Jung goes further. In his scheme, the subconscious, as in Freud, is a personal area. However, it rests on a vastly greater unconscious

38 See her obituary in the *Guardian*, 15 November 2004.
39 C.W. 9I.315.

mind that is not simply composed of life and death instincts but mental structures that reflect human experience over millennia or, if you like, the course of our evolution. These he calls archetypes. There are as many of them as there are typical human experiences. Just as animals instinctively flee from predators, mate with the healthy of their kind and mark a territory, so people fall in love, develop mental attitudes that reflect their physical age and follow a leader in a way that is influenced by the residue of instinct in their mind. Put another way, he explains that the potential of some human behaviour patterns is innate. Which is why similar situations give rise to similar ideas or similar responses.

Jung claims that the archetypes organise our responses in typical, but not necessarily predictable, patterns. That is particularly so where the mind is thrown into crisis. And, as we shall see in the next chapter, instances of mass murder tend to have their roots in catastrophic events that are either dishonestly manufactured or dishonestly exploited in order to shake a society to its foundations. The expression of our responses may differ from culture to culture but, he claims, the underlying form is the same.[40] Images are, for him, the foundation of how we react to events. Jung speculated that as our consciousness was developing at the beginning of human history, in order to try to think, people used to project images from their mind onto the external world.[41] There, they saw them and reacted to them, thus clarifying their thoughts. In a similar way, he thought that images actually in the outside world could satisfy a kind of instinctive craving to see them exist that the mind has. A weaverbird is satisfied when the nest that it makes fits into a certain pattern. All the nests of this bird are different. But when the conditions of tunnel, chamber and correct proportion are woven together with grasses, the image within the instinct is then satisfied. In the same way, the ant that grows fungus for

40 C.W. 8.440.
41 C.W. 9I 69, 120, 160.

food by cutting leaves and then storing them underground follows a pattern based on cutting particular leaves, transporting them and cultivating the harvest in the right conditions.[42]

Symbols reflect the visual power of instinct in the human world. There are many symbols that you can squarely base on the notion of instinct. A young man is attracted to a young woman, not to an old lady, is but one of almost endless examples. There are many others. The world of myth throws them up, as does the world of dreams. A hero has similar characteristics in the folk tales of many different cultures; he or she is made to undergo a series of trials that are differently expressed, depending on the origin of the story, but which are fundamentally the same.[43] A witch or goblin is usually his evil protagonist or opposite. It seems always to be the case that when you have an extreme on one side towards goodness, a character driven by opposite, and evil, qualities balances it. Examples of this occur throughout myth. For instance, in the Irish legend "The Wooing of Étáin", the hero is a beautiful and noble woman: she is destroyed through the treacherous sorcery of Fúamnach, her opposite, whose main weapon is the skilled use of lies.[44] We have all met people like Fúamnach, and we know it. But too many of us believe we are heroes without fault like Étáin or Fionn.

The shadow is our aboriginal bad side. For Jung, it is more than a one-sided Freudian death instinct because it may also fuel normal instincts, creative impulses and realistic insights. For him, no mental structure based on instinct could ever be completely bad. Experience perhaps suggests that it is when the mind is allied to deceit then it, the shadow or death instinct, becomes a source of danger in everyone. When you lie to yourself, you create a personal shadow. Going on everyday life experience alone, people who smugly pretend that they are only good make up a lot more of the population than the repulsive

---

42 C.W. 8.398.

43 C.W. 9I. 267.

44 J. Ganz, *Early Irish Myth and Sagas* (New York, 1981), pp. 37-59; G. Murphy, *Saga and Myth in Ancient Ireland* (Dublin, 1955).

15 per cent who Fromm thought were predominantly necrophiles. The personal shadow, Jung says, links into the archetypal shadow. Your greediness, for instance, may be the link to goading you into assisting in genocide in order to get a displaced person's possessions. For tens of thousands of years, perhaps more, people have been lying about their enemies. They lie about what they are and what they have done. The shadow aspect of our personality distorts. This justifies all manner of wrongs.[45] Once evoked, any archetype generates a stream of mental energy out of proportion to its apparent cause, just as a cornered animal responds with an energy that seems to take hold of its physical being.[46] We then may seem to be out of control. To some degree, this phenomenon might explain what murderers have claimed is the automatic nature of aggression.

Jung differs radically from Freud in his concept of the archetypes. But, just as Freud eventually saw human nature in dualistic terms, a similar viewpoint is part of Jung's view of the unconscious mind. It is both good and bad: life enhancing and life denying. In so far as archetypes reflect life's experiences, these also have a duel aspect. Let me take a few examples. Everyone has a mother. She influences our development even beyond her death. Not all experiences of a mother's love are positive. She cherishes, protects and nourishes her children but she can also be emotionally suffocating. As well as teaching her children to love, she can also teach them to hate, passing on prejudice from generation to generation. A mother's love sustains and fosters optimism; while her emotionality can overwhelm a developing personality, crushing its independent strength under the weight of her own unresolved fears. Within the experience of life and age is a depth that reaches through a mother's wisdom into the wellspring of creativity; but instead of warmth and light to sustain a child in the exploration of what lies within the mind, triviality, fear of the opinions of others and a refusal to relate emotionally may crush the will of the child to do anything other

---

45 C.W. 9II. 423.
46 C.W. 9I 152-152.

than bite off and chew a tiny morsel of life. Thus the way that Jung explains the mother, as a symbol, means she has a favourable meaning as well as an unfavourable one:

> *The qualities associated with it are maternal solicitude and sympathy; the magic authority of the female; the wisdom and spiritual exaltation that transcend reason; any helpful instinct or impulse; all that is benign, all that cherishes and sustains, that fosters growth and fertility. The place of magic transformation and rebirth, together with the underworld and its inhabitants are presided over by the mother. On the negative side the mother archetype may connote anything secret, hidden, dark; the abyss, the world of the dead, anything that devours, seduces and poisons, that is terrifying and inescapable like fate.*[47]

Male relatedness to the feminine can be characterised through extremes of emotion running from the polarity of misogyny through to that of "boundless fascination, over-valuation and infatuation".[48] The feminine can be both maiden and mother, whore and divinely chaste.[49]

As a symbol, the snake can represent the most primitive form of mental life. Its image mirrors the lowest functions of the reptilian brain and the spinal cord. In consequence, it can be a symbol of evil lurking within the psyche and creating opportunities for corruption; but as the carrier of those aeons of experience that shaped instincts through evolution, the serpent can herald that power which heals through the wisdom of healthy functioning.[50] On the one hand, it appears in the Bible as the personification of evil and, on the other, it is the symbol of healing in medical science. The archetype of the child looks forward to what is to come and backwards to what was. The archetype of the self is both "male and female, old man and child, powerful and helpless, large and small".[51] In the same way,

---

47 C.W. 9I.158.
48 C.W. 9I.141.
49 C.W. 9I.356.
50 Aion C.W. 9II.369, 402; 9.I.567.
51 Aion C.W. 9II.355.

the concept of God in primitive thought embraces both that which is to be worshipped and that which is to be feared.[52] This concept is reflected to a degree in the Jewish tradition; since with absolute justice all would perish under the weight of divine retribution for sin, but with divine mercy all might be spared, and chaos might reign, the world is in fact held between survivable polarities. When we enter the Christian era, we encounter the concept and person of the Saviour, from whom, in the words of the liturgy, "all good things come". The figure of Christ is the personification of divine love but, in setting up that extreme, the antichrist is brought into Scripture as an adversary and figure of ultimate dread. Jung would explain the figure of the antichrist as a psychological necessity: the proclamation of the "all good" has to be balanced by the appearance of the "all bad". This is not a contradiction of divine revelation but an instance of how the mind balances everything according to its own internal laws. When people proclaim themselves to be the elect of Providence, the air is pregnant with the potential for violence against those opposed to them.

Perhaps it really is the case that in life you basically have two choices. You can live either in reality or in a myth. You can either live honestly or dishonestly. In Jungian terms you could say that you can either acknowledge your shadow-side or you can reject it. A classic Freudian narcissist will do the latter. This may account for his sense of rage when events beyond his control prod him into remembering it. Living with your shadow means a life of some discomfort. When things go wrong, any part in it that is your fault will be clear. Other people will acknowledge no wrong at all. Every single day the law courts have plenty of such cases.

Living without your shadow is a distortion of nature, and one that cannot succeed. Here is where one aspect of Jungian theory tends to fit the experience of both criminal practice and mass murder. The shadow will have a life. Where a person sees

---

52 Aion C.W. 9II.191.

himself as spotless, he will see his opponent as vile. Denial awakens the most primitive state within us where we project our hidden self onto the world, distorting reality. Our shadow is in our neighbour: lying and scheming. Our enemy is not simply wrong: he is demonic. This is a concept apart from any explanation based on narcissism. It leads us beyond defending our image and into a realm where we are pursuing phantom images of the unholy. Not in every case, obviously. But there may be a scale of balance in opposites. The more vicious you become, the more your distortion of other people will turn them into monsters. Our self-deceit fosters these emotions. What we see through this unconscious influence confronts us with a precise, but unacknowledged, mirror image of ourselves.

You might analyse the examples in the first chapter by saying that Franz Stangl, MD, MG and PJ denied their shadow until it killed them or caused them to kill. You might say that KE and SO'R were unwittingly touched by their victims in some aspect of their hidden personality that evoked an outburst of the shadow within. However, life is life and I don't think that any one theory can be pressed into explaining all facets of human behaviour. Truth then ceases to have the upper hand and distortion replaces it.

Jung would argue that there is something more than the influence of narcissism, as identified by Freud, at work here. He claimed that the shadow could be spurred into action by false pride.[53] Certainly, threats to a person's self-regard are a common cause of violence. In historical terms, refusal to back off from a hopeless encounter, such as the Vietnam War, can be pride based.[54]

---

53 Jung claims that evil is an immense psychological power and that we are prone to be made into nothing more than its instrument through the action of the anima, in a man, and animus in a woman; C.W. 10.451; C.W. 9II.422.

54 See, for example, S. Karnow, *Vietnam: A History* (London, 1994) pp. 336, 337, 358, 377, 391, 419, 441, 592, 595, 615 and 659; and R. McNamara, *In Retrospect: The Tragedy and Lessons of Vietnam* (London, 1995) p. 124 quoting a statement from the CIA's Board of Estimates: "The loss of South Vietnam and Laos to the

Whatever proof that Jung offered in support of his theories, it was not enough for most of the scientific community. For them, what was impossible was the notion that thoughts seem to pass, as part of our genetic make-up, from generation to generation.[55] Jung never said this. He said that our mental inheritance made us human and that with it came the psychological drives that were specifically human. Our unconscious mind organises images and ideas in ways that reflect the experience of the human race, so it is to be expected that people respond to, and create, symbols that speak in the same way to all cultures and eras.[56] Even when people go mad, their craziest idea has to correspond to something within not just their mind but our own.[57] When a person becomes possessed by the image of an instinct, another way of describing an archetype, he becomes like an animal driven to react.[58] The more you are possessed by your shadow, the image of evil within, the more precisely will you construct the right lie in order to create the situations that cause other people to hate like you do. Does any of this explain the myth of child murder that dominates the worst demonising fantasies?

The symbol of the ass can relate in mythology to the false god of a treacherous people. Jung notes that it occurs in myths about a people on whom evil fantasies are projected, even as far as falsifying confessions. It occurs in Roman fantasies about the early Christians and in Christian fantasies about the Jews and

---

Communists would be profoundly damaging to the US position in the Far East, most especially because the US has committed itself persistently, emphatically, and publicly to preventing Communist takeover of the two countries. Failure here would be damaging to US prestige, and would seriously debase the credibility of US will and capability to contain the spread of communism elsewhere in the area"; and see also McNamara. Pp. 106, 136, 106–7, 136, 146–7.

55 A striking example of this is S. Pinker, *The Blank Slate: The Modern Denial of Human Nature* (London, 2002), which contains no reference to Jung despite dealing with the issue of the inheritance of forms of ideas.

56 C.W. 8.440; 9I.89–90; 9II.12; 8.397–404.

57 C.W. 9I.496.

58 C.W. 9I.97–99; 9II.192.

also in Egyptian mythology.[59] The murderous game of ball with a living child he identifies as the recurring motif for a secret rite that is always connected to an accusation, against an excluded group, of child sacrifice.[60] Throughout human culture, patterns occur which are directed to the expression of the same underlying ideas, but which are not solely explicable on the basis of borrowings from one culture to another.[61] Jung would also point to the fact that Christ was prefigured in the early legends of pre-Christian groups, that the Virgin birth as the sign of the arrival of a great hero is part of human mythology and that the Eucharist, as the receiving of the body of a divine, being occurred in Central American culture prior to the arrival of Christian missionaries.[62]

Jung offered very little in the way of proof for his theories. He asserted that his theory of the universal contents of the unconscious mind was based on the study of myth and on dream analysis from divergent world cultures, including that of African Americans. He claimed that he was driven to conclude that his idea of an internal force for organising images was inescapable when in 1906 a schizophrenic patient told him of a fantasy that precisely corresponded to an ancient religious liturgy. The patient could have known nothing of this.[63]

---

59 Aion C.W. 9II.128-129; 9.I.463; Cohn, pp. 1-5.

60 C.W. 9I.323-324.

61 For instance see Aion C.W. 9II.176-177; 9.I.643 and 516. Examples of these include the mandala symbol as the expression of a desire to order a disturbing experience, and the fish symbol as an expression of the archetype of the self and the medium in which it moves, namely the unconscious. See C.W. 9I.627-714, 645, 711; 9II.59-60 and C.W. 9II.127-226. These images occur despite our lack of any conscious knowledge of them.

62 On the prefiguration of Christ see C.W. 9II.130, 147. On the Virgin birth see C.W. 9II.164-165. On the Mass see C.W. 11.339-375. On the universality of the symbols of religious experience see C.W. 11.1-168.

63 This patient asked him to look directly at the sun and to blink and to waggle his head from side to side. In the context of delusions that the patient was God-the-Father and God-the-Son, he believed him-

In an attempt to validate Jung's concept of archetypes on the level of natural science, Anthony Stevens, one of his followers, reordered any awkward aspects of the theory. As proof of the repetition of the form that ideas tend to take on, he gives an example of how finches inherit a fear of birds of prey. Most finches live in proximity to predator birds and so appear to learn to fear them partially, at least, on the basis of experience. Is it possible to react to an internal image without being taught that it represents danger, and without ever having seen it before? There are no birds of prey on the Galapagos Islands. Finches there have evolved from an original single species into fourteen different species, each successfully occupying different ecological niches. Their success in survival, adaptation and propagation has been due, in large measure, to the absence of any bird of prey in the remote environment to which storms blew their ancestors hundreds of thousands of years ago. Because a main predator was not reducing the finch population, it increased in numbers. That, in turn, increased competition for the food and shelter to be found in the same environment. That intra-species competition resulted in multiple adaptations to different microenvironments, which displaced the struggle for survival, through over-population by the same

---

self to control a divine wind that streamed from the sun through a phallus. This notion came to him unprompted in visions and it was this image that he wanted his doctor to see in order to confirm his own greatness. Years after this encounter, Jung came across a book describing visions which were induced through participation in the Mithraic liturgy, first published several years after the committal of the patient, and about which he could not have been aware. See C.W. 5.149-154, 223-224; 9I.104-110. It contained this passage: "Draw breath from the rays ... the path of the visible gods will appear through the disc of the sun, who is God my father. Likewise the so-called tube, the origin of the ministering wind. For you will see hanging down from the disc of the sun something that looks like a tube. And towards the regions westward it is as though there were an infinite east wind. But if the other wind should prevail towards the regions of the east, you will in like manner see the vision veering in that direction". This is quoted in C.W. 9I.105. For other examples see C.G. Jung, *Man and His Symbols* (London, 1978) pp. 58–64.

species, into distinct and less competing functions. Did these new species also adapt away from fear of predators? In 1939 an ornithologist sent thirty finches from the Galapagos Islands to California. Despite the passing of many thousands of generations since their ancestors had encountered a predatory bird, the finches brought in cages to America cringed and gave out alarm calls when put in sight of a raven or hawk.[64] The point is that the animal responded immediately to an image: a symbol locked in its mind though unused over many generations since that image was last seen. There is only one other example that I have been able to find to add to this. Deer can be deterred from visiting garden areas in Britain by the deliberate placing of lion and tiger droppings around the periphery. This response of fearing a prime predator remains innate, despite a gap to perhaps the last Ice Age since their ancestors were last preyed upon by big cats.[65] It is not learned by experience or from example.

I go back to the point where, it seems to me, Fromm's analysis takes his theory a step too far. Whether in individual or group narcissism, there is no foundation for saying that an enemy can be seen as demonic.[66] Fromm says that the narcissist attacks any pricking of his self-regard defensively. He says that it is like invading the space of a territorial animal. But it isn't. The animal will chase you off. The notion does not explain how a person can be seen as an enemy: as loathsome, despicable, vile, devilish and incorrigible. Nor does it help us understand how it becomes necessary to murder people en masse, to treat them worse than animals and to indulge, apparently, in enjoying their suffering. I do not think that it is enough to explain this, as Fromm does, on the basis that torturing another person makes us feel more alive. Why

---

64 This example is taken from A. Stevens, *Archetype: A Natural History of the Self* (London, 1982) p. 48.

65 See the *Independent*, 11 February 1994, 22L. Temple Grandin's work on the primacy of images in animal thinking can be argued to support the dynamism of visual symbols in instinct: T. Grandin, *Thinking in Pictures: And Other Reports from My Life with Autism* (New York, 1996) pp. 19–42.

66 Fromm, p. 276.

not torture a dog in private? No, I think that it has something to do with an image in the external world that may correspond to something that is already inside our minds.

I mentioned the mythological nature of the worst fantasies that people have about other people simply because I cannot see any other way of explaining the vicious images that hate throws up. Myth, after all, is also bound to have a dual function, good and bad. It warns us about life's dangers and teaches us about how our minds work. It also produces the most fantastic nonsense about the greatness of our group and our leader and the devilish nature of anyone who opposes our plans. Allied to truth, myth is an aspect of human wisdom. Allied to lies, myth distorts and carries the dynamic of hatred towards cruelty and murder.

CHAPTER 3

Inverted Thinking, Mythical Thinking

O NCE THE NAZI PARTY took power in Germany in 1933 it began to incarcerate anyone who disagreed with it. Concentration camps for "Enemies of the State" were established on a similar model to those for "Enemies of the People" in the Soviet Union. After that came "euthanasia institutes", where the mentally ill were murdered, and eventually extermination camps where the dominant task was death. Anyone entering a concentration camp was bound to witness, if not suffer, ugly scenes of cruelty. Physical punishment had been abolished in Germany in 1918 with the collapse of the monarchy. As soon as it became necessary for the Nazis to concentrate, as they put it, their enemies, they reintroduced it. Since their official line was that labour under military discipline would rehabilitate the inmates, flogging was applied to the tiniest breach of discipline: endurance in the beneficial influence of work would make them fit to be freed. Hence "Arbeit Macht Frei", the vile slogan first placed over the concentration camp in Dachau and then over the death camp in Auschwitz.

One of those sent to Dachau in 1934 saw a flogging for the first time. For an infringement as petty as the theft of a few cigarettes by two prisoners, the camp was assembled to see the punishment. The duty officer read the sentence. The prisoners' hands and head were held and he was spread-eagled across the punishment bench. The first man reacted without a sound to twenty-five lashes of a rod across his back by two bloc leaders striking him alternately. The second man was a political prisoner. He screamed wildly and, all through the punishment, tried to tear himself free. It was horrific to watch, as the witness explains:

> *I stood in the front rank and I was, therefore, forced to watch the entire procedure in detail. I say forced because if I would have stood further back, I would not have looked. Hot and cold chills ran through me when the screaming started. In fact the whole procedure, even the first beating, made me shiver.*

When Dachau was changed from a prison to a concentration camp, many of the original prison staff remained on. The witness to the beating also made the acquaintance of the official who had the task of flogging prisoners under the monarchy. He provided this picture:

> *This coarse and depraved man always smelled of alcohol and to him all prisoners were only numbers. One could very well imagine him as a person who liked to beat people. In the solitary confinement area of the basement I once saw the punishment bench and the canes that were used. My skin crawled as I imagined the "bonebreaker" using them.*

Naturally, he learned to avoid scenes of violence as much as possible and, if forced to watch, he retreated to the back row.

So, who was this sensitive person? He was Rudolf Höss, member of the SS, officer in the guard at Dachau, adjutant to the governor of Sachsenhausen and, ultimately, Kommandant of Auschwitz.[1] After the Second World War, he was captured in Poland and, while awaiting the death sentence, he wrote his memoirs, which I have just quoted.

---

1   S. Paskuly (ed.), *Rudolf Höss Death Dealer: Memoirs of the SS Komandant of Auschwitz* (New York, 1996) p. 82.

Rudolf Höss, as commandant of Auschwitz, was the final authority within a camp that murdered hundreds of thousands of people. But, he writes, it was not his responsibility. In his 1947 memoir, he emphasises his own qualities of personal kindness by describing his relationship with his family in glowing terms.[2] When they visited him, he arranged picnics and horse riding with his wife and children. They enjoyed the idyllic countryside that surrounded the death factory. As a recreation from this work he found peace among the horses in his personal stables: "my darlings", is how he describes them.[3] He declares that he hated cruelty and details how he shunned scenes where prisoners were violently treated. He avoided any "trouble". The "consignments" of people who were to be murdered arrived by train. "Trouble-makers" were identified immediately upon their arrival. On his orders, they were taken behind a nearby building and shot in the head. This avoided the kind of nastiness that he could not bear to witness.

There was, as he describes it, the strain of killing women and children, the difficulty of avoiding questions from prisoners about their families, and the grim duty of presiding over executions.[4] So, according to himself, he was a victim of a kind. In reality, he was a ruthless killer. Höss was promoted to Chief of Concentration Camp Inspectors and transferred to Berlin to administer the system. When Himmler wanted the Hungarian Jews exterminated in 1944, he was posted back to Auschwitz to oversee their murder.[5]

Is self-inflation a basic component of evil? If it is then self-inflation, and the degradation of others that apparently goes with it, should be found in the memoir. And it is. He describes how in 1923 he had been convicted of killing a man and sentenced to ten years imprisonment. The victim had been a fellow member of a Freikorps unit, one of a number of right-wing

2 Paskuly, p. 186.
3 Paskuly, pp. 160–4.
4 Paskuly, pp. 28,82–3,100, 137, 156, 162.
5 See the epilogue by the editor in Paskuly, pp. 196–205.

groups that attacked communists. Höss claims that the deceased had betrayed their group and been sentenced by "a tribunal" to be beaten to death. The prosecution accused Höss of being the ringleader and the actual killer. He knew, according to himself, that he was not but, in order to protect the killer, he took the blame while his murderer comrade was freed. What greater nobility is there than this? While his memoir avoids Nazi ideology, beyond blaming it for inciting cruelty in the guards, not in himself, there is no doubt that he was committed to their worldview. His demons were the enemies of his ideology. They were as mythically evil as his group was good.

Some theorists have said that mere belonging to a group identifies all outsiders as less human, but this seems to me to be wrong. A group that recognised its limitations and acknowledges its faults is the same as a person with basic humility. Neither is likely to generate mythological language to glorify themselves and denigrate their enemies. Deceit is also likely to be kept in check.

It is revealing how Höss writes about the Jews. From his time in Dachau, Höss observes that the Jewish prisoners "protected themselves in a typically Jewish way, by bribing their fellow prisoners".[6] In general, he observes that his Jewish victims had a strong sense of family; clinging to each other "like leeches", is how he describes a quality that is usually a compliment. He also claims that they betrayed the hiding places of those who had escaped capture.[7] At the end of his memoir, he writes that the mass extermination of the Jews was "absolutely wrong", not for any moral reasons but because it had put back the cause of anti-Semitism and brought the hatred of the world on Germany. Because of this, he claimed, the "Jews have come much closer to their final goal" of world domination.[8]

In February 1943, when the murder of the Jewish people was at "maximum efficiency", one of the propaganda directions

---

6   Paskuly, p. 139.
7   Paskuly, p. 160.
8   Paskuly, p. 183.

issued by Goebbels to Nazi officials for their public statements, made this claim:

> *If we lose the war, we do not fall into the hands of some other states, but will all be annihilated by world Jewry. Jewry is firmly decided to exterminate all Germans. International law and international custom will be no protection against the Jewish will for total annihilation.*[9]

Hitler and his group set out to create a society based on their own distorted view of reality. Yet, they could not prevent themselves, in speaking about others, from describing their own character. Their faults appeared in others, fantastically magnified as in a nightmare.[10] As the Nazis were building up a society based on self-aggrandising aims, lies, arbitrary arrest and murder, Hitler complained that outside Germany: "Something should be done to prohibit the poisoning of public opinion among nations by irresponsible elements orally or in writing, and in the theatre or the cinema".[11]

Bauer, in his analysis of the Holocaust, writes that the Nazis "accused the Jews of wanting to do what they, the Nazis, were out themselves to do: control the world and annihilate their enemies". The Nazi leadership were the directing force of injustice in occupied Europe, yet, continually, this process was blamed on the Jewish people. Dawidowicz writes that what the Germans hated and feared most in themselves "they projected on to the Jews, endowing the Jews with those terrible and terrifying attributes they tried to repress in themselves". Even in his last military order on 15 April 1945, Hitler blamed the "Jewish Bolsheviks"

---

9 Deutscher Wochendienst, quoted in R. Hillberg, *The Destruction of the European Jews* (Chicago, 1961) p. 655, in turn quoted in N. Cohn, *Warrant for Genocide: The Myth of the Jewish World Conspiracy and the Protocols of the Elders of Zion* (London, 1996) p. 228.

10 C.W. 10.45.

11 Speech by Hitler 21 May 1935, quoted in W. Shirer, *Berlin Diary* (New York, 1941) for the same date. References here are to date entries and not page numbers. See also the article by Breda O'Brien "Outrage is no response to unpalatable truth" the *Irish Times*, 5 February 2005.

for the war and claimed that it was the aim of this phantom group "to reduce Germany to ruins and to exterminate our people".[12] Of course, it was nothing to do with him. It is useful to label the phenomenon of projection as an "inverted picture".[13]

Having split up Poland with Hitler, in August 1940, Stalin at last achieved the murder of Trotsky; his former comrade and rival for the leadership of the Communist Party. He had him followed to his exile in Mexico and killed. Since fleeing Russia, Trotsky had remained a thorn in Stalin's side, constantly writing that he had betrayed the ideals of communism and exposing his show trials as frauds. He then began work on an uncomplimentary biography of Stalin. This was intolerable to the dictator. An agent of Soviet power was dispatched to deal with him. His killer posed as a supporter. He gained Trotsky's confidence to the extent that he was admitted to his study. There, he smashed in Trotsky's head with an axe, spattering his blood over the manuscript.[14] Stalin celebrated the murder and had it publicised as justice in the State-controlled media. The dictator was shown the draft of an article that was to be published in the Soviet press. It was entitled "The Death of an International Spy". This met his approval, but only with the addition of a number of his own amendments. These described his former rival for the mantle of Lenin as "an organiser of murders", and someone who had "taught people how to murder behind one's back". Stalin had, by this time, murdered so many of the early founders of the Soviet Communist Party that by the eighteenth Congress, in the year before Trotsky's death, less than one-fifth of the delegates had joined the party before 1920.[15] Yet, his amendment to the pen portrait of Trotsky described the

---

12 L. Dawidowicz, *The War Against the Jews 1933–1945* (London, 1983) pp. 210, 211.

13 Y. Bower, *History of the Holocaust* (1982) pp. 83–5.

14 I. Deutcher, *Stalin: A Political Biography* (London, 1982) pp. 379–82.

15 A. Antonov-Ovseyenko, *The Time of Stalin: Portrait of a Tyranny* (New York, 1981), quoted in F. Chalk and K. Jonassohn, *The History and Sociology of Genocide: Analyses and Case Studies* (Yale, 1990) pp. 305–309.

deceased as having "organised the villainous murders of Sergei Kirov, Vilerian Kubyshev and Gorky". Stalin added a curious detail: Trotsky, he wrote, "has the stamp of an international murderer and spy on his brow".[16] The notion that an enemy is evil because his badness is a physical part of him is an aspect of demonic projection. We will return to it.

Example can be piled on example of inverted thinking. How it happens and what causes it to drive on violence is what is more important. The inversion of thinking in the cases of Stalin, Hitler and their henchmen was of the most extreme kind. There was a precision in their statements that looks ironic because it describes themselves. Any sense of self-deprecation was, however, absent from their personalities. Instead, deceit was the trait that most defined how they acted. However, they saw themselves as having a mission. Hitler and Stalin had, they fantasized, a special task in the world; the ultimate burden of changing the face of civilisation. Heaven was to replace earth: each had the necessary formula, if only opposition could be crushed. Apart from hiding and projecting their vicious plans of extermination, another dynamic was at work. They acted as part of movements that pursued a mission of transforming society permanently. As the sense of mission of any group becomes elevated to mythological proportions, the history of genocide suggests that anyone who does not agree is seen as despicable. Examples of this imbalance can be found in the worst instances of mass murder.

In societies moving towards aggressive war and mass murder, evil is never seen as arising from within but is projected onto a victim group. The flawed nature of our human state is rejected: good and evil are sundered. Myth seems to reign supreme. Reality, especially that touching on the self, is disregarded. Those intent on destruction can never allow themselves to believe that the wrongs that motivate them may have arisen, even in part, through their own fault. The inflated self-regard of some individual murderers is mirrored in the behaviour of aggressive groups. They are entirely

---

16 Quoted in D. Volkogonov, *Lenin: Life and Legacy* (London, 1995) p. 270.

good even though they are intent on bringing their enemies to a bloody end. All unrighteousness resides in the other and all right-eousness resides in the self. Abbot Robert's account of Urban's II's preaching of the first crusade in 1095 has the pope advocating the invasion of Palestine in exactly this way. In the crank philosophy of the Nazis, the so-called "Nordic race" was the originator of all the advances of civilisation, the bringer of culture to all nations. That "race" was believed to embody in its genetic makeup a supe-rior disposition that made it Nature's overlord of all other races. Its genetic superiority was inherent. It could only be diluted through interbreeding with the so-called "inferior races". "Blood" was the ultimate treasure to be protected at all costs. All Germans, there-fore, could believe that they were a priceless gift to the entire world. Any people, or group, who opposed them were hated. Ordinary people who happened to be Jewish, Slav, socialist, homosexual or Roma became the objects of savage rage. In the philosophy of Turanism, which dominated the thinking of the organisers of the Armenian genocide, the Turkish people were dis-tinguished by their equivalent to "Nordic qualities".[17] Their char-acter was described by one of their principle ideologues as embracing: "open handed hospitality, modesty, faithfulness, courage, [and] uprightness. Especially praiseworthy was their atti-tude to the peoples subdued by them. Strong was their love of their own people ... they did not oppress other people".[18] The Armenians were the opposite of this. To true believers they were treacherous and disloyal; a grasping people determined to destroy a golden future. To the organisers of the Rwandan genocide, the Hutu were industrious, religious and law-abiding; members of a properly organised, democratic and peace-loving society.[19] A lead-ing Hutu "thinker" described his own people as being "modest,

---

17 For a reference to the attitude of the Khmer Rouge see E. Staub, *The Roots of Evil: The Origins of Genocide and Other Group Violence* (Cambridge, 1989) p. 199. For the crusades see C. Tyerman, *An Eyewitness History of the Crusades: The First Crusade 1096–1099* (London, 2004) p. 2.

18 U. Heyd, *Foundations of Turkish Nationalism: The Life And Teachings Of Ziya Gökalp* (London, 1950) p. 29.

open, loyal, independent and impulsive" while the Tutsi were con-
demned as being "masters of deceit ... dictatorial, cruel, bloody ...
arrogant, clever and sneaky". More generally, the majority group
were able to feel they were the victims of bloody aggression by the
opposition Rwanda Patriotic Front, all of whose actions were seen
as being designed to smash the harmony that was achieved when,
as leaders of the Tutsi minority, they were expelled from
Rwanda.[20] Who expelled them and was it right? They never asked.

Projection seems integral to organised destruction. The historian Alan Bullock offers an observation which points up this
dynamic. He wrote that Hitler, in his speeches, habitually placed
himself on the defensive, as if it was him and his people who were
the victims. His custom was "to accuse those who opposed or
obstructed him of aggression and malice, and to pass rapidly from
a tone of outraged innocence to the full thunder of moral indignation". Germany was never to blame: "It was always the other
side that were to blame, and in turn he denounced the
Communists, the Jews, the Republican government, or the
Czechs, the Poles and the Bolsheviks for their 'intolerable' behaviour which forced him to take drastic action in self defence."[21]

Conflagrations of violence do not happen accidentally, no
more than an individual can accidentally become a murderer.
When people unbalance themselves to mythological proportions
of self-good and opponent-evil, they become dangerous on an
individual level. For a mass conflagration to take place, society
must be carried along. The instrument of this ultimate crime is
deceit.

Carl Jung thought that people who shared a fundamental
ideal identified unconsciously with each other to the degree that
they lost their individual identity.[22] Freud had similar ideas. Both

---

19 G. Prunier, *The Rwanda Crisis: History of a Genocide* (Columbia,
    1997) p. 157.
20 Colonel Bagasora in "Yaoundé", 30 October 1995, p. 7, quoted in
    A. Des Forges, *Leave None to Tell the Story: Genocide in Rwanda*
    (London, 1999) p. 123.
21 A. Bullock, *Hitler: A Study in Tyranny* (London, 1954) p. 344.

appear to have been influenced by the work of Gustav Le Bon, his *The Crowd: A Study of the Popular Mind* of 1895.[23] Both were wary of groups. Jung's view was that sharing an emotion could, more easily than with an individual, transform people into beasts.[24] The presence of many people, he wrote, increased the suggestive emotive force of emotion making it easier for the members of the crowd to shed their moral responsibility. Such group experiences took place on a lower level of consciousness than with an individual. People en masse sunk to their lowest level of functioning where there was an innate tendency to savagery.[25] Unconscious forces could then take over, he thought, archaic tendencies that the veneer of civilisation only disguises. Le Bon wrote that even a cultured individual would, in a crowd, become a barbarian: "a creature acting by instinct".[26]

I do not believe that savagery is the inevitable result of a group experience. It could equally be a sense of belonging, or religious ecstasy, which results from a crowd emotion. Of themselves, these do not lead to violence. There is typically a dynamic based on self-inflation and despising others. In this respect, the behaviour of criminal gangs reflects what can happen to larger groups. Criminal gangs are enclosed societies.[27] All share a common purpose, and often a common mythology that is isolated by deceit and secrecy from wider society. Whether that is, or is not, a cause of mental disturbance, I cannot comment. What a criminal gang does is to create an inflation of the living standard of its members. As a result, the self-regard of its members becomes dependant on their enhanced status in the criminal underworld and their abili-

---

22 C.W. 10.852.
23 J. Waller, *Becoming Evil: How Ordinary People Commit Genocide and Mass Murder*, pp. 29–49; and S. Freud, *Group Psychology and Analysis of the Ego* (London, 1921) passim.
24 C.W. 11.23,25.
25 C.W. 9I.225–228.
26 G. Le Bon, *The Crowd: A Study of the Popular Mind* (1895) quoted in Waller, p. 30.
27 R.D. Laing and A. Esterson, *Sanity, Madness and the Family: Families of Schizophrenics* (London 1964, Pelican reprint 1986) pp. 224–5 offers a possible parallel.

ty to adopt a lavish lifestyle. All of this is artificial. It is vulnerable to discovery should anyone, police or journalist, break through the membrane of silence and so burst the bubble. From what I have seen, a decision to kill, or to turn to other forms of savagery, is made by a gang leader when his world is put at risk. He will not be discovered because the entire foundations of his existence depend on what he has created. Nor will another criminal usurp his authority or deal with him dishonestly. If they do, his status and self-regard will burst. The precipitating event can be a double-cross, an invasion of his area of operations, a defection by a gang member or an enquiry by an outsider. It is then that the savagery will erupt. All loyal members of the gang will share the aggressive intent because all of them stand to loose everything. You can blame the result on archaic emotions, if you like, but savagery does not just burst up out of nowhere and for no reason. It is not just a question of sharing a group experience. You have to lower the conscious controls of people. In particular, in a context where they become desperate to protect themselves. The problem is that societies can be manipulated when their ordinary foundations are put under threat. In the worst cases of aggression, the events that draw people into supporting aggression are lies.

Archaic emotions can dominate our thinking when leaders create events that shake people to their core; so that they demand that someone will make the decisions that will relieve them of their fear. Then, they will be more ready to believe that the destruction of an internal or external enemy is justified. Their leaders will act under the appearance not only of "avenging violated rights", or some other justification. They will also typically promulgate "skilfully camouflaged lies ... the results of which have already been calculated" in order to promote conflict and mass murder.[28] The other side is always to blame. This process is deliberate. The enemy always acts in the most savage way, always

---

28 Pope John Paul II in a speech to Ex-Combatants for Disarmament, Rome, 1979, Observatore Romano, November, 1979, quoted in J. Kwitny, *Man of the Century: The Life and Times of Pope John Paul II* (New York, 1997) p. 321.

in an unprovoked situation, while the aggressor's every action is a necessary response to aggression and terrorism. Hate breeds hate and, at some stage, they may both be right. At its worst, two sets of enemies may believe the most vile things about each other while angrily shaking off any notion that the responsibility for the conflict is to be in any way attributed to their own side.

In each of the three most visible genocides of the twentieth century, in Armenia, in occupied Europe under the Nazis and in Rwanda, the conflicts under the cloak of which such mass murder was perpetrated were commenced through deceit. This suggests that it is through lies that our worst aspect assumes dominance. If it gains complete control it can run its course unhindered in aggressive war and mass murder. The describable qualities of our worst side incorporate tendencies to inverted thinking as the product of projection; touchiness in defence of an unreal sense of group mission; the abuse of real events; or the creation of apparent wrongs that are described as proof of the evil character of our enemy. But can it be said that mythical thinking can replace ordinary sense?

Normally, logical thinking seems to have the upper hand in an educated society. However, things are not always normal. There can be circumstances, as Stephen Runciman remarks, "in which dreams and visions" thrive. A situation may evoke an unconscious response simply because its emotional impact over-whelms a rational response. In Irish folklore, extreme positive and negative events, an escape from danger or the death of a loved one, are often ascribed to supernatural influences.[29] Is this because these are situations that are so emotion-charged that they

---

29 S. Ó Catháin (ed.), *Scéalta Chois Cladaigh: Seán Ó hEnrí* (Dublin, 1983) number 5 for a negative experience and number 9 for a positive, are examples. Another instance is the appearance of the cattle-killing prophetesses on the defeat of the Xhosa which is paralleled elsewhere, see N. Mostert, *Frontiers: The Epic of South Africa's Creation and the Tragedy of the Xhosa People* (London, 1992) pp. 1181–26. For Runciman's view see S. Runciman, *A History of the Crusades: The First Crucade and the Foundation of the Kingdom of Jerusalem* (London, 1944) pp. 199-216

just cannot be dealt with any other way? In the 1930s a Romanian folklorist, Constantin Brailion, recorded a ballad of tragic love in the Transylvanian mountains. The verses told how, a few days before his marriage, a young suitor had been bewitched by a mountain fairy who, through jealousy of his human love, had flung him from a cliff where shepherds found the body caught in a tree and carried it back to the home village of his bride-to-be. There, on seeing her betrothed dead, she poured out a funeral lament rich in mythological allusions to the evil spirit who had stolen her beloved. This became the core text of the ballad. Despite the fact that the occurrence giving rise to the ballad was said to have taken place "long ago", Brailion was able to discover that the event had occurred about forty years previously. The heroine, and originator of the ballad, was still living. Brailion found her and spoke to her. He discovered the prosaic truth of her tragedy. Shortly before their intended marriage, her betrothed was in the countryside alone and had slipped and fallen from a cliff. He had not died immediately, but had been discovered by mountaineers who had carried him to the village where, shortly afterwards, he expired. The lamentations, which she had uttered on his arrival, had conformed to the customary rituals of the area and with no allusion to a mountain fairy:

> Almost all the people of the village had been contemporaries of the authentic historical fact; but this fact, as such, could not satisfy them: the tragic death of the young man on the eve of his marriage was something different from a simple death by accident; it had an occult meaning that could only be revealed by its identification with the category of myth. The mythisisation of the accident had not stopped at the creation of a ballad; people told the story of the jealous fairy even when they were talking freely, "prosaically", of the young man's death. When the folklorist drew the villager's attention to the authentic version, they replied the old woman had forgotten, that her great grief had almost destroyed her mind. It was the myth that told the truth, the real story was already only a falsification. [30]

---

30 M. Eliade, *The Myth of the Eternal Return* (New York, 1991) pp. 44–6.

Mythological thinking can sometimes emerge even when peoples' emotions are not stretched beyond breaking point. The potential seems to be there in all of us to identify with individuals and situations on a mythical level. The Canadian writer Robertson Davies gives the example of the Challenger Rocket crash of 1986. Suddenly in a country that prided itself, then, on the division of Church and State under the US constitution, schools were full of children praying to God for divine mercy[31]

In a few of the cases in which I participated as a lawyer, the public imagination was so enthralled that the courthouse trying a murder was full in the middle of the night with people awaiting a verdict, and similarly on a Sunday afternoon. In one instance they were gripped by the perceived personality of the killer and in the other by the nature of the victim. But what did either mean to them? Nothing, certainly on a personal level. What is striking is the degree of identification with something outside of their own lives. Is modern society still prone to thinking in mythical terms, as were the Transylvanian mountain people?

No one should really be much affected by the death of someone that they never knew, or even met. Perhaps there is a logical exception to this. If, for instance, a singer whose records helped you to sort out the emotions of your adolescence dies, you might feel in some way that you shared something and so feel vaguely sad on their passing. But the potential for being overcome by mythical emotion goes much wider than that. The responses seem hysterical: a question of vast emotions evoked by very little. If I think of the three deaths of people whom I never knew that made the most impact in my culture in my time, I come up with President John FitzGerald Kennedy, Diana Princess of Wales and Pope John Paul II. I can remember the moment when my parents told me about Kennedy's death and how I felt stunned. What did he represent to me, or to

---

31 R. Davies, *Happy Alchemy: On the Pleasures of Music and the Theatre* (London, 1997, edited by J. Surridge and B. Davies) pp. 299–321.

many millions more like me? When Princess Diana was killed, it caused a huge wave of emotion in Great Britain and beyond. And when John Paul II died, millions travelled to his funeral, with no real hope of attending, but with apparently real grief to assuage. What did those figures represent to these people, with their flowers and their tears? A representation is an image. Did they correspond to some pattern in the human mind: the young hero; the eternal feminine; the wise old man? I also wondered about the victims of childhood sexual abuse. By far the greatest number of abusers were fathers, uncles and other male family members; people with authority. Threats by an adult figure kept many of them silent for years after the abuse, and the threats supporting it, had stopped. In a good number of cases, well into adulthood. If not some reaction to authority, what else had been activated in their thinking? Was there something in their minds, as well as in their bodies, to be abused?

What happens if some symbol that is fundamental to the life of a people is destroyed? In an individual the result can be a resort to mythical thinking in an attempt to explain the inexplicable. Jung writes that mental fatigue, bodily illness, violent emotions and shock can cause a loss of conscious function.[32] Repressing the shadow, he says, requires considerable energy. Thus, if people are stirred to violent emotion by events such as the destruction of a symbolic building, the murder of a head of State or an atrocity against someone of their number, then we may find ourselves pulled towards violence against those who we previously merely despised. In these circumstances, Jung might reason that unconscious drives had taken the place of conscious thought.[33]

Mass murder has been given a free reign where these plunges into emotion have been deliberately engineered, or exploited, by a controlling group. If the worst documented occurrences of human destruction can be taken as evidence of a general tendency, the population was, in each case, carried

32 C.W. 9I.213–214.
33 C.W. 9II.53.

along by deceits that now make it almost impossible to define what happened. This is not surprising. Lies conceal and distort reality. It is hard to sort out the present or to tell precisely what happened in the past, but you cannot tell the future. Murderers sometimes do. The enormous tension of holding back on planned violence can make a person speak where it is unwise to. In one case, BN, a person later convicted of murder told a plumber that visited his home that his spouse might soon die in a house fire. Exactly that happened the next day. One might feel safe in making an inference, as a lawyer might say, that deliberation is behind any event that sets the scene for destruction where those who demand violence have exactly predicted how it will happen. Characteristically, in such circumstances reality is suppressed and the control of all thought is channelled in favour of a general and violently enforced obligation to believe lies. In 1969, the government of Iraq required the population to believe that elements within the country were moving to smash the revolution, which founded the Ba'ath party state, and to take power. In a totalitarian state, that kind of situation justifies repressive measures. That is why such things are said. It is also why events are organised to paint them up as the truth. Total control is the objective. The "traitors" referred to, "fifth columnists", as they were called in Iraq, were supposed to have embarked on a reign of terror against the civilian population, randomly attacking the centre of Baghdad with car bombs. However, some of these car bombings had actually been announced in the daily newspapers before they had even occurred. If these car bombs had exploded before they had been reported on, mere suspicion as to the cause of them would have replaced certainty.[34]

Suspicion is all that we now have in relation to the key events that allowed the seizure of power in Germany and Rwanda. Those actions set the scene for the mass murders that followed. When the worst side of our nature controls us we are

---

34 See S. Al-Khalil, *Republic of Fear: The Politics of Modern Iraq* (London, 1991) pp. 51–2.

liable to commit murder. When the worst of our kind control society, then mass destruction can happen. Is this why aggressive groups tend to be totalitarian? Hitler's first cabinet meeting as Chancellor of Germany dissolved itself after passing a resolution to call further elections. Characteristically, the stated reasons were a combination of the touchy inversion of blame and deceit: the centre party leaders could not be worked with because they had made "impossible demands". The communist and socialist parties, with 221 seats out of the available 572 in the Reichstag, compared to the Nazi's 196, were the main stumbling block to their ambition for total dictatorship. The complete abrogation of power to Hitler required a major polarising event that could make it come to pass: one that would both turn the people against the communists and justify ultimate measures against anyone who was not openly on their side.

On 27 February 1933, the Reichstag burnt to the ground. Rushing to the burning building, Hitler proclaimed that the fire was "something really cunning, prepared a long time ago".[35] What did he mean? Four weeks before, writing on the day after the first Nazi-led cabinet meeting, Josef Gobbles had confided a prophecy to his diary: "In a conference with the leader we arrange measures for combating the Red terror. For the present we must abstain from direct action. First the Bolshevik attempt at revolution must burst into flame. At the given moment we shall strike"[36]. The main fires at the Reichstag were set with large quantities of chemicals and were seated in many different places in the building. Expert evidence, at the later arson trial, put this feat beyond the command of a person acting alone. A Dutch communist arrested at the scene was blamed. He

---

35 The account that follows is mainly taken from W. Shirer, *The Rise and Fall of the Third Reich* (London, 1964). Modern historians are not inclined to refrain from passing judgment on the cause of the fire. For example, see I. Kershaw, *Hitler* (1998) pp. 456–62. Jung in his essay "After the Catastrophe" was of the view that the fire was caused by the Nazis: C.W. 10.409.

36 Quoted in Bullock, *Hitler*, p. 237.

apparently had managed on his own to start some small fires peripheral to the main conflagration. He had earlier been arrested for fire setting elsewhere, but was then carefully ushered by members of the Nazi militia towards the Reichstag. He claimed that he had acted alone. Even if that was the truth, the idea of one individual setting fire to the Reichstag as a protest did not fit with Nazi plans. It suited them to proclaim the event as "the beginning of the communist revolution". This gave them a justification to arrest all communist officials, to ban their publications and to institute a reign of terror through the device of "protective custody"[37] under the emergency law "for the protection of the people and the State".

Inside Germany, the electorate were subjected to a barrage of deception. With the media resources of the State at their disposal, the Nazis proclaimed the discovery of evidence, which was never published, of a planned "communist uprising". Adolf Hitler was presented as the defender of the German people. He was to be their saviour against the demonic plans of the communists to destroy government buildings, to use children as a shield for terrorists, and to unleash civil war. [38] Apparently acting reasonably in the face of these plans, Hitler proclaimed that after the elimination "of the communist danger" things would get back to normal.[39] The reality was that the Nazi leadership, in speaking about the supposed plans of the communists, precisely described their own. Why did the German people not resist these lies? The answer of Sebastian Haffner, who lived through this, is that the German people suffered a collective mental collapse. As he puts it, the result was "a unified nation, ready for anything" that became "the nightmare of the rest of the world".[40]

Every event under the Nazis was a crisis, manufactured or

---

37 See Bullock, *Hitler*, p. 329.
38 Statement of the Prussian government, 28 February, 1933, quoted in Shirer, *Third Reich*, p. 244.
39 See Bullock, *Hitler*, p. 330.
40 S. Haffner, *Defying Hitler: A Memoir* (London, 2002) pp. 79–127.

misrepresented to allow aggression. Every subsequent statement by the German government was a lie. In his *Berlin Diary 1934 –1941*, the historian William Shirer recorded the bizarre newspaper headlines that accompanied the events that led to the Second World War. Always, someone else was to blame and always Germany was justified in aggressive action. Hitler had instructed the German minority leader in the Sudetenland that he should "always demand so much that we can never be satisfied".[41] The German newspapers presented the German minority in Czechoslovakia as being subject to gross provocation with stories headed: WOMEN AND CHILDREN MOWED DOWN BY CZECH ARMOURED CARS – EXTORTION, PLUNDERING, SHOOTING – CZECH TERROR IN SUDETEN GERMAN LAND GROWS WORSE FROM DAY TO DAY – and – POISON GAS ATTACK IN AUSSIG?[42] No matter what solution was offered to the German minority it was refused as inadequate "after the events of the last few days". When, five months after bullying the rest of Europe into bullying the Czech government into ceding the Sudetenland to him, the Nazis wanted the rest of the country, the German media carried the same fictitious stories in almost identical terms.[43] "German blood" was flowing and "German honour" was being trampled on. There was the "beaten up student" and the "pregnant German woman" who was walked over. Plans drawn up on Hitler's orders in October 1938 had specified that "to the outside world it must clearly appear that the ... liquidation of the rump Czech State ... is merely a peaceful action and not a warlike undertaking".[44] When Poland's turn came in 1939 they were accused of doing all the things that the Nazi leadership were adept at: aggression against Germany; mobilising for war; oppressing the German minority

---

41 Bullock, *Hitler*, p. 405; and D. Kagan, *On the Origins of War* (London, 1997) p. 391.
42 Shirer, *Berlin Diary*: 19 September 1938.
43 Bullock, *Hitler*, p. 433.
44 General Kietel's Supplemental Directive, 21 October 1938, quoted in Shirer, *Third Reich*, p. 535.

in Posen and Upper Silesia by atrocities extending to castration. These were "barbaric actions of mal-treatment which cry to heaven".[45] Of course, the Poles were also "utterly unreasonable" in refusing German demands. The newspaper headlines included: COMPLETE CHAOS IN POLAND — GERMAN FAMILIES FLEE — POLISH SOLDIERS PUSH TO EDGE OF GERMAN BORDER — THREE GERMAN PASSENGER PLANES SHOT AT BY POLES and IN CORRIDOR MANY GERMAN FARMHOUSES IN FLAMES.

Again, there was a prophet of the forthcoming events. This time it was General Halder, the chief of the General Staff. He confided to his diary, on 29 August, that on 30 August the Poles would come to Berlin to "negotiate"; that on 31 August the negotiations would collapse; and that on 1 September the Germans would use force.[46] Earlier in the month, on 17 August, Halder had made an apparently inexplicable entry in his diary: "150 Polish uniforms for Upper Silesia". On the predicted day for war, at the frontier post of Gleiwitz, a dozen conveniently chosen German criminals, who had been dressed in those Polish uniforms, were shot and left for the Press to photograph. SS men in Polish uniforms seized the German radio station. Over an emergency transmitter the "invaders" broadcast a speech in Polish declaring that Poland was attacking.[47] In a proclamation to the German Army, Hitler announced "a series of violations of the frontier". He claimed "in order to put an end to this lunacy I have no other choice than to meet force with force".[48] The Poles defended themselves as best as they could. Even in this, they were wrong. The German media claimed that, as a lying propaganda scheme, the Poles had bombed their own capital.[49] When Great Britain declared war in defence of Poland a newspaper headline screamed: ENGLAND'S

---

45 Shirer, *Third Reich*, p. 698.
46 A. Bullock, *Hitler and Stalin: Parallel Lives* (London, 1995) p. 677.
47 Shirer, *Third Reich*, p. 719.
48 Proclamation of 1 September 1939 quoted in Shirer, *Third Reich*, p. 723.
49 Shirer, *Berlin Diary*: 11 September 1939.

RESPONSIBILITY — FOR THE OUTRAGEOUS PROVOKING OF WAR-
SAW TO DEFEND ITSELF.[50]

Like the Reichstag fire in 1933, the murder of President
Habyarimana of Rwanda in 1994 cannot be definitely proved
to have been a manufactured event. How an event is used, however, can be more significant than its authorship. The German
people as "victims" of the communists were required to strike
back because the Reichstag fire had been attributed to them. In
the same way, the murder of the President of Rwanda made
him into a symbol of the supposed victimisation by the Tutsi of
the Hutu majority.[51] A constant refrain of justification during
the subsequent organised slaughter of the Tutsi was: "they killed
him".[52]

Of the competing theories as to the attribution of
Habyarimana's death, the most compelling is that his own
entourage killed him in order to assure the retention of Hutu
supremacy in Rwanda.[53] He had finally been forced to sign an
agreement to implement the earlier Arusha Accords; drawing
back into the government the opposition Tutsi-based Rwanda
Patriotic Front, which had been displaced as a refugee group by
earlier conflicts. The percentage of Tutsis in the population
prior to the massacres was estimated at between 9 per cent
(officially) and 14 per cent (unofficially). In terms of political
power, the minority had negligible representation. Of one hundred and forty seven bourgmestres, three were Tutsi; of eleven
préfets one was Tutsi; there was one Tutsi in the entire diplomatic corps, one minister in government, and two out of seventy two members of parliament. The Arusha Accords required
a complete reversal of the policy of exclusion. They provided
for the resettlement of refugees; the integration of the RPF into
the Rwandan army; the stripping of most powers from the

---

50 Shirer, *Berlin Diary*: 4 October 1939.
51 Des Forges, p. 81.
52 Des Forges, pp. 252–3.
53 For the theories see Prunier, pp. 213–29; Des Forges, pp. 5–6, 666;
African Rights — Rwanda, pp. 95–105.

Presidency; the reform of all government institutions by bringing the opposition into power sharing; and the creation of a separation of powers constitution based on the rule of law.[54]

The only certain fact about the event that ostensibly set off the genocide is that the President of Rwanda, travelling in an executive jet with the President of Burundi, was killed at 8.30 on the evening of 6 April 1994 by a ground to air missile that shot down his aircraft as it approached Kigali Airport. He had just been forced at a regional summit meeting in Tanzania to promise the immediate implementation of the Arusha Accords. This reluctant promise had been made in the face of threats from the International Monetary Fund and the World Bank to cancel promised funds. The United Nations had also threatened to withdraw its assistance mission. In effect, the nature of the society enforced by the Hutu power gang behind President Habyarimana was about to collapse.

Within an hour of the plane crash, the Hutu special militia, the Interahamwe, had set up roadblocks and commenced house-to-house searches throughout the capital. On that evening, one of the main organisers of the genocide contacted the U.N. special envoy to Rwanda and told him that they were going to save the nation: "don't worry, this is a coup, but everything is under control".[55] During the week previous to the plane crash, on the 2 April, the government-backed radio station, Radio Télèvision Milles Collines, had announced that a group of military officers had met with the Prime Minister to plan a coup.[56] The next day the station announced: "On the 3rd, 4th, 5th heads will get heated up. On the 6th, there will be a respite, but 'a little thing' might happen. Then on the 7th and 8th and the other days in April, you will see something". This was not the only prediction. Others were even more explicit. The hate-filled and government-financed newspaper Kangura

---

54 Arusha Accords quoted in African Rights, *Rwanda: Death, Despair and Defiance* (London, 1995) p. 35.
55 Quoted in Prunier, p. 225.
56 Des Forges, p. 171.

had predicted in March that, just like President Ndadye of Burundi who had been murdered the previous October, their own head of State was about to die:

> *There is nothing as bad as knowing that bad things [are] about to happen without being able to do anything about them. Last month we saw undeniable signs showing how Habyarimana is going to be killed. And that he would not be killed by a Tutsi, but by a Hutu hired by a Tutsi ...*[57]

In Burundi, the government response to the death of their president in the plane crash was to broadcast appeals for calm.[58] Burundi did not explode into violence. Rwanda did because the event was seized upon to implement detailed plans for the murder of all the Tutsis within the country.[59] Historically, people in Burundi knew about mass murder, they knew how to make it happen and they knew how to prevent it.[60]

Prior preparations included the training of a militia outside the command of the army or police, built around a core of young Hutu males displaced by the ongoing civil war (the Interahamwe); [61] the distribution of weapons, including in particular the importation of enough new machetes for every third adult male in Rwanda (over half a million); [62] and polarising the

---

57 March, 1994 edition of Kangura, quoted in *African Rights – Rwanda*, pp. 73, 74.

58 P.Gourevitch, *We Wish To Inform You That Tomorrow We Will Be Killed With Our Families: Stories From Rwanda* (London 1999) p. 113.

59 African Rights, *Rwanda*, pp. 95–9.

60 In 1972, thousands of Hutu people were massacred in Burundi. It is generally accepted that there was a small Hutu uprising which, however, was taken as an excuse to launch a series of massacres. On that occasion, President Micombero declared that his army had found lists of "Hutu plotters" on the defeated rebels. These, he claimed, were used to track down and execute "only the guilty"; see Stanley Meisler, *Holocaust in Burundi 1972 in Case Studies in Human Rights and Fundamental Freedoms: A World Survey*, edited by Veenhoven, quoted in Chalk and Jonassohn, pp. 384–93.

61 Des Forges, pp. 1–21, 56, 106, 128.

62 Des Forges, pp. 127, 98.

population by lying propaganda against the Tutsis. These plans were implemented immediately the command of the army had been seized.[63] The swift elimination of all opposition leaders, moderate Hutus and prominent Tutsis, created a power vacuum into which the organisers of the genocide stepped. All the while, they proclaimed that the killings were "spontaneous" and that the true responsibility for the slaughter lay with "those who had killed the President". Three weeks after the plane crash, and in the teeth of what he knew was the systematic massacre of hundreds of thousands of people, the chairman of the ruling MRMD government party declared at a press conference in Nairobi:

> It is easy to speak of militias of the MRMD. They are accused of everything. I am scandalised that when two Presidents die ... [the media] don't talk of the death of the two Presidents, but of the behaviour of the militias. People killed on their own, without any authority ... The fundamental problem is that this is a war ... the armed forces had to go to war [against the RPF] and did not have the time to control the population.[64]

On the border with Burundi a notice, posted up entirely without irony the year before the genocide began, proclaimed:

> The Tutsi assassins are out to exterminate us. For centuries the ungrateful and unmerciful Tutsis have used their power, daughters and corruption to subject the Bantu. But we know the Tutsi, that race of vipers, drinkers of untrue blood. We will never allow them to fulfil their dreams in Kivuland.[65]

This theme became typical of the lies justifying murder during the 1994 genocide. Thus, the préfet of greater Kigali referred in

---

63 For the army connections see Des Forges, pp. 56, 146, 150–80, 222, 377, 499.
64 Quoted in African Rights, *Rwanda* pp. 62–3.
65 Leslie Crawford, "Hutus see France as their Saviour", *Financial Times*, 27 June 1994 quoted in *African Rights – Rwanda*, p. 64; see also pp. 41, 69 and 58–85.

newspaper interviews to the "murderous nature of the Tutsis".[66] In the early days of the massacres, many leading members of the minority community were exterminated on the basis of written lists proscribing them for slaughter. Yet, an exponent of the mass murder could declare that the "Tutsis were preparing to kill all of us, they had lists. We were ahead of them by some days".[67] In the immediate aftermath of the genocide, the perpetrators claimed that the huge number of dead bodies in Rwanda could only be explained as the product of massacres that their opponents, in the Tutsi-dominated Rwanda Patriotic Front, had committed. In the refugee camps in Zaire, the perpetrators of the genocide warned their camp-followers not to return to Rwanda, claiming that within the zone controlled by the RPF only five thousand people could be found alive.[68]

A lie is deliberate. The lies used to justify the genocide of the Armenian people are considered in Chapter 8. It suffices to record here that these deceptions practiced on the Turkish people by the Committee of Union and Progress, as the Turanists called themselves, were similar in their brazenness and in the depth of hatred that they managed to evoke. Do the mythical nature of fantasies acted out as facts, in the Nazi, Hutu and Turanist schemes of mass murder suggest that perhaps lies unbalance the mind? In these three instances, the deliberate nature of the process cannot be doubted. It all looks very sane but very cunning.

If a plausible excuse for aggression does not exist, it can always be invented. Retribution seems the most suitable pretext. Governments, which act in this way represent human nature, mired in deceit. When Hitler decided in 1938 that he was strong enough to dismember Czechoslovakia he assured

---

66 Interview in the *New York Times* with Jane Perlez, date not given; quoted in African Rights, *Rwanda*, p. 124.
67 Laurent Bijard – "Tourquoirse, l'operation sans boussole", *Nouvelle Observateurs*, 30 June, 1994 quoted in African Rights, *Rwanda*, p. 915.
68 Gourevitch, 161.

that country that it had "nothing to fear from the Reich".[69] In fact, Hitler had earlier told his military commanders that it was his "unalterable decision to smash Czechoslovakia by military action in the near future": the political leadership was to bring about "the suitable moment".[70] This was explained as "a convenient apparent excuse and with it adequate political justification". Plans for this operation made explicit the deceptive nature of the game about to be played out:

> *Operations preferably will be launched either: (a) after a period of increasing diplomatic controversies and tension linked with military preparations, which will be exploited so as to shift the war guilt onto the enemy; (b) by lightening action as the result of a serious incident which will subject Germany to unbearable provocation and which, in the eyes of at least a part of world opinion, affords the moral justification for military manoeuvres.*[71]

You find a similar lie in the creation of the circumstances for the Armenian genocide. In an order circulated in April 1915 to all local Ottoman authorities with an Armenian population in their jurisdiction, the Committee of Union and Progress spelt out the lies that were necessary to protect their plan of genocide:

> *...The government ... and Committee intending to forestall the presentation of the Armenian Question in any place and in any matter ... has decided to end that question once and for all, by deporting the Armenians to the deserts of Arabia, exterminating that spurious element ... The following serve as an excuse to implement that plan: (a) the Armenian voluntary forces, serving in the enemy armies; (b) the existing [Armenian] parties in the interior of the country, which have organised to give a body blow to our Army; (c) the unaccountable number of firearms and war material discovered and confiscated everywhere in the country.*[72]

---

69 Quoted in Bullock, *Hitler*, p. 394.
70 Quoted in Bullock, *Hitler*, p. 408, address of 30 May 1938.
71 "Case Green" draft dispatch to Hitler from General Kietel on Friday, the 20 May, 1938, quoted in Shirer, *Third Reich*, p. 443.
72 Document quoted in D. Boyajian, *Armenia: The Case for a Forgotten Genocide* (New Jersey, 1972) pp. 318–20.

Nothing the Armenians could do would ever have extirpated their "guilt". Like that of those who confessed under the Inquisition, it did not exist.[73] Furthermore, when the Armenians were attacked then every action in proportionate defence of their rights was to be officially "interpreted" as a vicious and treasonous rebellion.

This process is not that of a sleepwalker. It is a deliberate process made up of secrecy, deceit and self-protection: like a criminal gang. Just as criminals create the conditions for a fraud by drawing on gullibility and greed, leaders can exploit the human tendency for panic to draw them into a net of deception. In a memorandum discovered in Butare after the Rwandan genocide, the anonymous author advocates two techniques for preparing the general population to support "action" against the Tutsi minority. Firstly, events should be falsely created to be attributed to the enemy. The memorandum cautions that the authorship of such events should be concealed, otherwise they would be ineffective. Definite examples of this were given. They included the fictitious RPF invasion of Kigali in 1990 (used at the time to arrest and torture several thousand opponents of the government), and the alleged discovery of caches of arms and of radio communications equipment "for guiding in the RPF". The media reiterated these lies during the genocide as a justification for the slaughter. Secondly, the writer of the memo proposes the inversion of Hutu-supremacist plans. He, or she, called this scheme "accusations in a mirror". In other words, that the enemy should have attributed to them precisely the plan of violently dismembering the Hutu people which was proposed as the only way of dealing with the Tutsi/RPF threat: "In this way the party which is using terror will accuse the enemy of using terror."[74] In the years of tension leading up to the genocide in 1994, the exiled RPF, in seeking a share of power in the government of Rwanda, were continually described in the government-

---

73 Chalk and Jonassohn 260, 268, 282; Walker 201, 214, 221, 232, 235.
74 Quoted in Des Forges, p. 66.

sponsored media as having plans of extermination against the majority population.[75]

While the Butare document was mimeographed, it is impossible that all of those who participated in the genocide, or who urged it on with statements about the Tutsi that seethed in hate, used it as a master plan. The consistent theme in the execution of mass murder is the invention and projection of myths that demonise the victim group and render their destruction legitimate. Is this a natural manifestation of the ideas that the unconscious mind projects when people choose the path of mass murder?

Lies are integral to the disasters humanity engineers to destroy itself with. During the Cuban missiles crisis, President Kennedy rejected a suggestion by his brother, who was later a strong advocate for an honest approach, that an incident should be manufactured that would justify the USA invading Cuba. Robert Kennedy stated: "Let me say, of course, one other thing is whether we should also think of whether there is some other way we can get involved in this, through Guantanamo Bay or something. Or whether there's some ship at ... you know, sink the Maine again or something."[76] The most destructive wars begin with a manufactured excuse, or the abuse of the first plausible justification, for launching disproportionate violence directed towards a repulsive, and therefore secret, aim. Japan's conquest of Manchuria began with a staged attack, supposedly "an act of outrageous violence by Chinese soldiers", on the railway line under Japanese "military protection" in northern China.[77] Mussolini directed Italy into the conquest of Ethiopia by acting on the

---

75 For examples of this see Des Forges, pp. 65–95.

76 Transcript of Tuesday, 16 October 1962: Quoted in E. May and P. Zelikow (eds), The *Kennedy Tapes: Inside the White House During the Cuba Missiles Crisis* (Harvard, 1997) pp. 100–1.

77 On this see L. Young, *Japan's Total Empire: Manchuria and the Culture of Wartime Imperialism* (Berkeley, 1998) pp. 31, 40, 58, 121, 122; P. Duus (ed.), *The Cambridge History of Japan, Volume 6* (Cambridge, 1988) pp. 282–302.

pretext of the necessity "to repulse an imminent threat".[78] Austria was invaded by Hitler's Germany, supposedly "to restore order". Stalin's armies invaded Poland during the Nazi attack "because it no longer existed" and in order to "help" the socialist system's Ukrainian and Byelorussian "brethren".[79] Hitler attacked Russia because the USSR had "combated the German attempt to set up a stable order in Europe" by using "sabotage, terrorism and espionage".[80] Hitler had already invaded Holland and Belgium "to save their neutrality" from a "French invasion".[81] Earlier, Stalin had attacked Latvia, Lithuania and Estonia "to put an end to all the intrigues by which England and France had tried to sow discord and mistrust between Germany and the Soviet Union in the Baltic States".[82] These are but examples of a deadly and timeless pattern.[83]

We may reason that the worst side of human nature is characterised by the projection of our own worst motives onto others, by inflated posturing requiring the defence of prestige and by the selection of deceits that are most likely to plunge societies into armed conflict. However, this does not of itself show that people turn to destruction because of unconscious drives. Inverted thinking may not really exist. Like the individuals who planned the destruction of the Armenian, Czech and Tutsi nations, those who kill could just be coldly calculating. Hatred could, after all, be no more than a logical process: you want something from your enemy and you invent the excuse to destroy him and get it. Is destruction the product of logic, or is myth in some way dominant?

---

78 Quoted in Shirer, *Berlin Diary*: 4 October 1935.
79 See Shirer, *Third Reich*, p. 755.
80 Quoted in Shirer, *Third Reich*, p. 1013.
81 See Shirer, *Third Reich*, pp. 770–83.
82 Quoted in Shirer, *Third Reich*, p. 949.
83 For further instances from the ancient and modern world see Chalk and Jonassohn, pp. 68, 87, 184, 191, 199, 213, 260, 268, 340, 383, 387.

Patterns of Des~~truction~~

DESTRUCTION IS an emotion-charged activity. The emotions that drive hatred happen to people in describable circumstances. Emotions put the position of the conscious personality and the unconscious mind upside down; submerging our will to control our actions beneath an eruption of feelings. When this happens, it is as if our emotions compel us to act according to their will, not ours.

Feelings declare themselves. The process of destruction is not just about murder victims and concentration camps. It is about what people say so as to whip up hatred in themselves and in others. It is about how we create lying justifications for murder. Secretly, we are calculating. We may think that we are in control when we lie to ourselves. But lies infect our emotions so that hatred and unreality are merged. Our lies to others are about the age-old process of whipping up a mob. We declare our hatred so that others will join in it. There are recurring patterns: "Look at our history, the riches of our spirit and our civilisation, that are threatened by them"; "Their latest atrocity proves that there is only one way to deal with these people"; "We have tried only to do good and yet we are victims of aggression"; "Our comrades have been slaughtered but now those who did this will hear from us"; "Negotiation and compromise have failed – there is now no other answer". All the while the focus is on appropriate lies to bolster our own self-worth. When a suitable crisis comes along, people will begin to believe lies such as these. Even

who invent them seem to believe them on some
ey are like the corrupt policemen who "know that the
used did it" and set out to invent appropriate evidence. If that
is so, does it mean that there is no unconscious pattern to how
hatred acts, but only cold cunning?

I believe it is both. The link between unreasoning hatred
and reasoned calculation is deceit. The lies that evoke hatred
may well be thought-through but in those that plan and in
those that kill, you will find weird mythological justifications.
What I want to explore here is whether it really is possible to
explain a recurrent pattern of violence only by logic.
Alternatively, you could ask if the pattern of apparent logic
hides a deeper myth that it serves.

Reason is reflection that is not driven by emotion. It is
detached in time and space from the necessity of immediate
response. Feelings are akin to an instinct. Emotions demand that
we act. They grip us into an urgency of response because the survival of a species, or an individual faced with a deadly danger,
depends upon a total response. A terrified beast is possessed by an
emotion that conditions all of its responses into dealing with the
cause of its terror and that alone. The animal becomes its instinctive response to fear. It cannot express its terror in language. It has
no response except in fleeing or in aggression in defence of its
life. If it had language with which to express itself then it would
speak in the most exaggerated way. Instinctive behaviour is
charged with the most extreme emotions. Since instincts are
preservational patterns of behaviour, only language that reflects
their ultimate purpose in defying annihilation would be adequate. Instinctively driven language, like instinctively driven
behaviour, is extreme in the emotion that it reflects. Like the
alarm cry of the finch, instinctively driven language declares, and
also has the capacity to evoke, extreme emotions.

Mythology also exaggerates. It reflects the otherwise inex-
pressible energy driving the mind. It turns people into royal or
divine beings, protagonists into the servants of absolute evil or
unsullied goodness, and real situations into magic. It speaks in

extreme terms that amplify reality beyond reality. Enemies are demons, heroes are endowed with divine luck, people are all very good or very bad, very old or very young and each character expresses the essence of central human situation as mother, maiden, king, dunce or self-satisfied fool. Human conduct in two different places, or in two eras separated by a long time, can be similar because it may be practical for people to do the same thing in order to achieve the same end. You murder leaders, for example, so that you are not faced with a concerted uprising from an entire people. That makes logical sense. It that as far as any explanation needs to go? Human behaviour patterns, however, are unlikely to be merely based on the cold choice of reason where the declarations that accompany them express reality through dramatic mythological images. The states of mind that characterise those who are intent on aggression boil with emotion. Their declarations seem to reflect the unconscious energy that drives them. When the quality of myth invades the realm of reason, it becomes almost impossible to detach actual events from the overlay of projections streaming from the unconscious. Then you are entitled to wonder: is there something more than the coincidence of the forms of aggression with the aims of an attacking group? Negative myth seems to drive the emotions behind mass murder. There are many aspects to this pattern. Fundamentally, is behaviour in extreme aggression a logical choice or a dynamic based on myth? The main patterns considered here are revenge; the murder of leaders; the murder of children; rape; theft; and victimhood. All of them can be explained as occurring for the nasty, but thought-through, interests of the aggressors. Yet, all of them generate warped justifications: myths and lies in an unholy alliance.

The desire for revenge is an emotion universal throughout human society. In one case in which I appeared for the defence, the family of a girl who had been raped, kidnapped the suspect assailant and held him in a cargo container where they set an Alsatian dog on him. In societies based on the rule of law, revenge behaviour is controlled by systems of justice. The accused is made to suffer retribution, but humanely and only after a proper trial. In popular culture, scenarios are easily presented where we are made to feel that there is such a creature as "an enemy", and that the enemy should get what is coming to him. In the film *The Green Berets*[1] we are drawn into identifying with the emotions of newly arrived American recruits to the Vietnam War in the 1960s. Initially, they are queasy and reluctant to support the behaviour of seasoned veterans in, for example, their methods of questioning Vietcong suspects by torture. When, however, they come to realise the nature of the enemy against which they are fighting, their restraints evaporate. The Vietcong are portrayed as killing and maiming in a vicious and cowardly fashion. Fellow soldiers search for the hidden enemy in the jungle. He never shows himself. Instead of a fair fight, the "greenhorns" witness their fellow soldiers pierced by poisoned spears hidden underfoot or catapulted by the legs against concealed impaling spikes. Because the Vietcong use "inhuman" methods of terror, instead of fighting honourably, they re-define themselves. Our responses are artfully guided into regarding them as a group who deserve the severest retribution.[2] In watching such a film we can feel our emotions re-direct themselves according to a predictable and innate pattern. This is only a film. It is invented; but events are also manufactured.

Stories of the atrocities perpetrated by the enemy are a constant currency of societies engaged in warfare. The barbarous conduct of the enemy evokes innate ideas as to how the enemy should be violently dealt with.[3] It has the power of a myth. Barbarous conduct towards people within one's own group has

---

1   Warner Brothers (1968).
2   In fact the film is not unrelated to actual experience; see J. Sack, *Lieutenant Calley: His Own Story* (New York, 1971) pp. 85, 106, 123; and see S. Babuta and J.C. Bragard, *Evil* (London, 1988) pp. 112–117.
3   For examples see H. Thomas, *The Spanish Civil War* (London, 1990) pp. 144, 201, 279–281; and L. Young, *Japan's Total Empire: Manchuria and the Culture of Wartime Imperialism* (Berkley, 1999) pp. 94, 39, 86–7.

the capacity to evoke the impulse to reprisal. Harold Lawton, a veteran of the First World War, recalled to an interviewer that the intention of the men in his company in shooting the enemy was always to disable, and not to kill them. They hoped that stretcher patrols would later recover the wounded. When, emerging from his trench he was charged by a German, he shot him in the leg. Weeks after this, three of his friends were killed in a bomb blast. It changed his attitude: "If that had happened before I met that German, I would have killed him."[4] Most combatants in the Second World War came from societies with a wide range of attitudes towards violence, but none could be said to be exclusively peaceful. When appropriately inflamed, people found it easy to slip into a pattern of revenge. Of two and a half thousand Australian and British prisoners who were captured by the Japanese only six survived the prison camp at Sandakan. A combination of disease, malnourishment, torture and forced marches accounted for the rest. When the opportunity presented itself, with the defeat and capture of the Japanese combatants, the prisoners' comrades took their revenge. This is how one of them explained his emotions:

We'd beaten up the unarmed Nip working parties lined up on the Sandakan Wharf after the surrender. Rolled quarter-ton drums of petrol over them as they lay there ... that was the way to find criminals. Some of them had done nothing, of course, but what did that matter? A Jap's a Jap. And the embarkation of the sick and wounded, about 2000 of them. When they couldn't climb the ladders we hauled 'em up the ... side with a rope. The lads with the lifeboat paddles were waiting for 'em on deck. Sounded good, the crack of wood on their skulls... Those that fell were kicked in the face; if they couldn't get up, overboard they went ... They died like flies on the trip back ... We tied weights to 'em and cheered as we slid them overboard ... And then the fellow we made dig his own grave. He'd been given a hell of a belting, but he still said he

---

4   Max Arthur – "Lest We Forget", the *Guardian*, 1 November 2005; and see M. Arthur, *Last Post: The Final Words From Our First World War Soldiers* (London, 2005).

*knew nothing about the Sandakan march, wasn't even there. But you
know you can't take a Nip's word for anything ...*[5]

The origins of the Spanish civil war took place against a backdrop of the murder and then the revenge assassination of
prominent individuals from each opposing ideology. The mutual thirst for vengeance came to echo through towns and villages
throughout Spain unleashing emotions that could only be satisfied by engagement in a chain reaction of endless violence.[6]
These are but examples of a behaviour trait in societies that
already contained varying levels of hatred. But what is there to
show innate, or unconscious behaviour?

In the early 1950s the British had to deal with a communist
insurgency in Malaysia. They were advised not to recruit soldiers from among a stone-age group called the Samai. Local
inhabitants knew them as a completely peaceful people who
fled any aggressive encounter rather than run even the risk of
fighting. Over many generations their culture had deliberately
targeted violence as unacceptable: children were rarely struck,
and then only mildly, and animals were killed only for food.
Hostility was culturally unacceptable. Violence was cut off
before it began. Strangers described the Samai as "timid" or
"weak". Those with a passing acquaintance thought of them as
"jolly" or "carefree". Even drunkenness, associated in Europe
and America with a major percentage of crimes of violence, did
not increase their levels of aggression, but was instead manifested in talkativeness or noisiness.[7] These are the observations of
the anthropologist Robert Dentan:

> *Many people who knew the Samai insisted that such an unwarlike peo-
> ple could never make good soldiers. Interestingly enough, they were*

---

5   Clifton, *The Time of Fallen Blossoms* (London, 1950) quoted in J.
    Lewis and B. Steele, *Hell in the Pacific* (London, 2001) p. 239. For
    further examples see pp. 159–240.
6   Thomas, pp. 159–333.
7   Murdoch – Int J Addiction 25, 1065–1108 (1990).

wrong. Communist terrorists had killed the kinsmen of some of the Samai counterinsurgency troops. Taken out of their nonviolent society and ordered to kill, they seemed to have been swept up in a sort of insanity which they call "blood drunkenness". A typical veteran's story runs like this "we killed, killed, killed. The Malays would stop and go through people's pockets and take their watches and money. We did not think of watches or money. We thought only of killing. Wah, truly we were drunk with blood." One man even told how he had drunk the blood of a man he had killed.[8]

The Samai were trained to be fighting men by the British military elite. I do not believe in the notion, so often put about by the leaders of inhuman regimes, of "spontaneous mass murder". All the evidence shows that someone has to organise it.[9] Similarly, leaders need to take charge of a society under threat and organise its defence. You need to lie about that less, perhaps.

When a society is conquered then its leadership needs to be "dealt with". Every human society generates an elite. Some people take over the direction of the organisation of society on behalf of all of its members. The method whereby such an oligarchy is chosen, or imposed, varies with the tradition and history of a people. Nevertheless, in all groups some individuals are looked to for advice or direction; a process whereby the complexity of interpersonal relations is simplified. In this way, large numbers of people are enabled to move beyond the consensus

---

8   Taken from R.K. Dentan, *The Samai: A Nonviolent People of Malaya* (New York, 1979) pp. 58–9.
9   On this, in respect of Armenia see V. Dadrian, *A History of the Armenian Genocide* (Providence, 1997) pp. 145–57; C. Walker, *Armenia: The Survival of a Nation* (London, 1980) 171; H. Morgenthau, *Ambassador Morhenthau's Story* (Ann Arbor, Michigan, 2000) p. 233: on the Holocaust see L. Davidowicz, *A Hollocaust Reader* (New, Jersey) pp. 89–96; on Rwanda see A. Des Forges, *Leave None to Tell the Story: Genocide in Rwanda* (London, 1999) pp. 21, 56, 89–90, 106, 127–8, 144–80, 192, 222–62, 341, 370, 377, 499; and African Rights, *Rwanda: Death, Despair and Defiance*, pp. 454,518,769,361,431,477,511; and for suicide bombers see D. Gambetta, *Making Sense of Suicide Missions* (London, 2005) p. 260.

planning possible with smaller groups and so attain a uniformity of action that benefits the survival of a large society. Human society is stratified according to criteria based on blood relationship, education and a multitude of other factors that are variable with the culture of a society. These factors, in turn, establish qualities that are particularly prized. If a group intends to fulfil an ideological or territorial ambition and another society stands in its way, it makes sense to devise a strategy that undermines that rival. Killing its entire leadership group is, on the face of it, logical. If such a pattern exists in human history then it appears unnecessary to resort to any explanation based on something akin to myth. However, the element of rhetoric accompanying such actions and its relationship to possible instinctive patterns cannot be ignored.

It has been argued that in the ancient world the common people did not count in warfare. If one group conquered another, the subjects of the defeated oligarchy were transferred into the ownership of the victors. Because they counted only as chattels of burden or service, successive overlords may have come and gone leaving their anonymous lives unchanged. With the eradication of its own ruling class the people would have no choice, and might even be glad, to submit to a new regime on its own terms.[10] In the present day, the strategy of leader-eradication in order to weaken an enemy people continues.

Apart from the viciousness of Darfur, according to the human rights organisation, African Rights, the Sudanese government has been engaged in a long-standing campaign to conquer the people of the Nuba Mountains. One primary focus of government efforts is the eradication, or control, of all those who are or might be looked to for leadership. People of the educated or influential sector of Nuba society, have been disappearing through organised campaigns of abduction by the Sudanese military. As well as chiefs and educated people, Nuba

---

10 E. V. Walter, *Terror and Resistance: A Study of Political Violence* (1969) pp. 137–43.

culture reveres traditional wrestlers. As a result of their stature they have become prime targets in this homicidal campaign. A defector, formerly in charge of organising the government strategy, has said that it has been centred on "taking the intellectuals [and] taking the professionals, to ensure that the Nuba were so primitive that they could not speak for themselves".[11] This echoes the determination of the Nazi leadership, on their invasion of Poland in 1939, to liquidate the upper class of that nation, "particularly the nobility and the clergy". They planned to prevent the Polish intelligentsia from ever "establishing itself as a governing class"; those who attempted to take the place of "those capable of leadership" were not to "burden the Reich" but to be "eliminated in their turn". Hitler's purpose in Poland and in Russia was that in the absence of leadership the "Slav sub-humans" would become "cheap slaves".[12] Under Soviet communism we find the same strategy of "beheading the community"; focusing on the eradication of army officers, landlords, clergy and those with an education.[13] The Soviet action was consistent with a strategy of removing all those who might resist the Communist Party's plan of total ideological domination. Within Russia the elimination of the educated, the middle classes, the landlords and the better off among the farming community, had been at the cutting edge of violence since the Bolshevik revolution. On the Nazi invasion of Soviet occupied Poland and of Russia, the Jewish people, who were mythically identified as "carriers of the

---

11 Khalid Abdel Karim al Husseini, Interview with the BBC in Switzerland, 13/6/1995, quoted in African Rights, *Facing Genocide: The Nuba of Sudan* (London, 1995) p. 109, and see pp. 2, 90, 95–109 and 197–99.

12 Document drawn up for Heinrich Himmler, "Some Thoughts on the Treatment of Alien Populations in the East", May, 1940, quoted in A. Bullock, *Hitler and Stalin: Parallel Lives* (London, 1993) 707. See further W. Shirer, *The Rise and Fall of the Third Reich* (London, 1964) pp. 792–9.

13 Bullock, 709. For an individual account of this process by a survivor see E. Wood and S. Janowski (eds.), *Karski: How One Man Tried to Stop the Holocaust* (New York, 1994) pp. 13–25.

Bolshevik bacillus", together with the administrators of Soviet society, were singled out for immediate murder.[14] These plans seem "logical". But, at the same time, a weird rhetoric invades declarations supposedly founded on reason.

If a conquering group plans genocide, it is also logical to lie to its leaders so that the common people will be persuaded by them to submit. A community under attack is compelled to reason that co-operation with the enemy may undermine the anger directed against it. Under Nazi overlordship, the Jewish tradition of service to the community was abused in order to force the setting up of Jewish councils. These, through terror and deceit, became a prime focus of pressure, whereby the coercion of those forcibly appointed leaders in turn influenced those whom they represented.[15] But this process only went so far. The Nazis did not want to deal with real leaders. It made sense to kill all Rabbis first. The Rabbinate was a symbol of cohesion in religious worship and was the court of justice in secular disputes.[16] Without their Rabbi, a Jewish community was leaderless and more inclined to look to the artificial structures set up by the Nazis. Similarly, when the government of Turkey set out in 1915 to eliminate the Armenian nation they first decapitated it. Where the leadership was already known, they were arrested on the basis of lists circulated by the central authority.[17] A strategy of requiring leaders to confess to plans of rebellion was used. In order to identify influence, a demand was made for specified numbers of hidden weapons. When these were produced, the leaders of the Armenian community were identified as those who had acted as spokesmen. They were arrested on a charge of conspiracy against

---

14 On the origins of this myth see R. Pipes, *Russia Under the Bolshevik Regime* (London, 1994) pp. 99–114.

15 See generally L. Dawidowicz, *The War Against the Jews – 1933–1945* (London, 1977) pp. 276–96.

16 For an example see D. Kahane, *Lvov Ghetto Diary* (Massachusetts, 1990) pp. 5–84. On the liquidation of the Jewish intelligentsia see M. Gilbert, *The Holocaust: The Jewish Tragedy* (London, 1990) pp. 166–72.

17 Dadrian, p. 221.

the government. When arms were not available for surrender, the charge was of withholding arms.[18] This indicates something obvious: to kill a leader, you have to identify a leader. Is this process cold and unemotional?

Both in the Rwanda genocide of the Tutsi people in 1994, and in the massacres of the Hutu people in Burundi in 1972 which preceded it, the prime focus of the organisers was in first eliminating the elite of the group under attack. In the earlier massacre, all Hutus with government jobs, with enough wealth to be considered as potential leaders and, eventually, all those with more than basic education, were murdered.[19] Lists of selected targets were a feature of the methodology of both slaughters. Sitting down and drawing up a list of people slated for murder is, on the face of it, a reasoned action. A 1992 memorandum from the Rwandese Ministry of Defence on "identification of the enemy" targeted, in particular, Tutsi who had "managed to infiltrate ... international organisations as officials". In this mythical world a Tutsi could not just take a job. No, taking a job was "infiltration". In pursuit of slaughter, educated people were the first to be killed pursuant to exhaustive lists circulated by local and central government around the country.[20] Where, as might be expected, those listed refused to come forward, or were not betrayed by

---

18 See Melson, "Provocation or Nationalism" in R. Hovannisian (ed.), *The Armenian Genocide in Perspective* (New Brunswick, 1998) p. 63; Dadrian, p. 221. For a personal memoir see H. Riggs, *Days of Tragedy in Armenia: Personal Experiences in Harpoot 1915–1917* (Ann Arbor, 1997) pp. 48–78.

19 Meisler. "Holocaust in Burundi, 1972" in Veenhoven (ed.), *Case Studies on Human Rights and Fundamental Freedoms: A World Survey, Volume V* (The Hague, 1976) pp. 227–32, quoted in F. Chalk and K. Jonassohn, *The History and Sociology of Genocide: Analyses and Case Studies* (Yale, 1990) pp. 384–93. Further references in Chalk and Jonassohn are at pp. 61, 218, 266–7, 268, 291, 339, 404 and 410.

20 See G. Prunier, *The Rwanda Crisis: History of a Genocide* (New York, 1995) pp. 222–4 and see P. Gourevitch, *We Wish To Inform You That Tomorrow We Will Be Killed With Our Families: Stories >From Rwanda* (London, 1999) p. 83.

their neighbours, the killers had to see if they could spot who was educated, rich etc. One survivor of the stadium massacre in Cyangugu described the process:

> *Since they did not know the faces of the people they wanted, people were able to hide ... Absolutely no one responded to the names they called out. They became furious. The called for all men to come out and form lines ... They looked closely at the faces, seeking out educated men or those who "looked" wealthy. They asked between twenty and thirty men to step aside. No one could refuse because the orders were given at gunpoint. They were taken to Gataranda, about one kilometre away, and killed by the militia with machetes.[21]*

How did the militias scouring the faces and hands of captives in Rwanda or Poland actually feel? This kind of work cannot be undertaken with polite diffidence:"Regrettably we must kill you because we need the services of the ignorant workers whom otherwise you might enlighten as to our true nature and who would then be a nuisance to us". In human destructiveness, I have been unable to identify any pattern of logic that emerges isolated from an ideological background. Illogic and myth dominate that landscape. Evil becomes heroism, deceit becomes justification and murder gets painted-up in the colours of the weirdest euphemisms. Heinrich Himmler, leader of the SS militia, which was the vanguard instrument of leader-genocide, and genocide in occupied Europe, felt compelled to remind a gathering of his murder squads one year after the invasion of Poland, that violence in the service of the ideas which they served had done them no inner damage. Rather, "carrying out executions, transporting people away, taking away howling and weeping women" had ennobled them.[22] It was the

---

21 African Rights, *Rwanda*, p. 729. Further references are at pp. 481, 515, 517, 527, 491, 604–23, 729, 733 and 791.

22 Quoted in J. Fest, *The Face of the Third Reich: Portraits of the Nazi Leadership* (London, 1985) pp. 177–8. The documents therein quoted are in turn taken from Trial of the Major War Criminals before the International Military Tribunal (Nuremberg, 1947–1949).

unpleasant duty of "suppressing a rebellious population at a low level of culture". Within the mental world that made these deeds possible, Himmler declared that theft from the booty stolen from his victims was a capital offence. Murderers, after all, had to have standards:

> ... We had the moral right, we had the duty to our own people, to kill this people that wanted to kill us. But we have no right to enrich our-selves by so much as a fur, a watch, a Mark, or a cigarette or anything else. I shall never stand by and watch the slightest rot develop or estab-lish itself here. Wherever it forms, we shall burn it out together. By and large, however, we can say that we have performed this task in love of our people. And we have suffered no damage from it in our inner self, in our soul, in our character.[23]

A group cannot turn itself to the task of mass murder by reason and logic alone. A form of possession must first be made to take a hold. Structures of coercion are indispensable within any society. Societies within the scale of sane values do not need non-sense justifications for the ordinary objectives of common order. A society turned towards aggression is different. The perpetrators of destruction act against a profoundly disturbed backdrop of the most extraordinary ideas. Is the ostensible rationality of an action a sufficient explanation for organised murder?

An apparently rational goal can arise from a mythical ideal. The situations encountered in this work are based upon non-rational schemes of ideas. A community of shared thinking is necessary before people can be moved to dispatch another group. Even where an apparently rational justification is offered for mass murder, a question needs to be answered. What does the rational idea serve, itself or a deeper pattern? It is not right to kill a person. It is wrong to organise a machine integrating military discipline into an engine of mass destruction. A person

---

23 Quoted in Fest, p. 182.

who is a sole murderer is not, in rational human terms, a hero; nor can the scale or objective of homicide change this. It cannot be sane to construct a system of ideas, such as that referred to by Himmler, which underwrites mass murder as service to an ideal. Nor can it be in accordance with reason or logic that anyone should attempt to turn reality on its head in extolling destruction as a virtue. Yet, like individual murder, the process of mass murder is replete with these inverted declarations: the enemy is evil and we are noble; the victim is a thief and we are reclaiming our heritage. Speaking in Poznan in October 1943, at a time when the mass murder of the Jewish people in occupied Europe was nearing completion, Himmler said this:

> *I speak to you here with all frankness of a very serious subject. We shall now discuss it absolutely openly among ourselves, nevertheless we shall never speak of it in public. I mean the evacuation of the Jews, the extermination of the Jewish people. It is one of these things which it is easy to say "the Jewish people is to be exterminated" says every party member "that's clear, it's part of our programme, right, we'll do it". And then they all come along, the eighty million good Germans, and each one has his decent Jew. Of course the others are swine, but this one is a first-class Jew. Of all those who talk like this, not one has watched, not one has stood up to it. Most of you know what it means to see a hundred corpses lying together, five hundred, or a thousand. To have gone through this and yet – apart from a few exceptions, examples of human weakness – to have remained decent, this has made us hard. This is a glorious page in our history that has never been written and never shall be written.*[24]

One wonders where the rationality is in this. He was speaking about murdering an entire religion: men, women and children.

Children are the least empowered group in any society. They are also the most malleable. They can "forget" the past, learn new languages and swear to new allegiances. Children are capable of being re-identified with those who have disposed of their parents. While leader-genocide can be advanced as a logical step in

---

24 Quoted in Fest, pp. 177–8.

the control of a conquered nation, the eradication of the entire population, down even to small infants, is a defiance of reason. After all, they can be used as sources of labour; according to the perverse logic that is becoming so familiar. Reason can be dressed up to justify the total eradication of a population. It can be presented as an aid to the attainment of an objective. Himmler spoke of the need to protect his rule against vengeance. Stalin, late in his life, became worried about the children of those enemies of his whom he had already destroyed: they might be harbouring "vengeful thoughts". Even years after the removal of their parents, the children of purged army commanders, and some of the children of Trotskyites, were arrested.[25] The Zulu chief Shaka justified an order to exterminate an entire tribe of his enemies by denying that women and children were innocents who could cause him no injury. He said: "Yes, they could, they can propagate and bring children, who may become my enemies. It is the custom I pursue not to give quarter to my enemies, therefore I command you to kill all".[26]

The total eradication of the Tutsi population during the Rwandan genocide of 1994 was government policy. The danger of vengeance was also presented as an ostensible rational. The much-touted revolution of 1959 had toppled the Tutsi minority from its traditional position of power and sent many of them into exile. Their children had formed the Rwanda Patriotic Front. It demanded the return of the exiled population to Rwanda and the kind of power sharing promised by the hated Arusha Accords. All Tutsi children were to be killed in the genocide so that this could never happen. The Interahamwe militia, pursuing the murder of an entire population, were exhorted to kill young children. The hate-rhetoric of the government told them that because the RPF invaders of today were the children of yesterday's refugees, the same would happen in a new generation. In an apparent display of logical

---

25 A. Solzhenitsyn, *The Gulag Archipelago* (London, 1974) p. 90.
26 Walter, pp. 137–43.

thought, one group of killers justified the murder of twenty children. Their leader pointed out that the military commander of the RPF had once been a child, one who had been shown mercy in 1959 and allowed to become a refugee: " ... Paul Kagame was three when he left Rwanda. Like him, these ones will come back and bring problems for us. We cannot let them live".[27] This was repeated uniformly throughout the country in ostensible justification of the genocide.[28] The mass media, a prime weapon of this genocide, continually reminded people that to have allowed anyone to escape in 1959 had been "a fatal error".[29]

Logic is not the trigger than unleashes the human destructive drive. Children are murdered en masse out of an inner imperative; a desire to annihilate a line down to the last survivor.[30] The killers are possessed of a warped belief that their hated enemy is constructed of an essence that is ineradicable in him. The myth they follow is that this essence is passed to his progeny, in his blood. That, in the words of one destroyer of Native-American peoples, "a nit would make a louse".[31] Similarly, the German justification for murdering the entirety of the Jewish people was that their nature would never change. The "reasoning" underlying the eradication of all Jewish children in Europe was, according to the Nazis, that anyone of "Jewish blood" was an enemy. There was no thought given to the influences of environment or education. Any Jew had to be regarded as an incorrigible destroyer. Himmler urged that, "Even the brood in the cradle must be crushed like a puffed-up toad".[32] The rhetoric supporting this bizarre notion will be examined later. Recently declassified CIA archive documents

---

27 African Rights, *Rwanda*, p. 560.
28 Des Forges, p. 297, and see pp. 550, 569.
29 African Rights, *Rwanda*, pp. 77, 79.
30 Khemer Rouge slogan quoted in Chalk and Jonassohn, p. 404.
31 Quoted in Chalk and Jonassohn, p. 198.
32 Quoted in M. Burleigh, *The Third Reich: A New History* (London, 2000) p. 613.

reveal the contents of secretly recorded conversations among German prisoners of war in Britain. On a tape recording, from 22 April 1945 made in an allied prison camp, Admiral Engel, Commander of the North Sea fleet is asked whether he believes stories about the Holocaust. He says: "Yes, of course. I have known myself for a long time it was like that. We were at Posen when that man told me how he killed the Jews. I can well remember how he said: 'When I am asked did you kill children as well? I can only reply that I am not such a coward that I leave to my children a job which I can do myself'."[33]

This is an emotion talking. It is far from dispassionate, and far from logical, despite the reiteration of the "guard against vengeance through total eradication" argument. Lieutenant William Caley, convicted in 1971 of the pre-meditated murder of twenty-two Vietnamese villagers, out of between 175 and 400 killed by American troops in My Lai three years earlier, repeated this argument to his biographer. In justifying his actions, he said:

> *"God", people say. "But these were old men, and women and children". I tell you: I didn't see it. I had this mission, and I was intent upon it: I only saw, they're enemy ... And babies. On babies everyone's really hung up. "But babies! The little innocent babies!" Of course, we've been in Vietnam for ten years now. If we're in Vietnam another ten, if your son is killed by these babies you'll cry at me, "Why didn't you kill those babies that day?"*[34]

His underlying attitude is the same as that of Talaat Pasha, one of the architects of the Armenian genocide. He declared that no distinction could be possible between the guilty and the innocent; an entire race must be destroyed because "... those who were innocent today might be guilty tomorrow".[35] He ordered

---

33 See the *Observer*, 20 May 2001, Vulliamy, "Jail Small Talk Reveals Holocaust".
34 Sack, pp. 101–2, original emphasis.
35 Quoted in Morgenthau, p. 223.

the army to kill Armenian children because they could "serve no other purpose than [to] become dangerous in the future".[36] The fact that this was untrue is irrelevant. Are lies the foundation of hate?

In the grip of hatred, people express their destructive urges in symbolic language that reflect the mental state that drives it. A baby can be described as a "snake".[37] A child can be slaughtered "like a chicken".[38] Those descriptions express a mythical idea. Myth reaches through reality to change facts into the mirror image of emotion. In that state, the mode of expression is symbolic and exaggerated because only that kind of language can reflect something which changes a person into a negative essence. The common form of the ideas does not arise from reason, but from the expression of unconscious forms that wait, like an instinct, for the visual and verbal signals that draw it forth. The expression in symbolic language of mythical ideas about the evil of the enemy signals that the speaker is himself possessed by evil.

The killer does not interact with the victim on the basis of logic. Lieutenant Caley's feelings for the enemy he saw himself as fighting in Vietnam were far removed from reasoned dispassionate emotion:

> As for me, killing those men in My Lai didn't haunt me. I didn't, I couldn't kill for the pleasure of it. We weren't in My Lai to kill human beings, really. We were there to kill ideology that is carried by — I don't know. Pawns. Blobs. Pieces of flesh. And I wasn't in My Lai to destroy intelligent men. I was there to destroy an intangible idea. To destroy communism ... it's evil. It's bad.[39]

How can this be explained? The escaped victims of mass

---

36 Telegram to the Governor from Talaat, 2 January 1916 quoted in D. Boyajian, *Armenia: The Case For a Forgotten Genocide* (New Jersey, 1972) p. 331; and see p. 229.
37 African Rights, *Rwanda*, pp. 614, 641, 787.
38 Dadrian, p. 121.
39 Sack , pp. 104–5.

murder should be listened to. They alone can tell us about the behaviour of people who justify their actions on the basis of apparent logic. Their testimony refutes the notion that mass murder is nothing more than a calculated strategy. Individual murderers have explained away their actions many times in court as something that took hold of them. Can people be overcome by emotions driven by myth? Whatever it is that drives viciousness operates at the furthest extreme of human action where the intensity of the hatred involved admits of no mercy. Compassion is the very negation of this emotion. Here is an extended quote from a survivor of the genocide in Rwanda who, on the commencement of the organised murders in her sector, witnessed mothers being given machetes and ordered to kill their own sons. Despite being pregnant, she decided that she had to run away:

Somehow, I managed to flee with the children. We headed in the direction of our home. But, before we got there my labour pains started. I took another woman to help me. We went into the bush and I delivered a baby boy. I could only regard this as unfortunate under the circumstances. The other woman was afraid to hide with us in the bush as the baby's cries would alert attackers. I continued hiding in the bush the whole day with my children. In the evening, an old woman, a neighbour, passed by on her way to fetch water. As I knew her, I greeted her. I also hoped that, as a grandmother, she would understand my predicament. She asked me about the delivery. I told her that I had had the baby, not wanting it known that it was a boy. She asked me about the child with a lot of sympathy in her voice. She requested that I let her see the baby. I was afraid, but what could I have done? When she saw it was a boy, she commented, "Aha, so you have given birth to another Inyenzi? You are not going to live yourself". She picked up a stick and hit the child. He groaned only once and then he was dead. He was ten hours old by then. She then added, "The other ones you have will do. After all, I hear they do well in school". She then told me to bury the child. But I refused. I told her "the blood of my child is on your hands. You bury him yourself". She went back to her house and unleashed her sons on us. When her sons arrived they set upon my seven year old son,

Emmanuel Mugiraneza. One of them commented "this future Inyenzi, he has to go, otherwise he will be ruling over us when he is older". They dug a small hole first. Then they pierced him with a sword and while he was still groaning, they threw him into the hole. It was now after-noon, and I was left with my daughter, eleven year old, Immaculée Mukandahiro and my four-year-old son, Théogène Uwiringiyimana. They pointed to me, saying, "Come on, let's kill you. We don't want the cockroaches marrying you". In fact I was still bleeding from the birth. One of the attackers gave me a slap and hit me with a masu on the arms. At the same time they started macheting Théogène on the head. I literally saw his brains spill out of his head. Immediately after-wards, they gave me a major blow ... I passed out. My daughter and I were taken to a pit latrine. First they threw in Théogène's body, then Immaculée and then me ...[40]

This account is not an aberration.[41] It finds precise parallels with other situations where one group is intent on the total eradication of a group designated as appropriate victims.[42] What can possibly lie behind such perverse behaviour?

Even within this simple narrative, the possibility emerges for finding elements that show the expression of an underlying pat-tern. The old woman uses deceit, a show of parental sympathy, to manipulate her chosen victim. The children of the adult vic-tim, whose name was Liberata Mukasakindi,[43] are invested with the quality of being an "Inyenzi", a "returning cockroach", that is a refugee whose purpose of undoing the 1959 revolution can-cels out every one of her human qualities. Unreality pervades

---

40 Quoted from African Rights, *Rwanda*. The story of this victim appears on pages 624–627.

41 I. Chang, *The Rape of Nanking* (London, 1998) pp. 35–59; See also the article by Robert Fisk, "Cleansing Bosnia At A Camp Called Jasenovac", the *Independent*, 15 August, 1992.

42 For instances of similarity see N. Davies, *God's Playground: A History of Poland* (Oxford, 1981) II, pp. 458–61; Bilton and Sim, pp. 180–2; Morgenthau, pp. 200–16; Boyajian, pp. 352–5; Chang, passim.

43 In Rwanda, family names are typically not given. Hence her chil-dren have individual names that do not follow those of the victim or her spouse.

this narrative, and not just from the nightmarish horror that overtakes us as we read it. Children are killed because they have political allegiances. Their nature is seen as already formed by the group to which they belong. The children are murdered because of the stated reason that this makes them evil. This is a myth. A child of four or seven can have no fixed destiny of being, or becoming, a creature of unassailable evil that requires it to be exterminated for the safety of its killers. That is a fact. Therefore, what the grandmother and her sons believe about the children must be a reflection of what is within their own minds. To believe an unreality in the teeth of the plain appearance of the truth is a state of mind incompatible with consciousness and consistent with possession by, or surrender to, a mythic unreality. Apart from the qualities ascribed to the children, another factor emerges: the killers declare that unless they murder the children they will come into their own as adult rulers over an unjust society. It is in serving a higher ideal, that of preventing evil, that the killers justify their actions. The children lose the quality of childhood and instead become enemies. At the same time, from what the killers say, the children give off a sheen of evil. This is nonsense. In fact, it must be the mind of the murderers that is reflecting back at them the hate which they project.[44]

The human ability to project a myth can only be part of any answer to the problem of destruction. It is what the deceitful myth can do that matters. The human mind must contain some structure of indescribable evil: call it the shadow, or the death instinct, it does not matter. We can comfort ourselves about our sympathy with suffering children all we like. The symbols of evil demand violence. The myth-driven push to eradicate evil overrides all human fellow feeling. Similarly, for ideas to be more worthy than respect for life itself, the human mind must be able to put certain ultimate goals at the summit of our mental values. Is this process that of accepting an ideology? It displaces, or restructures, conscience into a new form of morality.

---

44 C.W. 14.129.

Finally, male children, in this instance, are particularly targeted as the carriers of the quality of violent enmity. It is also hinted that it seems possible to see their mother as a kind of empty vessel, waiting to be impregnated, and for that progeny to carry in their blood the quality of the male rapist.

It is commonplace to read and hear horrified reactions in the media to the slaughter of women and children. The eradication of men evokes less revulsion, perhaps because the male of our species is more aggressive. In ancient times, warfare often followed the pattern of killing the men and enslaving the women and children of the conquered people. A grave insult, or one perceived as such, such as the killing of a leader among the aggressor group, could provoke wholesale slaughter.[45] In the early twentieth century, the mass slaughter of Armenians commenced with all adult and teenage men being separated out from the general population and killed.[46]

In the Rwandan genocide, men and boys were the first to be destroyed among the Tutsi population.[47] In many areas, women and children survived the early phase of the slaughter as, following the custom of past conflicts, they were spared. Educated women, as representatives of the elite from which the enemy leadership was drawn, were treated with particular venom and sought out from the earliest stages.[48] As a result of a later government decision, all Tutsi women were sought out

---

45 For references see Chalk and Jonassohn, pp. 58–64, 65, 73, 76, 105. Similarly, see I Samuel, pp. 30, 15; Duteronomy II: 26–37 and 3:1–11 for incidents of male destruction only; Joshua 6 (destruction of Jerrico); 7, 8, (destruction of Ai); and II Kings 10 (the destruction of the worshippers of Baal) see also M. Lings, *Muhammad* (London, 1988) 229–233. For a bizarre modern judicial use of biblical authority as justifying universal slaughter see Bilton and Sim, pp. 356–7.

46 Hovanissian, p. 29. See also Boyajian, pp. 114, 118–19 quoting Lepsius, *Deutschland und Armenien* (Potstam, 1919).

47 For references see African Rights, *Rwanda*, pp. 597–604, 625, 777, 787, 794, 815.

48 African Rights, *Rwanda*, pp. 515, 748, 717, 782.

and killed.[49] Here, another pattern emerges: some women were more likely to be allowed to live than others. By the end of the genocide, a large proportion of the survivors were young women in their teens to thirties.[50]

More than from feelings of tenderness, any decision to spare women's lives was grounded in a view of marriageable-age females as the spoils of war. This is primitive thinking indeed. With the elimination of their husbands, brothers and fathers, these women became chattels to be distributed among those in the aggressor group who wanted them for their sexual needs.[51] By removing the male element of the population their ethnicity became neutral, following the custom of assigning identity through the males.[52] Marriage within the aggressor group thus re-identified the woman from being a Tutsi to being a Hutu.[53] Rape and abduction are used as weapons of aggressive war. The sexual abuse of women is a form of ritual humiliation that degrades them from their natural position of dignity.[54] Its purpose is to leave women mentally broken. Aggressors move from some deep-seated drive that is at its most virulent when they succeed in visiting on their victims the internal mental picture they hold of them. If that image is of an incorrigible evil, mirroring the internal drive that they project in order to deny their own evil motives, the humiliation and rape of women may be followed by murder.[55] Resistance to rape is not, of itself, ordinarily demonstrated to provoke murderous violence.[56] In

49 Des Forges, pp. 296, 565 and see African Rights, *Rwanda*, p. 773.
50 African Rights, *Rwanda*, p. 748.
51 Des Forges, pp. 215, 296.
52 Des Forges, p. 296, African Rights, *Rwanda*, pp. 297, 692.
53 For an example see *African Rights*, pp. 774–7.
54 Of considerable interest is the International Commission of Jurists publication U. Dolgopol and S. Paranjape, *Comfort Women: An Unfinished Ordeal* (Geneva, 1994) passim.
55 For instances of this kind of behaviour see J. Rickert (ed.), *The Good Man of Nanking: The Diaries of John Rabbe* (New York 2000) passim and Chang, pp. 50–3, 89, 86, 118–19.
56 S. Brownmillar, *Against Our Will: Men Women and Rape* (New York, 1993) p. 207.

Rwanda, women were regarded as being capable of serving the ethnic group of those who forced them into pregnancy or marriage. Thus, they were regarded as desirable acquisitions.[57] The choice was between death or marriage to a Hutu Interahamwe militiaman.[58] Similarly, the women of the Armenian nation were faced with either continual rape, coupled with a slow death through attrition, or abduction into sexual slavery.[59] The mad "blood theory" of the Nazis ruled out sexual contact with "inferior races". I cannot explain this exception. Human nature, however, had to be fought against on this front through an elaborate, and savagely enforced, legal code. Sexual congress with Jewish people was punishable by death or imprisonment.

A definite pattern emerges that links rape to the domination of one people by another.[60] The nature of any possible dynamic is less clear. Rape is an instrument of genocide and war. It fundamentally undermines the enemy group. It attacks the relationship of fidelity between spouses, puts in doubt the origin of subsequent progeny and marks out ravaged women as having been possessed by a hated enemy. When hate dominates a situation, people want to sate their hatred in destruction. Something in the human mind demands total satisfaction. This can only be achieved if complete dominion over the enemy is established. Conquest may be regarded as having been completely achieved where there is no male line to uphold the identity of the vanquished people; where all of their women are forced into sexual servitude. The inevitable result of this will be the generation of children to an alien identity. There are echoes of this attitude in the systematic exclusion of girls of marriage-

---

57 For instances of humiliation through giving women to vagabonds see African Rights, *Rwanda*, pp. 763, 754.

58 African Rights, *Rwanda*, p. 754.

59 For instances see J. Bryce and A. Toynbee, *The Treatment of Armenians in the Ottoman Empire: Documents Presented to Viscount Grey of Culloden* (Princeton, 2000) pp. 45, 96, 112, 126, 193; Morgenthau, pp. 209–12; Walker, pp. 203, 213–14; Riggs, pp. 120–1, 139–40.

60 See Brownmillar, pp. 31–113, 410–18.

able age from the slaughter of their people in both the ancient and modern world. Similarly, random acts of rape could be seen as expressing a dynamic that is opposite to that of destroying the ineradicable qualities of the enemy. If the conquering people are driven by a myth of their own superiority then the impregnation of enemy women will redefine the nature of the conquered society in their own image.[61]

Rape, can be seen as being the worst aspect of violent plunder. The other aspect of plunder is theft. An unbroken pattern of plunder by the conqueror of the conquered unites human behaviour from ancient to modern times in the context of mass destruction. As an underlying dynamic, it manifests itself, apparently spontaneously, where one group is at the mercy of another. So strong is this drive that it must be controlled. It was the propensity for theft to which Himmler referred when he spoke of "a few ... examples of human weakness". In any quiet village in twentieth century Rwanda, Soviet Russia, Nazi-occupied Europe or the late Ottoman empire, two families of different ethnic, social or religious groups could live side by side, the one being successful according to the standards of the time and place, and the other less so. It becomes attractive for those who have less, to accept a system of ideas that brands those who have more as being unworthy. A plan to re-order society becomes very attractive if it involves their enrichment. Personal greed becomes the key to violence when it whispers to us: this field, this house, this woman could be mine. Add to this any myth that justifies "action" and violence can be predicted.

Prior to the revolution, the Russian aristocracy and well-off small farmers had become, according to the communist dogma of the time, "blood suckers" or "blood sucking Kulaks".[62] The Jews under the Nazi system were called parasites who did no

---

61 See Robert Fisk, "The Rapes Went On Day And Night", the *Independent* 8 February, 1993; Linda Grant — "Rape, Babies: What Do We Know", the *Independent On Sunday*, 10 January 1993.

62 See D. Volkogonov, *Lenin: Life and Legacy* (London, 1995) p. 70.

work themselves, but existed in luxury through swindling honest workers of the fruits of their labour.[63] The Tutsi in Rwanda were officially declared to be "dishonest in business" in order to ensure the "supremacy of [their] ethnic group".[64] And the Armenians in the Ottoman Empire were traditionally resented for their good business sense and thrift that was regarded as an affront to the sense of superiority of their Turkish and Kurdish neighbours.[65] A small trader or farmer in Rwanda knew that by immersing himself in "the work", as it was called, of slaughtering the Tutsi, a farm, animal, or business would become his by right of plunder.[66] Neighbours brazenly moved into the houses of the slaughtered families with whom they once affected to enjoy good relations. Looting was an integral part of the execution of mass murder. In Russia, the over-controlled and over-stratified farming community occupied the lands of those devoured by the revolution until they too became dispossessed when common ownership became the prevailing dogma. The houses, businesses and lands of dead Armenians were redistributed to their former neighbours as "abandoned property";[67] both in the era of massacres under Abdul Hamid at the end of the nineteenth century, and in the genocide of that nation at the beginning of the twentieth. In the swathes of Europe occupied by the Nazis, every single possession of those subjected to eradication was directed to enriching the central apparatus. Where the Nazis conquered, for instance in Poland, poor German families were moved into their houses and businesses. The owners were, literally, kicked out. Those Poles not reclassified as "ethnic Germans" were simply ejected without right of

---

63 Dawidowicz, *The War Against the Jews*, p.58.
64 The Hutu "Ten Commandments" quoted in African Rights, *Rwanda*, p. 42.
65 For an example see Dadrian, p. 173.
66 For examples see Des Forges, pp. 90, 227, 237, 321, 323, 374, 378–9, 408, 474, 492, 530, 562.
67 Dadrian, pp. 222–5. For further instances see, for example, Boyce and Toynbee, pp. 101, 124, 183, 204.

compensation or redress.[68] In all of these instances, those who were plundered of their property were themselves described as thieves. In all of these instances as well, people justified their crimes as furthering a future ideal state of mythical perfection.

A further process of inverted thinking emerges in the focus, by the aggressor groups, on the evil deeds of their victims. Atrocities, either invented, or ones that have actually occurred, are used as a one-sided means of creating a mass emotion that focuses on the enemy group. Abominations perpetrated in pursuit of aggression are either made out to be essential, due to the necessity of dealing appropriately with a duplicitous foe, or are shrouded in secrecy. Constantly, the black soul of the enemy is etched out. Events are created or distorted. Deception appears as such an integral part of this process that it is like an underlying cancer upon which other patterns feed. Upon the occurrence of a particularly repellent atrocity, the perpetrators invert their guilt by blaming it on the victims. As we know, according to the Nazis, the Poles bombed Warsaw, their own capital. They apparently were not alone in this crazy behaviour. In April 1937, during the Spanish civil war a squadron of German aircraft with incendiary, high explosive and shrapnel bombs attacked the Basque town of Guernica. Supporting fighters strafed the panicked crowds trying to flee the bombardment. The town was defenceless to this form of attack and, following earlier military setbacks, was full of refugees and retreating soldiers on the republican side. Despite the unimpeachable nature of the attribution of this action to the nationalist side by independent war correspondents, their news agency insisted that the Basques had destroyed the town themselves by planting bombs and setting fires in order, it was said, to inspire indignation. When a reference to the bombing was found shortly afterwards in the diary of a German pilot, captured after being shot down by the republicans, the nationalists insisted that republicans, motivated

---

68 For eyewitness accounts of this process see the BBC video, *The Nazis: A Warning from History* (London, 1997).

by some ulterior purpose to destroy their own side, had in fact piloted the attacking aircraft.[69]

We have become familiar with the cry "they have done this to themselves". Conflicts in the late twentieth century, as far apart as Sarajevo and Belfast, continued to echo with it. At the dawn of the new millennium, the patterns of delusion continue to weave on the same weft. In the aftermath of the atrocities in the United States of America on 11 September 2001, followers of a warped distortion of Islam were identified as the executants. Within the societies where this ideology found its breeding-ground, the conflict between just Palestinian aspirations and the rights of the state of Israel was linked to the equation. In the myth of the cause of all-righteousness, people blamed the attacks on the Jews. They could not accept that those whom they supported could be responsible. One reporter was told: "It was a very sophisticated operation to mount from a cave in Afghanistan. I heard four thousand five hundred Jews did not go to work that day because they knew something was going to happen. I think they did it".[70] He was told that this was a widespread point of view.[71]

Instances of individual recurring patterns of behaviour that emerge in the context of aggressive war and genocide only describe what has occurred in particular circumstances. As such, they are not necessarily predictors of future conduct. By examining such patterns together the hope would be to attempt to reveal some aspect of any underlying dynamic. However, what is seen on the surface is not necessarily illustrative of why an unconscious motivation exists. Nor does it define the key that unlocks its power. If it is possible, however, to isolate some fundamental attitude of mind that defines societies that embark on aggression and mass murder, then the substratum on which aggression rests may be partially illuminated.

---

69 These details are taken from Thomas, pp. 623–30.
70 The *Guardian*, 13 October 2001 "Strains Tell in US Bonds with Cairo" by Ian Black.
71 The *Guardian*, 18 December, 2001, Linda Grant in G2.

Just as there are factors that make people dangerous, there are factors that make a society particularly dangerous. They are not so different. All of these factors centre around our ability to lie to ourselves and about ourselves. Those who think of themselves as being victims are, on an individual level, prone to hatred. PJ, who killed his business partner, was, in his own mind, already a victim of the deceased before he killed him. He continued to think that way after he had bludgeoned him to death. Any society that defines itself in terms of the wrong done to it is similarly inclined. From the perspective of the seventh century, the abbot of St Catherine's monastery in Sinai characterised those who remembered the wrongs done to them as being possessed by "a dark and loathsome passion" which, he said, was the final point to which anger may be taken. He described it as the living, never-ending, parent of rancour and revenge. In his experience this, in turn, deceptively twists reality to the viewpoint that feeds what he calls "a pleasureless feeling cherished in the sweetness of bitterness".[72] Victimism is a dangerous mythical pattern in individuals and in nations.

Many societies that have committed the worst wrongs have

---

72 St John Climacus (579 – 649), *The Ladder of Divine Ascent*, translated by C. Lubhéid and N. Russell, (New Jersey, 1982) pp. 152–3. Here are the actual words of the author on "Step 9" of the ladder: "Remembrance of wrongs comes as the final point of anger. It is a keeper of sins. It hates a just way of life. It is the ruin of virtues, the poison of the soul, a worm in the mind. It is the shame of prayer, a cutting off of supplication, a turning away from love, a nail piercing the soul. It is a pleasureless feeling cherished in the sweetness of bitterness. It is a never-ending sin, an unsleeping wrong, rancour by the hour. A dark and loathsome passion, it comes to be but has no offspring, so that one need not say too much about it. A man who has put a stop to anger has also wiped out remembrance of wrongs, since offspring can only come from a living parent. A loving man banishes revenge, but a man brooding on his hatreds stores up troublesome labours for himself. A banquet of love does away with hatred and honest giving brings peace to the soul...Malice is an exponent of scripture which twists the words of the Spirit to suit itself".

launched themselves into destruction on the basis of an image of themselves as victims. In 1931, Japan initiated a series of military actions against China designed to consolidate and expand the annexation of Manchuria as a colony. Japan claimed that this aggression was lawful because China had ceased to be a nation due to civil war and banditry and, in consequence, had no central government to protect its people. Like other colonial adventures before it, the act of conquest was described as a humanitarian and civilising mission. China brought a case before the League of Nations. In response, Japan argued a set of pretexts that twisted the charge of aggression into a defence of their own righteousness. This included a claim that an independence movement had sprung up in "Manchukuo" which had then begged for Japanese aid. As it was put, in consequence of an attack by "Chinese bandits" they had no "honourable" choice but to assist those who were merely defending themselves. The report of the investigation by the League into Japan's actions rejected these arguments. It recommended the demilitarisation of the region so that new structures could be put in place to lead to the setting up of an appropriate form of local administration. Japan's actions against China had always been based upon a self-promulgated view of itself as the bringer of civilisation into chaos thwarted by the bullying interference of European powers.[73] Reacting to the condemnation of his country, Ambassador Matsuoka poured out religious imagery in claiming that Japan was the true victim:

> *Suppose public opinion were so absolutely against Japan as some of the people try to make out, are you sure that the so-called world opinion will persist forever and never change? Humanity crucified Jesus of Nazareth two thousand years ago. And today? Can any of you assure me that the so-called world opinion can make no mistake? We Japanese feel that we are now put on trial. Some of the people in Europe and American may wish even to crucify Japan in the twentieth century. Gentlemen, Japan stands ready to be crucified! But we do believe, and firmly believe, that*

73 On this see Young, pp. 140–55, 95–106.

*in a very few years, world opinion will be changed and that we also shall
be understood by the world as Jesus of Nazareth was*[74]

In Nazi mythology, they were the crusaders who pledged to
restore Germany to its former glory; of which it had been
stripped by a conspiracy of Jews, communists and freemasons. It
was these elements, they proclaimed, who had forced their
nation's premature surrender in the Great War. This traitor's "stab
in the back", explained everything: it divested Germany of military power, split the country in two on each side of Poland,
robbed sovereign territory, imprisoned millions of Germans
under the yolk of uncultured peoples masquerading as nations,
prevented unity with Austria and emasculated rightful territorial
ambitions.[75] This florid thought-system was the poisonous captivity of the self-conferred status of victimhood.[76] The Turkish
government launched its genocidal actions against the Armenian
minority on a refrain that they were traitors to the integrity of
the nation. According to this, the Armenians were a people who,
given a chance, would "jump on the back" of Turkey.[77] The
Armenians had violated the pact of surrender and protection in
Islamic law to which, as alien peoples, they had agreed.[78] In part,
the embarkation on their respective campaigns of mass murder
was launched by the Germans and the Turks from a platform of
restoring lost glories through the eradication of enemies fixed
with responsibility for their current woes.[79] According to the
hysteria created in Rwanda for the purpose of genocide against

---

74 Japanese Delegation to the League of Nations – The Manchurian
Question: Japan's Case in the Sino-Japanese Dispute as Presented
before the League of Nations (Geneva 1933) 166, quoted in Young
154, see also 95 –106, 102, 141, 148.
75 C.W. 10.426.
76 On this see Burleigh, pp. 268–77.
77 On this see Morgenthau, pp. 222–40.
78 On this see Dadrian, pp. 172–6, 185–99.
79 On Turkey see Kuper, "The Turkish Genocide of The Armenians
1915–1917" in Hovannisian, pp. 67–79; and on Germany see
Burleigh, pp. 75, 153.

the Tutsi people, all Hutus had been made into victims. In government, commerce, the ownership of land and above all else in their stubborn refusal to accept that they had been rightly displaced as the natural overlords of Rwanda, the Tutsi were portrayed as cheating the Hutu of their rightful inheritance.[80] It was only through clearing Rwanda completely of the Tutsi that harmony would be restored; a state, which according to this mythology, had already existed prior to the "arrival" of the Tutsi.[81] The myth of the lost golden age can be a very dangerous lie. [82] The self-conferred status of being a victim can be worse.

Where this sense of victimhood lurks, terrible eruptions of hatred can be expected. This is beyond even the perspective of which the abbot of St Catherine's Monastery wrote; his analysis deals with the mentality of people who, in truth, have suffered grave wrongs, but who chose to hold onto deep-seated emotions of bitterness instead of trying to be able to forgive. All the images created in pursuit of aggressive war and mass murder falsely characterise the target group with disgusting propensities of a nature appropriately dealt with only by conquest and slaughter.

Hitler was not alone in making speeches that according to William Shirer, who heard them, were typified by his "distortions of history".[83] Nor could Bullock's opinion that it was a psychological necessity that all Hitler's aggressive speeches began with a distorted list of the wrongs done to Germany be applied to him alone. I believe that the fundamental dynamic of this process is deceit. Blatant lies are at the black heart of every society that

---

80 On this see Des Forges, pp. 36–40, 73–74, 81–6, 105, 444–46.
81 On this see Prunier, pp. 5–54.
82 On the golden age see C.G. Jung , *Man and His Symbols* (London, 1978) pp. 72–5.
83 In a recording of Mozart's Requiem Mass made in Berlin in 1944 by the Berlin Philharmonic and Furtwangler, all Hebrew words are excised, as are all references to Abraham, Zion and the Christian inheritance in the Jewish faith. For a modern example of the modern Turkish government apparently removing all sign of the Armenians see W. Dalrymple, *From the Holy Mountain: A Journey in the Shadow of Byzantium* (London, 1998) pp. 77–88.

transforms itself into a weapon of violence on others. An aggressive society may have many factors but a false view of its own history is always a sign of danger.[84] This lie supports an elevated self-regard.

No reasoning based on reality can support the mass murder of another people. The orientation of any society geared up for mass killing is false. It looks to a golden past that, in turn, promises a future filled with plenty. Above all, the promised golden age shines with the absence of those that are blamed. In turn, a retrospective orientation that looks to the past as a source of myth, and not as a means of discovering the truth, may be expected to throw up religious forms and practices supportive of an ideology. According to Jung, secular ideologies are a regression to paganism.[85] Such societies resort to religious language in defining their central myths as received truth and substitute ritual forms in place of the dispatch of the business of the State as a secular function.[86]

Fundamentally, it is the myth of our own superiority that fuels the denigration of enemies. If there is any unifying factor to these recurring patterns of vile human behaviour it is false self-regard. If a form of mythical thinking emerges when deceit dominates our thinking, then the risk is that our enemies become as devils while our own leaders appear to be gods; reflections of our self-deceiving perfection.

---

84 For examples of this see S. Al-Khalil, *Republic of Fear: The Politics of Modern Iraq* (London, 1991) pp. 175, 177, 181, 193; Burleigh, pp. 51, 428, 535; Thomas, p. 639; Hovanissian, pp. 67–79; Prunier, pp. 80–92; Young, pp. 145–9, 382–92; Lambley, *The Psychology Of Apartheid* (Georgia, 1980) p. 271; D. Lindaman and K. Ward, *History Lessons: How Textbooks from Around the World Portray US History* (New York, 2002).
85 C.W. 6.124.
86 For examples of this see Al-Khalil, pp. 223–5, Burleigh, pp. 75, 100–17, 153, 152–155, 194, 196, 212, 252–77; Young, pp. 67, 108, 138, 148, 176–8, 251, 363, 364–9, 384.

CHAPTER 5

The Leader as God

IN 1894 ANTON CHEKHOV wrote a story called "The Black Monk". It is about the destructive effects of self-delusion. Andrey Kvorin, a psychology lecturer, spends fifteen years working towards, and eventually achieving, an associate professorship. Exhausted, he visits his legal guardian who runs a market gardening and orchard business. There, his mind seems to relax. That summer Kvorin marries his guardian's daughter and for a time all goes well. But, at the point of what appears to be his greatest happiness, his mind wanders to a legend that the spirit of a black monk haunts the local countryside. On a walk one evening the black monk appears to him. Over a series of encounters, the black monk tells him that he is one of the elect of God and that through him a brilliant future will be assured for all humanity: thousands of years in advance of its ordained time, "the kingdom of eternal truth" will be granted; sin and suffering will cease. One day his wife wakes up to find him conversing with the wall of their bedroom. She persuades him to seek medical help and to rest. This does not suit him. Shakespeare, Buddha and Mohammad did not seek a cure for their ecstasy, he reasons, and if they had, not a trace of their legacy would have been left after them. So, he deserts his wife and goes to live with a woman who panders to his every whim as if he were a child. Unable to work, he is frustrated by his inability to further his mission. The black monk no longer appears to him. One day, he receives an angry letter from his wife. She tells him that he has ruined all of their lives; the truth, if you like. Her father is dead and their orchard and garden have been taken over by strangers. "My curses on you", she writes. Already ill, he suffers a throat haemorrhage and dies, being assured by the last visitation of the black monk that he is one of the elect of God.

No one believed in Andrey Kvorin. Millions of people believed in Josef Stalin, Saddam Hussein, Adolf Hitler and a host of leaders who were thought of in their time, and thought of themselves as, "the chosen of God".[1] Obviously, that belief was misplaced and, it would be easy to say, a mere fantasy. But, wrong or not, the fact that people were prepared to follow them gave them the power to direct contagions of hatred. They did not establish God's kingdom on earth. Their purpose was total control and the destruction of all who opposed them. How did they succeed? Leaders do not work in a vacuum. Leaders who are unbalanced seem to have their worst effect when their people are both panicked and filled with an unreal self-regard. In despising their enemies, the people who pursued aggression adored their leaders. Entire nations have, apparently willingly, followed a succession of dismal leaders, people of ordinary talent who were regarded as giants. The result was catastrophy. Their power came not from what they could do but from the trust that "their people" reposed in them.[2] Unlike Chekhov's deluded hero, they left more then a trace behind them.

After a lifetime as a war correspondent, Martha Gelhorn concluded that it was leaders that made wars; that people need

---

1   For an observation on Pol Pot see E. Staub, *The Roots of Evil: The Origins of Genocide and Other Group Violence* (Cambridge, 1989) pp. 206–8.

2   Aion C.W. 9II.309; 310; 18.1570; 10.471, 475, 386. This idea is also expressed in Robertson Davies' novel, *The Manticore* (London, 1972) pp. 118–20. See also D. Shostakovich, related to S. Volkov, *Testimony: The Memoirs of Dimitri Shostakovich* (London, 1979) pp. 94–6.

to be organised into killing units because, without direction, they would never just rush off to destroy their so-called enemies: even in civil wars, there have always been aggressor leaders who inflame the masses with fear and hate. What, for her, was less understandable was why it was always so easy to get men roused to kill each other.[3] What people can believe about their leader suggests not an answer but a description of the problem. If he is a leader invested with divine attributes then his will can overcome human scruples. If it is really possible to believe that the leader is super human, then it follows that you could trust him with your life and with the justification for taking the lives of others. Rudolf Höss asserted that an order from Hitler was "holy".[4] That statement could very easily be a self-justifying lie. Can anyone believe that a leader has the power to turn evil into good?

Mass murder is almost always justified as a sacred mission. Very often, the inspiration for a wave of destruction is a leader whom his followers believe is the source of infallible wisdom. This does not always happen. No such leader appeared in Rwanda. On the contrary, President Habyarimana was disparaged in many of the publications of the Hutu-supremacists for giving the appearance of negotiating with the opposition RPF.[5] When it came to it, it is likely that they killed him rather than yield power. In Turkey, three men ruled during the Armenian genocide but none of them were elevated to super-human rank. It seems probable that the phenomenon of the divine leader needs particular conditions to appear.

Leaders exist in plenty in the world of organised crime. They do not help as illustrations of this problem. Any that I came across were the subject of investigation or prosecution. People rise in the criminal underworld because of their smartness and

---

3   M. Gelhorn, *The Face of War* (London, 1993) p. 368.

4   S. Paskuly (ed.), *Rudolf Höss Death Dealer: Memoirs of the SS Komandant of Auschwitz* (New York, 1996) p. 153.

5   J.P. Chretien, *Rwanda: Les Médias du Génocide* (Paris, 1995) see in particular the illustrations.

ruthlessness. Those are the qualities their peers respect. When you get caught, or your enterprise fails, you are despised. There is little time for luxuriant notions of divinity to grow around a crime boss and, anyway, his minions are likely to be too street-wise to entertain such thoughts. The world of crime differs from the law-abiding world but both camps need leadership. Democracies choose leaders on the basis of advertising campaigns and media promotions. Usually, the electors also have something real to go on as the candidate has often done a real job in politics before seeking the top position. They rarely meet him or her. Supporters write opinion pieces, books and academic articles in the leader's name so as to promote the idea of their competence. This may often be a lie, but it is usually within controlled limits. Most people are aware of the nature of the exaggeration that makes up a modern election campaign and, in any event, they are interested only in finding someone who can do the job of government well. In ordinary times, they are not looking for a saviour. That is the difference. Leaders on whom extraordinary stature is projected all tend to seize, or abuse, power in crisis situations.

Even in the midst of a catastrophe, there is a basic choice between reality and myth. In a small society you can be close both to the problem and to the leader who might show a way through it. Perhaps if there is the real possibility of a solution to a problem, then there is less need to grasp at a myth. Trusting a leader, whether a real or a phantom hero, means that all can act as one. You can speculate a reason based on instinct. Surrender to the will of one man, or one woman, may have been conditioned by evolution because, in our ancestors, it allowed a desert to be crossed or the Promised Land to be found despite all of the apparent obstacles. And real leaders do exist. They are a focus for the cohesion of a group because they are competent and, despite setbacks, they are mentally strong enough to radiate hope. Probably though, this is logic intruding into an area of human relations where it is what people feel that is paramount. What they feel, however, does not necessarily have to be a myth.

An instance of this emerges from Gitta Sereny's interviews with the Treblinka death-camp survivor Richard Glazer. His reflections evoke some feeling of the power of real leadership. The Jewish prisoners at Treblinka planned a breakout. Their only alternative was to wait, inevitably to be selected for death. To plan their bid for freedom they formed an escape committee, which obviously met in secrecy. One of the German guards "smelled something" during their preparations and, on a pretext of the disappearance of some clothing, had several of them beaten up and two others murdered on the spot. The escape committee's military expert, Zhelo Bloch, was moved away to another part of the camp. Glazer says this of the effect of the loss of his leadership on their group:

> *It was the most terrible blow to our morale, an anti-climax which is indescribable now. It wasn't only, you see, that he was so necessary in a planning sense; it was that he was loved. Contrary perhaps to some of us, he was very much one of the people. Don't misunderstand me, I only mean that, of all of us, he was the one person who could talk to anybody, give anybody a sense of faith in himself and his capacities; he was a born leader, of the best kind. The evening he went was the end of hope for us – for a long time. I remember that night so clearly; it was the one time in all those months that we really lost control; that we gave way to emotion. It could have been the end of us.[6]*

In the event, the desperate nature of the danger faced by the prisoners made it imperative for them to regroup and to refocus their efforts through other leaders.[7] All of these were chosen because they were people of real ability. In suffering with their fellow prisoners every day the nature of their physical, emotional and intellectual powers became a real presence within the

---

6   G. Sereny, *Into That Darkness: From Mercy Killing to Mass Murder* (London, 1995) pp. 210–11.

7   For a society unable to move out of crisis and the phenomenon of the appearance of "prophecy" as a response see N. Mostert, *Frontiers: The Epic of South Africa's Creation and the Tragedy of the Xhosa People* (New York, 1992) pp. 1181.

camp. It could be rationally decided, in choosing a particular person as a leader, that their attributes fitted them to the nature of that task. This is in marked contrast to the kind of leader who proclaims that he has the vision to accomplish wonders.

Jung asserted that the worst kind of leader is the one who is chosen when people have surrendered their individual will to a collective movement; true leaders are those who are capable of reflection.[8] In a crisis, those who believe that they have the answers may be the ones to shout loudest and thus seem full of the self-assurance needed. Jung claims that irrational individuals are falsely seen to be the best adapted to desperate times and that accordingly they tend to have disproportionate influence.[9] Clearly, breaking out of a death camp is a desperate measure. Equally, surviving that kind of crisis puts you in a crucible of emotions. But, it can be possible for rational thinking to triumph over myth; even in the worst circumstances. From what I have read of the survivors of the death camps, apart from good luck, they had an abundance of mental strength. They looked at their situation realistically. They had no delusions. When you examine the circumstances where myth supplants real leadership you find the, by now familiar, pattern of inflated self-regard. It seems that when you elevate your own group to inhuman proportions, the regard in which your leader is held reflects this. The danger takes off where the population throws their responsibility onto the leader they have created in their own imagination. Then the myth can go anywhere.

There is something fundamentally comforting in the notion of surrendering our responsibility to those who want to control us. Solzhenitsyn described his experience of being a military officer as "the happiness of simplification"; of not having to think and of being immersed in the same life as everyone else in the army.[10] And this feeling is not confined to wartime. There

8   C.W. 10.326.
9   C.W. 10.490.
10 A. Solzhenitsyn, *The Gulag Archipelago* (London, 1974) p. 162.

is a continuity of danger running from democratic to totalitarian societies that one person will demand complete control and
that passing over their responsibility to him will be a relief to
the people. It seems that every time our world is shattered by
the kind of events described in Chapter 3, our natural reaction
is to run around looking for a saviour. Whether the event is one
that is constructed so as to make it look like our world is being
attacked, or whether outsiders are truly seeking to destroy us,
the cry goes out for someone to step in and direct events. It is
no accident that the United States went to war in Vietnam in
the aftermath of the shadowy events of the Tonkin Gulf incident; unlimited powers to wage war were passed by the
Legislature to President Johnson because of an attack on
national prestige. Similarly, the US Legislature were inspired by
the "9/11" attacks to give President Bush the powers that led to
interventions in Afghanistan and Iraq. Where that will lead, no
one can now tell. It is as well to remember that, even in a
democracy, mistakes can be made when panic decimates
thought, allowing emotion to dominate. In a controlled society, all power probably already rests with the leadership and no
further delegation is necessary. Yet, as we have seen, even dicta-
tors will invent or exploit a crisis in order to galvanise people
towards a destructive plan.

Saddam Hussein, the former leader of Iraq, held power of
life and death over almost everyone in that country. In his book
Republic of Fear, Samir Al Khalil described a society that resem-
bled a mad family. Nothing was real.[11] Everyone feared for himself or herself against arbitrary arrest. Muttering any form of
private dissent could end in torture or death. No digression was
permitted from the dogma of the one party state controlled by

---

11 R.D. Laing and A. Esterson, *Sanity, Madness and the Family:*
    Families of Schizophrenics (London 1964, Pelican reprint 1986) pas-
    sim. The ideas that are attractive here are the model of an
    enclosed unit, unammenable to outside influence, and the
    requirement for members of the family within that unit to
    believe lies.

the supreme leader. The ordinary people should have hated him. Yet, it appears, they worshipped him. Or, at least, some did and the rest pretended. Saddam's image dominated the entire country. In Baghdad models of his hands held giant swords as a triumphal arch to a victory in the Iran–Iraq war that had never happened. He was called by a range of titles that could not ever have represented the truth: Perfume of Araby, Knight of Islam, The Leader–President, the Leader–Struggler, the Standard–Bearer, the Arab–Leader, the Knight of the Arab Nation, the Hero of National Liberation, the Father Leader, the Daring and Aggressive Knight.[12] Al Khalil reasons that because all of the people of Iraq lived "on the edge of a precipice", they desperately needed to believe in Saddam as their saviour.[13] What difference did it make that the saviour was a mass murderer? According to Al Khalil, when there is no hero to turn to in a crisis, our imagination will invent one.

Quoting the propaganda of a totalitarian regime proves little. All through the life of Kim Il Sung, North Korea produced a magazine called *Korea Today*. In garish colour photographs, it showed the "fatherly leader" inspecting rice harvests and power plants. The captions described him talking to everyone from farmers to nuclear scientists, to whom the readers of this publication were expected to believe he was giving "on the spot advice"; an expert on every subject. The state publishing firm produced, in addition, a series of dreary books on his thoughts together with works of fiction describing his greatness in the form of short biographies and long biographies. These were sent to every library that would take them. None of the sane recipients could have been expected to take these creations seriously. In one copy I consulted in the Berkley library, a student had crossed out Kim's name in a caption and substituted "Comrade God". Yet, when he died in 1994 millions wept,

---

12 Mostly taken from S. Al-Khalil, *Republic of Fear: The Politics of Modern Iraq* (London, 1991) p. 110.
13 Al-Khalil, pp. 116–17.

apparently spontaneously, and vast crowds of grief stricken people thronged Pyongyang for his funeral. Can an enclosed society make people believe in myth or did it suit a captive people
to put on an act? When an official Nazi publication similarly
proclaimed, "When you see our Führer, it is like being in a
dream; you forget everything around you, it is as if God has
come to you", [14] you might also suspect that it was a pure lie,
nothing to do with real emotion. Equally, you might think
"indoctrination" reading a private diary entry by Martin
Boorman's wife Gerda, where she wrote:"O Daddy, every word
which the Führer said in the years of our hardest struggle is
going round and round in my head again".[15] But what magic
could make such indoctrination work?

In September 1934, William Shirer attended the Nazi Party
rally at Nuremberg. Returning to his hotel one evening he
came upon a mob of thousands of people chanting outside
Hitler's hotel for him to show himself. For a few moments the
Führer appeared. Shirer was shocked when they "looked up at
him as if he were a Messiah, their faces transformed into something positively inhuman". From what he saw at Nuremberg,
he concluded that Hitler was able to unloose hidden springs in
his followers.[16] Contemporary films and photographs seem to
confirm this. When the leader appears, a huge outpouring of
energy is set off. Does this suggest some connection with the
Jung theory of archetypes being activated by symbols and
releasing disproportionate energy?[17] Could this be another
example of faked, or semi-conditioned, behaviour in a closed
society?

For the 1997 BBC television series on the Nazis, a series of

---

14 "Flamen und Deutsche", an article in *Das Schwarze Korps* newspa-
    per, quoted in M. Burleigh, *The Third Reich: A New History*
    (London, 2000) p. 196.
15 Quoted in J. Fest, *The Face of the Third Reich: Portraits of Nazi Leaders*
    (London, 1972) p.408.
16 W. Shirer, *Berlin Diary* (London, 1941) 4 September 1934.
17 C.W. 9II.423.

witnesses to, and participants in, the events of 1930–1945 were interviewed. What they said about the leader myth is likely to be true as they had nothing to gain, and much to be embarrassed about, in admitting any emotional captivation by Hitler and his gang. One person recalled being at a dinner party when Hitler's eyes rested upon his. He felt that he ought to return the gaze steadily because otherwise the leader might think that he had something to hide. Believing in this clairvoyance produced another effect:

> *And then something happened which only psychologists can judge. The gaze which at first rested completely on me, suddenly went straight through me into the unknown distance. It was so unusual. And the long gaze which he had given me convinced me completely that he was a man with honourable intentions. I can say only, aye that I am glad that I saw Hitler's most beautiful side. Surely there must have been dark sides but I saw his wonderful side and nobody can take that away from me.* [18]

Another witness to the Führer myth did nothing more than shake Hitler's hand. Yet, from that moment in Linz in 1938, she was transformed:

> *I just looked at him and I saw good eyes. And in my heart I promised him, "I always will be faithful to you because you are a good man …". That was a dreamlike time and later I kept my promise. All my free time, besides school, I gave to the work because he had called us …* [19]

Thirty years later, in another culture, people were having similar experiences. In her memoirs, Chang Jung recounts her journey to see Mao Ze Dong in 1966, at the height of the possession of the Chinese people by the phenomenon known as the

---

18 L. Rees, *The Nazis: A Warning From History* (London, 1997) p. 35. Note the second part of the quotation is reproduced from the BBC video.
19 Rees, p. 110.

"Cultural Revolution". There was nothing fake about the emotion of the pilgrims:

> I turned my eyes quickly away from him to the front of the motorcade. I spotted Mao's stalwart back, his right arm steadily waving. In an instant, he had disappeared. My heart sank. Was that all I would see of Chairman Mao? ... The sun seemed suddenly to have turned grey. All around me the Red Guards were making a huge din. A girl standing next to me had just pierced the index finger of her right hand and was squeezing blood out of it to write something on a newly folded handkerchief ... It had been done many times by the other Red Guards and had been publicised at nauseam: "I am the happiest person in the world today. I have seen our great leader Chairman Mao".[20]

Worship of the leader was what was expected of the pilgrims. Perhaps the expectations of a closed society explain this? It appears not. Educated, able people, it seems, can fall prey to this kind of thinking, just as the cleverest university students can fall madly in love.

Lenin was a clever person who surrounded himself with able people. He did not, apparently, discourage an atmosphere of worship directed at him while in exile.[21] Such worship may have become a basic expectation of party discipline by late 1917.[22] His comrade Anatoly Luancharsky wrote that the structure of Lenin's skull was "truly striking". In a bizarre passage, he described studying the leader's forehead and sensing "a physical emanation of light from its surface".[23] For centuries, Orthodox iconography had traditionally portrayed the saints of the Church with huge luminescent foreheads as an emphasis of their spiritual power. On 30 August 1919 Lenin, after delivering a speech on the defence

---

20 J. Chang, *Wild Swans* (London, 1993) p. 321. See also P. Short, *Mao: A Life* (London, 1999) p. 543.

21 O. Figes, *A People's Tragedy: The Russian Revolution 1891–1924* (London, 1997) p. 153.

22 Figes, p. 511.

23 A.V. Lunacharsky, *Lenin* (Moscow, 1987) p. 216, quoted in D. Volkogonov, *Lenin: Life and Legacy* (London, 1995) p. 77.

of the revolution in a Moscow factory, was shot three times at close range. Within a month, after being close to death, he was well enough to travel to an estate outside the capital to convalesce. In his history of the Russian revolution, Orlando Figes records that the Bolshevik press hailed the leader's recovery as a miracle. He was described as Christ-like, sacrificing his life for the masses. According to Pravda, "with his pierced lungs still spilling blood", Lenin had insisted on returning to work. In a pamphlet, mass distributed after the attempt on his life, he was called "the chosen one of millions. He is the leader by the grace of God. Such a leader is born once in five hundred years in the life of mankind". Another publication claimed that he could never be killed because Lenin was "the rising up of the oppressed".

Possibly these startling investitures of supernatural power in a human person could be grounded, as Figes explains, in the ancient cult of the Tsar as a divine figure. But, in themselves, these patterns are there to be explained. They did not grow up in a vacuum divorced from the human mind. Jung would say that they exist because they are part of our collective inheritance of the forms of ideas.[24] Symbols cannot be invented. Nor are these symbols, of the leader as a divine being, invented.[25] No doubt, manipulation and deception by the leadership can play a role in the formulation of these myths, motivated by a desire to retain power. Completely artificial ideas could not, however, evoke the response of awe and submission in people's minds. People have to have a capacity to believe. It is this that can be exploited. One might expect a tough military commander, such as Dimitry Os'kin, the leading Soviet defender of St Petersburg against the White Army, not to be moved by anything other than cold reality. Yet, when in October 1919 his leader telephoned him directly, he recorded: "I was literally caught for breath when a voice on the telephone said 'Lenin here'."[26]

---

24 C.W. 9I.496.
25 C.W. 11.339.
26 Figes, p. 674.

None of these witnesses to the notion of the great leader in various cultures were responding to their leader as a person. Instead they were caught up in a myth. Responses like these would be impossible were not the human race to have the capacity to project mythical elements on to people and situations.[27] In myth, an encounter loses the quality of an individual relationship and becomes something that we struggle to approach with words. We describe an inner experience, attempting to communicate a resonance that is internal. This is not just generated by the encounter, but is also projected onto it.[28] The resonance is vast, because it is a window into the power of the mind for investing energy into illusion. In that state, experience becomes akin to unconscious awareness. As in a dream, one hears a call; one responds to clairvoyance; one is suddenly within an apparently limitless world beyond the tangible. It seems unlikely, as Fromm would put it, that this is merely an expression of group narcissism.

Is unconscious response accidental, a random danger that can strike a panicked population? Those coming to see Mao were inspired by an ideology of which he was the leading figure. That was not all. Their extraordinary reaction to his appearance was deliberately encouraged by ritual. One aspect of the way the encounter was organised for maximum effect was that the first appearance of the Chairman coincided with the rays of the rising sun.[29] The medieval ideal of an all-night vigil as a means to enlightenment had resurfaced: deliberately.

However one looks at it, at the worst end of this spectrum, lies dominate the leader myth. This marks off that society a

---

27 C.W. 91.518.

28 Bullock observes that the exhilaration displayed by those submerging themselves in the supposed community of belonging through race and ideology projected onto the mythical figure of Adolf Hitler was an expression of something more than mere manipulation; "it was the sharing of a common experience deeply felt by leaders as well as followers": A. Bullock, *Hitler and Stalin: Parallel Lives* (London, 1993) p. 343.

29 Short, p. 542.

danger to itself and to whoever it chooses to regard as an enemy. The truth has no part to play, unless the truth serves the myth. For instance, whether in September 1931 Hitler flew into a jealous rage and killed his niece Geli Raubal is uncertain. Her bedroom was in his flat and even the thought in the public mind of his having such a sexual relationship would have been unwelcome to the Nazis. Officially, they lived separately; he in the admirable role of benefactor. In 1933, the Nazi leadership learned of an attempt to print and to publish a pamphlet attacking Hitler and the ideology of Nazism. The author was Fritz Gerlich, a Catholic monarchist. In earlier writings he had predicted that with the Nazis in power the result for Germany would be "international war, lies, fratricide and infinite trouble".[30] To buttress his arguments, the intended publication would have included what he had learned of the suspicions surrounding the death of Fraulein Raubal. The Nazis smashed his offices and destroyed his printing equipment. Gerlich was imprisoned and then murdered. Lies distort what is real. What is extraordinary is the desire by people who know the truth to destroy it in favour of a deeper myth that justifies manipulation. Are they like the Romanian villagers who were determined to believe in the malign influence of the mountain fairy, despite hearing that nothing supernatural had been involved?

During the early part of the Second World War, Lothrop Stoddard, an American racist writer, secured an audience with Hitler. On the appointed day, he was driven through enormous doors and into the inner stone courtyard of the new Reichschancellery building. He walked up a set of steps and arrived in a huge marble hall. From there he had to pass through a long mirrored gallery, set at an angle to the previous rooms, before turning along it into the grand antechamber of the office of the Führer. While waiting to be summoned, a thought flashed into his mind that he might find the German

---

30 This account is based on R. Hayman, *Hitler and Geli* (London, 1997) pp. 184–8.

leader inside the next room seated on a throne and surrounded by flaming swastikas.[31] He ascribes this mad thought to the psychic atmosphere created for those destined to meet the leader. He was conned.

In such confessions of weakness as Albert Speer allowed himself in his memoir *Inside the Third Reich*, he recognised that the style of his architectural projects for Hitler reflected the psychology of the Nazi regime. His designs were typical of the buildings that are produced by empires approaching their death phases.[32] He did more than unconsciously reflect an era through his designs. In the Chancellery building, constructed for Hitler over a period of a year so as to be ready for January 1939, people who came to be received by the Führer were required to walk through a route designed to evoke awe. As Stoddard described, the path to the leader included a series of huge rooms, together 175 feet long, before a visitor came to the personal reception hall of the leader. It was here, two months after the building was completed, that Hitler bullied President Hacha of Czechoslovakia, by threatening to bomb Prague, into surrendering the rest of his country. The building was a statement about the human mind. No one entered it to engage on a human level with its master. It was designed to overcome. Hitler told Speer: "On the long walk from the entrance to the reception hall they'll get a taste of the power and grandeur of the German Reich".[33] In plans for a replacement, due to be completed in 1950, Speer made the distance the supplicant would have to walk to meet the Führer, after being first received into the building, a quarter of a mile. Only then would he enter the "presence".

None of this speaks of a healthy attitude either in the leader or anyone assisting in the deliberate disproportioning of human life. Yet, for the people, it was all to be believed in as a

---

31 L. Stoddard, *Into That Darkness: Nazi Germany Today* (London, 1941) pp. 173–8.
32 A. Speer, *Inside the Third Reich* (London, 1979) pp. 203, 222.
33 Speer, p. 159.

confirmation of their surrender of self-responsibility to Hitler: he was the embodiment of their destinies and a leader beyond human stature.

Is this a limited example: a weird flowering of madness nourished by unique circumstances? Eight hundred years earlier, in 1167 the two emissaries of Amalric, the crusader king, who was seeking a sworn alliance with Muslim rulers, were brought into the presence of the sixteen-year-old Caliph in Cairo. The boy, as the successor of the Prophet of Islam, was treated as the guardian of divine revelation. The scene, as described by the historian Amin Maalouf, gives some idea of the projection of luminosity that can be made onto a human being:

> *Shawar led them to a superb, richly decorated palace ... ringed by a phalanx of guards. Then the cortege crossed a vaulted hallway that seemed interminable, impervious to the light of day, and finally came to the threshold of an enormous sculptured gate ... After passing through many ornamented chambers Shawar and his guests emerged into a courtyard paved with marble and ringed with gilded colonnades in the centre of which stood a fountain boasting gold and silver pipes. All around were brightly coloured birds from the four corners of Africa ... Again they passed through a succession of salons, then a garden stocked with tame deer, lion, bear and panthers. Then finally they reached the palace of al-Adid. Barely had they entered an enormous room, whose back wall was a silk curtain encrusted with gold, rubies and emeralds when Shawar bowed three times and laid his sword on the floor. Only then did the curtain rise and the Caliph approached, his body draped in silk and his face veiled. The vizier went to him, sat at his feet and explained the proposed alliance with the Franj ...*[34]

Solzhenitsyn claimed that if human nature changes at all, it changes "not much faster than the geological face of the earth".[35] If you go back to the titles of Saddam Hussein, a fair

---

34 A. Maalouf, *The Crusades through Arab Eyes* (London, 1984) p. 165.
35 Solzhenitsyn, p. 562.

parallel can be found in other cultures and eras, just as the multiple villas of Mao Ze Dong and the giant palaces of Nicolae Ceausescu and Kim Il Sung reflect the monumental sacredness of their person in their time. The twentieth century is not infected by the myths of the twelfth century by imitation. Al-Qualanisi, the chronicler of the Crusades, records that the Caliph conferred the following titles upon the Turkish general Imad al Din Zangi after the capture of Edessa from the Crusaders in 1144: the great, the just, the aid of God, the triumphant, the unique, the pillar of religion, the cornerstone of Islam, ornament of Islam, protector of God's creatures, associate of the dynasty, auxiliary of doctrine, grandeur of the nation, honour of kings ... victor over the infidels, rebels and atheists, commander of the Moslem armies, the victorious king, the king of princes, the sun of the deserving.[36] All that these titles do is reflect a warped magnificence beamed onto a human person. To his followers, Hitler was the only man "who never made a mistake". He was described as being lonely "like God", as being "greater than Jesus Christ"; in fact the "greatest of all Germans".[37]

Since Nazi ideology stood the German people above all others it becomes less surprising that their leader reflected their magnificence. Similarly, the abject devotion to General Franco, as victor in the Spanish civil war and as supreme authority, perhaps reflected the self-congratulation of his party. On the "Dia del Caudillo" in 1940, he received the diplomatic corps of other countries in a royal palace by having them parade before him seated in a throne-room on a raised dais. Several times, in attending the celebration of Mass on State occasions, he entered the church walking under a canopy; a distinction reserved for a king. His government proclaimed him, on the second anniversary of his rebellion, as "The man who, by divine plan ... had the inspiration and the wisdom and the courage to lift up the authentic Spain against the antipatria ... then ... personally and in unequalled fashion

---

36 Maalouf, p. 137.
37 Statements at the Nuremberg party rally of 1938 quoted in Fest.

direct[ed] one of the most difficult campaigns known to history".[38] One wonders about all this. Did those who upheld these insane visions really believe in them? And the leaders themselves, were they crazy enough to accept this homage?

Leaders can be like Chekhov's anti-hero and believe that they are the chosen ones of God. When you believe this kind of thing your personality has become unbalanced. If the leader chooses to believe that a unique mission makes him a source of absolute truth, then he or she is dangerous.[39] Napoleon in his autobiography wrote the following passage about the moment when he chose to believe in his "destiny": "It was precisely that evening in Lodi that I came to believe in myself as an unusual person and became consumed with the ambition to do great things that until then had been but a fantasy". In the personal copy of this work in Stalin's library this passage was underlined. Those who closely served him addressed him as "Master".[40] During his stewardship of the Soviet Union, "the Master" was publicly described by a litany of names. In their totality these appellations take on the religious air of the descriptions applied by Catholics to the Mother of God: Patron of Science; Leader and Teacher; Friend of Children; Greatest Strategist in History; Policeman's Best Friend; Great General; The Greatest Genius Who Ever Lived; Genius of Geniuses; Wisest Of Teachers; Greatest Man On Earth; Leader Elect Of God; Sailor's Best Friend; Great Railroad Engineer; The Wise Father; The Great Leader.[41]

Hitler proclaimed that it was his fate to lead the German people back to the state of "greatness from which they had fallen".[42] All couples marrying during the Third Reich were presented

---

38 P. Preston, *Franco: A Biography* (London, 1994) p. 309. See generally chapter 11 and chapter 13.

39 For Chingis Khan see J. Saunders, *The History of the Mongol Conquests* (London, 1979) pp. 50–69.

40 Shostakovich, p. 104.

41 These appellations are taken from, *inter alia*, A. Solzhenitsyn, *The First Circle* (London, 1992).

42 See R. Overy (ed.), *Interrogations: The Nazi Elite in Allied Hands* (London, 2001) pp. 235–6, 252.

with the leader's "masterpiece" Mein Kampf. The Nazi philosopher Alfred Rosenburg proposed a "National Church" for
Germany, cleared of "all crucifixes, bibles and pictures of saints",
but occupying "all churches, cathedrals and chapels".[43] Its guiding text was to be Mein Kampf, "to the German nation and
therefore to God the most sacred book", because it embodied
"the purest and truest ethics".[44] Hitler's public utterances centred on his own sense of providential destiny and on his personal sense of his own mission and achievements.[45]

By late in his life, if not earlier, Mao Ze Dong came to
believe that his writings ought to replace Confucianism,
Buddhism and Christianity.[46] The process of obsequiousness and
flattery to which he was continually subjected fed his ego-infla-
tion to gigantic proportions.[47]. Mao's thoughts were officially
declared to be "more precious than gold".[48] His deputy Lin Biao
asserted that he was more than a genius: "One sentence of his
surpasses ten thousand of ours".[49] This cult of the worship of a
living person assumed explicitly mythical form during the
Cultural Revolution in 1967. Throughout this period there was
constantly to be heard on the radio a dirge-like anthem which
proclaimed: "Born of the sun, the east glows red, from China has
come one Mao Ze Dong". His personal physician, Dr Li Zhisui,
noted that the Chairman was not disturbed by the veneration of
"his people". On one occasion, having assigned Dr Li to work
in a factory, he sent the works committee a present of a mango.
It was sealed with wax and set on an altar where all the workers
filed past, bowing to it. When it rotted, the mango from the

---

43 On whom see Fest, pp. 247–64.
44 Quoted in Shirer, *Third Reich*, p. 299.
45 For example, see the speech of 28 April 1939 quoted in Shirer, pp. 574–8.
46 J. Chang and J. Halliday, *Mao: The Unknown Story* (London, 2005) p. 471
47 Z. Li, *The Private Life of Chairman Mao* (London, 1994) p. 502; Chang and Halliday, pp. 568, 575, 589.
48 See Short, pp. 470–85.
49 See Short, pp. 522, 536.

leader was boiled and, in a solemn ceremony, everyone took a communion-like spoonful of the waters.[50] When Dr Li related this to Chairman Mao, he was amused and delighted. On another occasion, a greeting was sent in Mao's hand to a textile factory in Beijing. The revolutionary committee there were "ecstatic". The note was enlarged, by being photographed, and, in a huge size, hung at the entrance to the factory. The original note became an object of wondering stares when posted on the bulletin board. Such is the tragic comedy of people renouncing themselves to venerate the misplaced aspect of the divine in human nature.

None of these leaders objected to the fairy stories circulating about them. The reality must be that when you accept worship, you do so because you regard yourself as worthy of worship. The monuments of adoration, whether titles, palaces, or the sanctification of a leader's utterances, all testify to this. But what are the divine leaders really like? Are they exceptional people? Certainly, a lack of self-irony can be expected. But surely there must be real personality to inspire such utterances? When Franco died, his close personal circle published a series of reminiscences of him purporting to tell the truth about the Caudillo. Franco's biographer Paul Preston describes the portrait they presented of Franco as one of a person of astonishing personal mediocrity: "a sphinx without a secret".[51] His attendants, all holders of high office, were neither unaware nor acting unconsciously. That could reasonably be said about ordinary Spaniards. Few had ever met the leader and even fewer had any kind of human interaction with him. They were surprised that their leader did not possess the qualities they were encouraged to project onto him. Nor, we may infer, was the object of the organised projections lacking in reminders of his own fallibility. Why else would he take pleasure in the praise of sycophants and demand the subservience of all around him unless it was to

---

50 Li, p. 503; see also Short, p. 576.
51 Preston, p. 782.

repress the constant presence of the possibility of seeing reality? Dr Li's portrait of Chairman Mao is unappealing. However, he had no choice when appointed to be the Chairman's doctor. The portrait of Hitler that emerges from Speer is of a bore with no ability for productive work.

All of these leaders were the product of a combination of the panicked search for a saviour, by the ordinary people at a distance, and conscious manipulation, by those around the leader–saviour. Many people may be conned; but not those doing the conning. This is a paradox. An altar is set up and an idol is placed on it; a mere human being. Clouds of sanctity are disbursed to transform the ordinary into the divine. We know this. Yet, we still worship what we ourselves have made. How can this be? Is deceit a trap, liable to ensnare us once we evoke it? Certainly, leaders of this kind are both lied about and lied to. Though deceit is an integral part of the process of setting up the leader myth, the power of the divine leader continues.

Leaders who are not maintained by reality walk in fields of deception. In Mao's case, the mutuality of the myth between the leader, as the object of projections, and his subjects achieved a form of extreme purity. One does not know if it was only a product of vanity that had Mao, at the end of a conference in Moscow in November 1957 marking forty years of the Soviet revolution, declare that the socialist world would overtake the capitalist sphere in material conditions within fifteen years.[52] At the subsequent Nanming party conference, he accused provincial leaders of dragging their feet. This accusation was made in order to "goad, cajole and badger" into "consensus" the idea that industrial and agricultural production could be greatly increased.[53] In a document circulated early in 1958, Mao projected his elevated vision of the "continuing revolution", by proclaiming to party leaders:

---

52 J.D. Spence, *The Search for Modern China* (New York, 1990) pp. 574–83; Short, pp. 476–88; Chang and Halliday, pp. 444–99.
53 Li, p. 231; see also pp. 219–356.

Now we must start a technological revolution so that we may overtake
Britain in fifteen or more years ... After fifteen years, when our food-
stuffs and iron and steel become plentiful, we shall take a much greater
initiative. Our revolutions are like battles. After a victory, we must at
once put forward a new task. In this way, cadres and the masses will for-
ever be filled with revolutionary fervour, instead of conceit ...[54]

There was threat implicit in the accusation of "conceit". Anyone
opposing Mao was unsound from an ideological perspective.
Under a totalitarian leader, people fear the accusation of heresy.
During the subsequent Chengdu Conference he attacked anyone
who urged caution; to be against a rapid advance was to be an
anti-Marxist. The slogan was coined: "Go all out, aim high and
build socialism with greater, faster, better and more economical
results".[55] The threat of being labelled as "rightist" silenced those
who would have regard to reasoning based on ordinary sense.
Those most adept at toadyism advanced. Advancing the fiction
that production and agricultural output could increase exponentially, showed commitment to the abstract myth of "continual
revolution", in the form proclaimed by Mao, and so curried
favour with him. Manual labour was to be honoured as the people of China were bent towards Mao's purpose.

Thought was to alter fact. By a Politburo directive of August
1958, steel production was set to double within a year. This was
"achieved" by taking metal household implements and melting
them down in makeshift "backyard steel furnaces" into "ingots".
Even within the compound for top party leaders in Beijing, a few
of these furnaces sprang up. A cursory glance would have indicated to any of the party leaders around Mao that the operation of
the "steel works" was one of melting down metal implements and
not of steel production. No one spoke the truth to Mao: reality
had become heresy. Travelling south by special train from Beijing
in October 1958, Mao was met by an incredible scene: women
and old men working luxuriant fields; the young men rushing

---

54 Quoted in Spence, p. 577.
55 See Li, pp. 263, 236 and 276.

around "making steel" in makeshift furnaces; the night sky lit up by the smelting fires as far as the eye could see. Reports were made of astounding advances in steel and agricultural production. "Good news stations" were set up whereby the communes could vie with each other, in the production of statistics. Puzzled, his personal physician Dr Li, in Mao's absence, asked Lin Ke, one of the leader's political secretaries, to explain how there could be so many furnaces and such an abundance of agricultural production. In his memoirs, Dr Li records what, in fact, was happening:

> *What we were seeing from our windows ... was staged, a huge multi-act nationwide Chinese opera performed especially for Mao. The Party's secretaries had ordered furnaces constructed everywhere along the rail route, stretching out for ten li [about five kilometres], and the women were dressed so colourfully in greens and reds, because they had been ordered to dress that way. In Hubei, party secretary, Wang Renzhong had ordered the [farmers] to remove rice plants from far away fields and to transplant them along Mao's route, to give the impression of a widely abundant crop. The rice was planted so closely together that electric fans had to be set up around the fields to circulate air in order to prevent the plants from rotting ... The production figures were false ... No soil could produce twenty or thirty thousand pounds per mu [a sixth of an acre] ... What was coming out of backyard steel furnaces was useless. The finished steel I had seen in An Hui was fake, delivered there from a huge, modern factory ...*[56]

Taxed a percentage of reported production, rural areas were required to deliver close to all their true grain output to the State. Expert farmers were diverted into tending useless "furnaces". Famine struck at a time when people were especially unprepared. Millions died between 1958 and 1962. Children were particularly affected by malnutrition. The median age of death fell from seventeen years in 1957 to nine years in 1963; half the people who died in the latter year were under ten years old. When famine struck in 1959, Mao made another trip and continued to be welcomed by huge crowds. Dr Li explains that

---

56 Li, pp. 278–80; for a similar incident see Figes, pp. 186, 263, 391, 478.

the Chinese attitude was that the Emperor was never wrong, only misguided by his advisers.

When you have the attitude that the leader can do no wrong, he tends to be given increasingly unlimited powers. Mao's power may, at its height, have been sufficient for him alone to make a decision to go to war. This is the ultimate danger of the leader myth.[57]

When mass aggression breaks out, historians strive to find the cause. The genocide in Rwanda was initially widely considered to be an expression of "tribalism", whatever that might be. Theories about historical necessity forcing leaders into deciding to attack, and such like, may be seen as the answer to why one country suddenly invaded another. Sometimes wars, like the outbreak of the First World War in Germany and Russia, may be greeted with popular enthusiasm. That does not necessarily mean that the population of a country has forced their leaders into aggression. In a totalitarian society, or in a panic-stricken democratic society, leaders are well capable of making such decisions on their own, without any popular backing. On 1 September 1939, William Shirer observed the mood of the people in Berlin in response to Hitler's decision to attack Poland. Despite a host of propagandist lies, some already quoted in Chapter 3, no popular enthusiasm for the enterprise was generated. People acted as if they preferred to ignore what was happening, they "were simply dazed at waking up this first morning of September to find themselves in a war which they had been sure the Führer somehow could avoid. They could not quite believe it, now that it had come."[58]

After disposing of Poland and France, Hitler ruined whatever prospect of "success" he had by invading Russia. Historians again argue that social factors somehow caused this decision. This theory is advanced despite all the evidence of complete control over Germany by the Nazi leadership. Alan Bullock disposes of

57 See Li, pp. 270–71.
58 Shirer, p. 721; *Berlin Diary* for the same date; similarly see Figes, p. 252.

the argument that Germany was obliged in June 1941 to declare war on the Soviet Union to stave off the threat of an attack by simply ascribing that decision to the personal choice of Adolf Hitler.[59] Divine leaders can make god-like choices.

On 22 September 1980 full-scale war operations were launched by Iraq against the Islamic Republic of Iran. The official line of the Iraqi leadership blamed Iranian aggression. This was supposed to have taken the shape of "187 border incidents" in the months leading up to the declaration of war.[60] The Iraqi leadership never provided a detailed account of what these incidents were supposed to be or when, and in what circumstances, they were supposed to have occurred. According to Samir Al Khalil, the leader of Iraq, Saddam Hussain, had begun planning for that war since the early spring of that year.[61]

Efforts to understand the destruction of the Iran/Iraq War viewed the facts so as to allow their interpretation to conform to current thinking. This resulted in three theories as to the driving force behind the war: that deep seated hatred between the Persian and Arab peoples allowed surface incidents to draw on the existing tensions of underlying "ethnic loading"; that Shia unrest in a Sunni dominated Iraq forced the regime to calculate in favour of attacking Shi'ite Iran, the supposed sponsor of putative civil war; and that colonial injustices, reflected in the unacceptable position of the Iran/Iraq border, required to be revised by military action. Al-Khalil dismisses the ethnic hatred theory. He describes it as drawing on evidence of war rhetoric that is a deliberate simplification of underlying distrust. As is typical in any war, this rhetoric was promulgated by both sides to advance the necessary justifications for killing. He wonders why, if the ethnic tension theories are correct, Shi'i soldiers fought in the war against Iran and why Shi'i unrest was not crushed by the genocidal efficiency that the regime later used on the northern

---

59 Bullock, *Hitler and Stalin*, p. 782.
60 Al-Khalil, p. 265.
61 Al-Khalil, citing Stephen R. Grummon in *The Iraq/Iran War: Islam Embattled* (Washington DC, 1982) p. 16.

Kurdish minority. Finally, he regards the border dispute idea as the credulous trap into which commentators have fallen, unaware that it was set for them by Iraqi justifications of a kind that fit within a familiar pattern in these circumstances. Al-Khalil suggests a simple cause: the decision to go to war was "the action of the only genuinely free man in Iraq".[62]

Years later, on 2 August 1990, the Iraqi leadership had their army annex the small neighbouring state of Kuwait. This had nothing to do with inter-Arab hostility, social unrest or the sponsoring of ethnic division. The cause of the Kuwait invasion was probably the whim of one man. There had to be lies to justify this aggression, but those making the decision did not have to believe them. It was passed off, by Saddam and his close circle, as the righting of yet another injustice of colonial border setting. Al-Khalil advances apocalyptic vanity as the correct hypotheses for Saddam Hussain's motivations in his earlier declaration of war on Iran. In 1982 the non-aligned nations were due to meet in Baghdad. There, the leadership planned to glory in their victory that would have given them a conqueror's power over the wealth and territory of a disintegrating Iran. Had the victory ten years later over Kuwait been allowed to stand, that precisely would have been the reward for Saddam's further venture.

Throughout history, many people have closely participated in the lies that have justified aggression and have toadied favour with a sublime leader. Lying to him seems to be part and parcel of the act: falseness generating falsehoods.[63] How do they, the members of the court of the great leader, justify themselves?

---

62 Al-Khalil, p. 272.

63 Shirer describes the German Embassy in Washington under Hitler as grasping at straws in order to be able to make reports that would please the leader, describing the "Jewish dominated Roosevelt" and his fear of "the spiritual and, particularly, the moral superiority and purity of Colonel Charles A Lindeburg", one of the main opponents of intervention in Europe. They wrote: "The chorus of the Jewish element casting suspicion on Lindburg...merely served to underline the fear of the spiritual power of this man." Shirer 898–899.

Albert Speer's memoir, *Inside the Third Reich* gives some hint as to why people trap themselves into acts of false worship of the leader as saviour. Speer claimed to have been attracted to Hitler's ideology as the rational solution to the problems of Germany. Speer's initial encounter with Hitler, which led, he claims, to a desire to serve him personally, involved the Führer addressing a small gathering in a low voice and expressing what Speer describes as "reasonable" views. One might wonder what these views were, or how ideas of a return to German glory and pre-1914 borders could have been achieved without war being waged on at least five nations. Once seduced, Speer was loyal to the Führer to within weeks of the total collapse of Germany in April 1945. This loyalty, as close to friendship as Hitler could get, according to Speer, was maintained through the worst horrors of which the human species is capable. Why did he do it?

Speer describes what it was like to be at Hitler's side during the time of apparent peacetime "progress" prior to the invasion of Poland in September 1939. What tends to come through most strongly from his account is a sense of intoxication. In a way, it is similar to the overwhelming emotion of the ordinary citizens who worshiped their great leader at a distance. The difference is that in Speer's case, the intoxication was self-inflicted. He conned himself as he conned others. Personally, as a matter of his self-regard and status, the leader myth elevated him. It made him believe he was someone more than special. From 1934 to 1936, Hitler still took recreational walks in public areas. Speer was thrilled when the public recognised the Führer. He basked in the reflected glow of their adoration. The heady nature of Speer's service to his Führer is apparent in a passage that deals with a walk near the Königssee:

> On the last part of this walk we had to thread our way through numerous strollers who had been lured out by the lovely weather. Interestingly enough, these many people did not immediately recognise Hitler in his rustic Bavarian clothes, since scarcely anyone imagined he would be among the hikers. But shortly before we reached our destination, the Schiffmeister Restaurant, a band of enthusiasts began excitedly follow-

ing our group; they had belatedly realised whom they had encountered. Hitler in the lead, almost running, we barely reached the door before we were overtaken by the swelling crowds. We sat over coffee and cake while the big square outside filled. Hitler waited until police reinforcements had been brought up before he entered the open car, which had been driven there to meet us. The front seat was folded back and he stood beside the driver, left hand resting on the windshield, so that even those standing at a distance could see him. Two men of the escort squad walked in front of the car, three more on either side, while the car moved at a snail's pace through the throng. I sat as usual in the jump seat close behind Hitler and shall never forget that surge of rejoicing, the ecstasy reflected in so many faces ...[64]

Speer claimed to recognise that the nature of his interaction with Hitler was corrupting. He fails to acknowledge, or avoids, the recognition that it was a process of corruption through deliberate self-delusion.

Speer argues that the favour of the leader wins a special place of affection through affirmation of the subordinate's worth. This is because both have joined in the carrying through of the "great plan"; whatever that might be imagined to be. This reinforces the sense of self-worth that was dependent, in the first instance, on a commitment the follower made to a leader as the embodiment of an ideology. By favour, the value of that choice and the correctness of the leader's judgment is rein-forced. Speer claims to fail to understand the nature of this process, even though he describes it. He presents it as a univer-sal phenomenon of the relationship between a "magnetic leader" and those attracted to serving such a personage. In part, this lack of insight is due to his deeply deceitful involvement with war and mass murder from which he is later, by writing his memoirs, striving to distance himself. He claims that it is of the essence of every form of leadership that recognition by the leader is so desirable that servility is the price always paid for its

---

64 A. Speer, *Inside the Third Reich* (London, 1979) pp. 87–8; see also pp. 108–10.

favour.[65] By this process, he argues, the retainer corrupts the leader. That view is unreal. It is the negative nature of the leadership-myth, tapped into by deception that is the essence of this corruption.

The person whom Speer worshipped as an intimate, within his circle of reflected glory, was lacking in any constructive talent. At a distance, he was widely misunderstood; as evidenced by the fact that he was a leading contender for the Nobel Peace Prize in 1938. While foreign diplomats or statesmen may be understood to have been making a mistake as to Hitler's nature through distance, misunderstanding or ignorance[66], no such excuse was open to any of his intimate circle. His writings were full of hatred and aggressive intentions. They were written in a language that his close circle spoke. His intimate views were equally violent and his nature was unattractive. They had to know this. Instead of responding to Hitler as a person with qualities to be responded to in like human measure, they flocked around him as a projection of their self-aggrandisement as believers in racial superiority. Those who worshipped Hitler had sundered the wholeness within themselves. His image was glory. It was the opposite to that of his many victims. They were degraded into an infernal image. To them, as to the masses whose testimony we have touched on, their Führer was outside human limits. So, as we shall see, were their enemies. When this myth rules, the guiding light of consciousness is turned off. Deception becomes the dynamic that fuels the mutual relationship of leader and close client. That is the point at which corruption enters the equation.

But, despite this, can they still not say that they believed in the leader's mission?

---

65 Speer, p. 132.
66 C. Barnett, *The Collapse of British Power* (New York, 1972) p. 460 quoted in D. Kagan, *On the Origins of War* (London, 1997) p. 378.

CHAPTER 6

The Idea is Paramount

I F YOU ARE PITILESS you are very dangerous. An ordinary part of human nature is to empathise with other people. Because you feel for them you do not want to hurt them, much less to torture or murder them. It would be natural to think that those who enjoy seeing other people suffer are sick. Some may be. But those who are sick in this way are rare individuals: people with a borderline personality disorder that leaves them without a human connection of love and understanding to anyone. Erich Fromm would theorise that such people can only feel alive themselves through the reaction of their victims to their violence.[1] I think it more probable, for whatever reason, that they enjoyed seeing people suffer. Because their actions are so inhuman it would have been natural in another age to describe them as being possessed by the devil. Such notions are not entirely vanished. In one grim case of death and torture, a policeman told me that he thought that the accused was possessed. It was a tempting idea. From what I saw over the weeks of this trial, it was difficult to grasp how a person could have remained emotionless throughout all of the evidence, apparently without remorse. But, probably, this is how fairytales arise. The mind is confronted by something beyond its grasp and a myth emerges to fill the gap in understanding.

Pitiless murders ought to be rare in a small country like

1   E. Fromm, *The Anatomy of Human Destructiveness* (London, 1974, reprinted 1982) pp. 384–9.

Ireland. In twenty-five years, I dealt with only two killings where a psychiatric diagnosis was made of sociopathic disorder. In addition, there were several cases where people were found "guilty but insane": they killed but were mad at the time. Here, an unconscious rage seemed to replace coldness, driving the victims of insanity to destroy and sometimes to dismember. Whatever drove then on, they were genuinely unfortunate because they had no control over their actions. You could pity them because they were transformed by their madness and troubled by whatever small realisation intruded on their minds as to what they had done.

But the biggest number of pitiless murders over my lifetime has involved those with intact mental equipment. They took life for a cause. Their approach was impersonal. The murders happened for reasons that, as Lieutenant Caley the My Lai killer explained, involved destroying a person because he represented an idea.[2] We had thirty-five years of murder in the cause of Irish unity and counter-murder in the cause preserving the union of part of Ireland with Great Britain. Corruption spreads. It was never just a case of a group of isolated killers. A support organisation is essential. They need people to hide them, to secure their weapons, to raise funds for them, to promote the righteousness of their cause and to spread their lies. All of these people are criminals and all of them are pitiless.

All during the years of one inhuman outrage followed by another, the articulate voice of the killers kept appearing on radio and television in order to patiently explain to us how they were different.[3] It was not they who were to blame but the intransigence of the political system. A murder was not an injustice but a cry for justice. Anyway, it was not a murder but, in the language of those who claim to hunt down terrorists but kill many others on the way, collateral damage. They were not crim-

---

2   J. Sack, *Lieutenant Caley: His Own Story* (New York, 1971) pp. 104–5.

3   M. Dillon, all of the works listed in the bibliography.

inals but soldiers. Were they different? After one of the worst days of killing, where both military and civilian "targets" perished, a police operation was mounted that captured several people in circumstances that were referable only to their involvement. They were due in court and so was I, on another matter. As it happened, I had just come from a prison visit to KE, the young man mentioned in Chapter 1, who had murdered the girl he had met at a nightclub. This was not a happy professional encounter. He was crushed; unable to make any more than fleeting eye contact, bowed down and obviously under a terrible burden. It was as if, in killing his victim, he had also destroyed something in himself. This day, just before his case was called, the arrested individuals from the terror organisation were brought up from the holding cells underneath the court. They walked like people with a purpose. They were not eaten up by shame. I was startled. The memory of that day in court stayed with me through many similar cases. It was reinforced whether I was representing the prosecution or the defence. I saw people who were silly or clever or determined but not people who were regretful. The impression was inescapable. Speaking later to colleagues across the Irish border, I discovered that they had experienced the same disturbing impression when meeting the Unionist killers who made it their business to savagely torture and murder nationalists. When you acted for a cause were you not afflicted by what Hitler called "the chimera of conscience"?[4] Or, if you were, had you some way of dealing with it? All of these people looked and acted differently to the ordinary criminal accused. It seemed to me that Solzhenitsyn was right when he described the evildoer with ideology in this way: "His eyes remained clear and dry".[5] But how could this happen? If there was an answer it seems that it must have something to do with finding out how people could redefine themselves so as to supercede human feeling. That is all very well. But how does

---

4   Quoted in D. Volkoganov, *Lenin: Life and Legacy* (London, 1995) p. 229.

5   A. Solzhenitsyn, *The Gulag Archipelago* (London, 1974) p. 174.

anyone redefine human nature unless some part of that nature already allows for such a fatal split?[6]

I could scarcely imagine how I could have committed the crimes of some of my clients, child sexual abuse for instance, while recognising that I was of the same fundamental nature as them. These people, however, were in no way different to me. Some crimes tended to throw up similar patterns of behaviour that seem incidental, but almost linked, to the central act. Authoritarian dominance in the home and alcohol abuse strongly outlined the personality of most of the sexually abusive fathers that I encountered. That is but one example. In ideological murder, there was no apparent pattern. If there was anything, it was as if history had taken the place of personality. The ideological killers tended to be from grim housing estates, but not all, and some had friends or close relatives who had been imprisoned or died at the hands of the security forces. They all had a sense of belonging that comes from commitment to the cause. In itself, that passion for a cause was a mystery.

If you look at some of the conflict leaders who were among the most merciless in the treatment of their enemy, you will find that some of their savagery could possibly be explained as acts of revenge. Mao lost a brother to the nationalist forces, as did Lenin to the Czarist state and Serrano Súñer to the Republicans.[7] This is not a universal. Hitler had no such motivation and no real family. Some leaders in the Rwanda genocide might also have

---

6   The ethologist Irenäus Eibl-Eibsfeldt writes: "The growth of ideology is undoubtedly an expression of our tendency to form exclusive groups and this seems to be a constitutive character of our species. Perhaps in creating an enemy schema and clothing it in an ideology we are following certain thought processes quite involuntarily." *Love and Hate: The Natural History of Behaviour Patterns* (New York, 1979) p. 220; and see *The Biology of Peace and War: Men, Animals and Aggression* (New York, 1979) p. 19.

7   Volkogonov, pp. 12–17; for Serrano Súñer see H. Thomas, *The Spanish Civil War* (London, 1990) pp. 632–4; for Mao see P. Short, *Mao: A Life* (London 1999) p. 434 and J. Chang and J. Halliday, *Mao: The Untold Story* (London, 2005) p. 260.

made a personal case for reprisal against the Rwanda Patriotic Front, but I have no evidence for this. Even where there was a personal loss, the dynamic of that kind of revenge was not normal. It was directed at an opposing ideology and not at any particular killer. Mao, Lenin and Serrano Súñer hated an abstraction, and that hatred was intensified by a personal loss. Is it possible that when you commit to an ideological movement, all of the adherents become like your brothers and sisters? As an emotion, it seems that the desire for revenge can extend beyond those attached to you by blood and friendship to those you never met. Their death can speak to you personally. Or it can be made to. In the propaganda of the Nazis, a student dropout called Horst Wessel was turned into a shining hero. He had joined a Nazi terror group that used to provoke violence in left-wing areas of Berlin. Apart from doing no useful work, he was closely involved with prostitutes and pimps. He also had a serious dispute over a debt. When someone shot him dead, it suited the Nazis to make people believe that it was a communist plot. Vengeance became holy. On their way to commit their next murder, his comrades used to sing the song attributed to him: "Comrades murdered by the Red Front and Reaction, in spirit march among our ranks."[8] Another myth: the marching dead.

When that blood spills, the blood of the committed, then each side has its martyrs to be avenged. Ideological commitment may create unnatural priorities. In an incident from the Spanish civil war, the commander of the nationalist garrison in the Alcázar was threatened by the Republican government that if he did not surrender, his kidnapped son would be executed. On the telephone, his son confirmed that this was so. His father advised him to commend his soul to God and die like a hero.[9] That is what happened. The nationalists celebrated his sacrifice as an act

---

8   W. Shirer, *The Rise and Fall of the Third Reich* (London, 1964) pp. 185–6; G. Broderick, *Das Horst-Wessel-Leid: A Reappraisal,* in International Folklore Review (1995) pp. 100–27.

9   Thomas, pp. 324–5.

of heroism. Some on the commander's side had already taken as
their banner an immaculate white ship sailing on a sea of mar-
tyr's blood.[10] When an ideological conflict is ignited, each side
have their martyrs, and each will claim to sail in a spotless vessel. People will reach out to those they see as being like themselves. "Avenge, O Lord, thy slaughtered saints…in thy book
record their groans", wrote Milton in Sonnet XVIII on hearing,
in 1655, that an army of the Pope had slaughtered Protestants in
Piedmont. His connection to them was their shared Protestant
Christian faith. I heard a faint echo of the same attitude from an
English priest who, during the break-up of Yugoslavia, sought
prayers, but only prayers mind, for "Catholic Croatia". He might
also have reminded his congregation that a generation before
the Ustashi, Catholic Croatian fascists, felt it possible to butcher
their Serbian Orthodox neighbours.

One never hears about the wrong done to the enemy. That
is not why we commit ourselves to a cause. We are committed
because we believe. We believe because we define ourselves
through symbols. An historical event, and more importantly
how we are brought up to see an historical event, can become
a point of self-definition. When you find these events, and the
group orthodoxy about them, you may begin to have some
understanding of how a group of people see themselves. Deir
Yasin is not a name much mentioned in American and
European newspapers. Yet the massacre committed there, following on a demand to vacate the village, during the battle for
the foundation of the state of Israel, remains a constant symbol
to the Palestinian people of the wrongs done to them.[11] It is like
Lidice to the Czechs; only worse because the Czech people are
now at peace. For the Israelis, the crimes of the Nazis define
their determination to strive for security and Masada, where
the defenders took their own lives rather than surrender to
enslavement under the Romans, is the symbol of the heroism

10 Thomas, p. 149.
11 A flavour of this can be had from www.palestinehistory.com/
    mass01.htm.

of their ancestors. Every country has such symbols. When a country is in conflict, the currency of thought is never the symbols of their enemies, except the negative ones. Their atrocities on us. Is this all about education: catching children young enough and making them believe?

My recollection of the earliest ideological indoctrination to which I was subjected focuses on two images. In the first, from a Christian Doctrine primer, the Saviour rises triumphantly from the tomb, the astonished guards rendered unconscious by the sight. It was a simplification of Dürer's woodcut. The image contained no threat to anyone. The Christian faith would triumph, it said, not through violence but in the truth that had conquered even death. That is what we were taught. The second image was more sinister. Brian Ború, King of Ireland, defeated the Vikings at the Battle of Clontarf on Good Friday 1014. He had first conquered the Viking settlement in Limerick. We were told that he took their ships and sailed on Dublin, winning a decisive victory through the superiority of this brilliant manoeuvre. In our history books there was a drawing of the king in his tent, on his knees giving thanks to God after the battle. We were told he had unified Ireland and secured peace. But in the picture, a fold of the tent was lifted and a sinister Norseman, clutching a knife in his raised fist, prepared to advance and stab the king in the back. The whole story of Ireland at that time and the ambitions of the king was more complex than we were ever taught. The fact that in the Book of Armagh he had styled himself Emperor of Ireland would now make me wonder if he was in control of his vanity. King Brian was certainly killed in the aftermath of the battle, but this interpretation of his death spoke of the victimisation of Ireland at the hand of a cruel invader. As the savagery on our island intensified, many historians, "revisionist" as they were called, preferred to try to see what each successive wave of invasion and settlement had given to, rather than taken from, the Irish people. This was the counterforce to the feeling of martyrdom that might have become state policy if Ireland had become a fascist state: a place where mass murder becomes easy. The view taught to me prevailed in the Green Book; the version of history that was the primer for the self-styled Provisional IRA: those who believed that violence would bring unity and perpetual happiness.[12] It was the text of the men that startled me in the court with their coldness. The Unionists had their own myths too. They defined themselves differently.[13] This one-sided self-definition also facilitated a vast self-elevation in those of them caught up in that myth.

However, I do not believe that myths create destruction of themselves. Myths certainly have a negative tendency when they are false, but that is not enough. Since people are not naturally merciless, it requires plenty of effort to turn them into beasts. An evil leadership, operating in a situation of general panic, can do that. Ideologies can thrive within closely regulated systems that promote one-sidedness and violence. This has levels. Before stepping on the first rung it is as well to ask: where does this ladder bring me?

Maybe the lowest level of ideological action is the simple exclusion of an enemy: discrimination. In May 1914, a year before the Armenian genocide began, an Armenian merchant accompanied Dr Nazim Bey to a part of Turkey where the government wished to organise a boycott of Greek businesses. They were then, like the Armenians, prominent in commerce and an important minority. This action was organised in order to strike a blow against them. Dr Nazim Bey was a prominent "philosopher" of Turanism and a leader of the Committee of Union and Progress. Their conversation was chilling:

> The Doctor said that the work of the Turkish government was very complicated, and he laid all the fault of it on the ancestors of modern Turks, who, in spite of being victorious and defying all Europe, nay all the world, had not been far-sighted enough to cleanse all the country they ruled of the Christian element, but had yielded to their chivalrous feel-

---

12 The Green Book is an appendix to M. Dillon, *The Dirty War* (London, 1991).

13 See www.theulsterscots.com.

ings and allowed the Christians to live. Had they done this bit of clean-
ing up at a time when nobody could protest, there would have been an
easy task now ...[14]

Worse was to come. In February 1915, the Doctor addressed a closed session of the Committee and told them how they were to achieve the "progress" that the country needed. The Armenians were a problem that had to be eliminated. The "solution" was planned to be as "final" as that of the Nazis or the Hutu-supremacists. As a concept, Armenia was to be elim- inated: children, the elderly and the sick had to be included in the campaign of murder because anything less would leave the "problem" alive. He called for brutality: "I beg you, gentlemen, don't be weak. Control your feelings of pity. Otherwise those very feelings will bring about your own demise".[15]

This cry for pitilessness echoes through other major cases of mass murder. Before embarking on their campaign of terror, Mao's Red Guards contemptuously dismissed "human feelings", promising instead to be brutal and to strike their enemies "to the ground and trample them".[16] The Hutu "Ten Commandments" prescribed a similar remedy for reaching their aims. Those who believed in Hutu-supremacy should cut off all commercial, friendly and sexual, including marital, relations with any Tutsi. That was one step, a bit like Dr Nazim's boycott. The next was: "The Bahutu should stop having mercy on the Batutsi."[17] That is

---

14 Quoted in J. Bryce and A. Toynbee, *The Treatment of Armenians in the Ottoman Empire 1915–1916: Documents Presented to Viscount Grey of Culloden* (Princeton, 2000) pp. 58–9.

15 T. Hoffmann, *Der Volkermord an den Armeniern vor Gericht: Der Prozess Talaat Pascha* (Berlin, 1921 and Vienna, 1980) quoted in G.S. Graber, *Caravans To Oblivion: The Armenian Genocide 1915* (New York, 1996) pp. 87–8. See further the documents quoted in D. Boyajian, *Armenia: The Case for a Forgotten Genocide* (New Jersey, 1972) pp. 317, 322, 329, 331, 334.

16 Chang and Halliday, pp. 535–7.

17 Quoted in African Rights, *Rwanda: Death, Despair and Defiance* (London, 1995) pp. 43–4.

all very well but brutality is not a pill that works on demand from a leader. You have to believe in your own side, and unquestioningly at that. To an ideological movement a sceptic is anathema. Someone uncommitted is useless. Sceptics are to be despised for that reason alone. As Hitler pronounced, a leader whose followers questioned him "could not conquer the world; with them one cannot storm either a kingdom of heaven or a State".[18] The demand to resort to violence requires that all feelings of natural empathy should be set aside so that judgment should surrender itself to the aim of "the cause".

To merely cry out that people should believe is not enough. Demanding brutality will only appeal naturally to brutes. In order to make people do the minimum, and turn aside, while the enemy is smashed to pieces, there must be a greater goal. If you look at these instances, you apparently see a pattern of a leader bringing people to the point where they see that mercilessness is necessary. Could this process of persuasion be seen as logic? There is that appearance but it is illusory. Does the apparent logic hide a myth? To my mind the examples that stand out are Lenin winning the revolution through "war communism" and Hitler promoting "the rights of the German people".[19]

Before attacking Poland in 1939, Hitler called together his generals and demanded that they "close their hearts to pity", acting "brutally" and "with the greatest harshness". He told them that his objective was to secure the existence of "eighty million people" by "obtaining what is their right". [20] That right was supposed to be the overturning of the partition of

---

18 Quoted in J. Fest, *Hitler* (London, 1974) p. 331.

18 See also the account of the genocide in Cambodia in E. Staub, *The Roots of Evil: The Origins of Genocide and Other Group Violence* (Cambridge, 1989) pp. 188–209.

19 Notes of General Halder on 22/8/1939 quoted in A. Bullock, *Hitler and Stalin: Parallel Lives* (London, 1993) 671 and affidavit of General Halder 22/11/1945 quoted in Shirer, *Third Reich* p. 993.

20 *Hitler's Table Talk* (London, 1953) 17 October 1941 quoted in Bullock, *Hitler and Stalin*, p. 757.

Germany through the destruction of Poland. In effect, the restoration of German pride. Two years later, he gathered his field commanders together again for orders on the invasion of Russia: they were to conduct a campaign of "unprecedented, unmerciful and unrelenting harshness". Why? Because this was a fight of one ideology against another. However much one tries to see logic in this statement, it is still driven by Lieutenant Calley's myth that an ideological opponent is "a blob" and worthy of as much respect. Because the members of the Communist Party were "the bearers of ideologies directly opposed to National Socialism", Hitler, as the leader of that movement, required them to be "liquidated". There was a "necessity for such means of waging war". The natural "comradeship between soldiers" must be forgotten in a "war of extermination". That war was not being waged "to preserve the enemy". The Steppes of Russia were to be "depopulated"; the soldiers carrying out such orders were to remember that they were "absolutely without obligation as far as these people were concerned". The most important factor was that they were to be without remorse: they were to "go straight ahead, cold bloodedly".

On the field of combat, the soldiers needed convincing to get them to commit cold-blooded murder. In a secret order of October 1941, Field Marshall von Reicheneau used unassailable Teutonic reason in support of genocide. This was not a war, he wrote, but a "campaign against the Jewish-Bolshevist system". The Wermacht objective was the "extermination of Asiatic influence in the European cultural region", a task going beyond the "onesided routine of conventional soldiering". Commanders should make soldiers feel that they were the "avengers of all the bestialities inflicted on the German people and its rational kin". No one stopped to ask what these bestialities might be, since it was the Nazis who were intent on destroying everyone in their way. Nor was it questioned how it was right to proclaim that these German soldiers carrying out such orders were "not merely fighters according to the rules of war, but also the bearers of an inexorable national idea". It was everyone else who was supposed to be irrational; those who needed to be murdered. The negative power of myth can stand the world on its head. But, indoctrination in the myth system was necessary, and that is what the Field Marshall offered his troops: to "improve" their "understanding" and so diminish their pity. Therefore the soldiers:

> ... *must have full understanding for the necessity of a severe, but just atonement on Jewish sub-humanity. An additional aim is to nip in the bud any revolts in the rear of the army, which, as experience proves, have always been instigated by Jews. The fight against the enemy behind the front line is not yet being taken seriously enough. Treacherous, cruel partisans and unnatural women are still being made prisoners of war; the snipers and vagabonds, only partly in uniform or in civilian clothes, are still being treated as decent soldiers and taken to the prisoner-of-war camps ... the feeding at army kitchens of natives and prisoners of war who are not working for the armed forces is as mistaken a humanitarian act as giving away cigarettes and bread. Items which the home front must forego under great self-abnegation and which the leadership brings to the home front under the greatest difficulties may not be given to the enemy by the soldier – not even if they originate from booty. They are an indispensable part of our supply.*[21]

Reading this now, it seems demonic. The tempting idea of possession can intrude on our supposedly rational minds. That is not how the killers saw themselves; as people with black souls. They thought of themselves as being rational, consumed by a national ideal and full of culture. The demonic was not acknowledged as part of them. Rather than do that, they saw the devil over there; in the innocent Jewish people and in Slavs and homosexuals and freemasons and the Roma people and communists; anyone who was not classified as one of them and who did not believe in the myth of their mission.

Again, if one looks at the Reich economic staff, highly edu-

---

21 Reproduced in L. Dawidowicz, *A Holocaust Reader* (New Jersey, 1976) pp. 70–2.

cated administrators all, one might expect logic to predominate in their plans. After all, they did not have to deal with burning flesh and screaming children. Not seeing these unpalatable results, they did not have to invent mad justifications in order to live with themselves. They only had to sit down and map things out on paper. Myth, however, is never far away from brutal plans. These planners mapped out the future, or rather lack of it, of those regions that mercilessness was to capture for Nazi over-lordship. The plan was mass murder.[22] It was described as its opposite, as a form of order. It was decided in Berlin that the population of the Ukraine would have to migrate to Siberia, on foot and on empty stomachs, or they would die. They planned to make extinct "a large percentage of human beings in the hither-to deficit areas of Russia". They saw this as justified: "Efforts to save the population from starving to death by bringing surplus food from the black soil region can only be made at the expense of feeding Europe. This would undermine Germany's ability to hold out in the war and to withstand the blockade. There must be absolute clarity on this point".[23] This process of mass starva-tion was described by the planners as a "process of reordering" and presented as "a systematic loosening-up and restoration to health of our entire social and economic order".[24]

Defeat prevented the complete implementation of these plans. The Nazis, nevertheless, managed to control vast areas of the Soviet Union before they were driven back. Their treat-ment of the population was utterly brutal. Their "reasoning" was that harsh measures were needed for the purpose of order. Because of the enormous size of the occupied areas, and the paucity of the manpower for occupation, the leadership ordered

---

22 G. Aly and S. Heim, *Architects of Annihilation: Auschwitz and the Logic of Destruction* (London, 2002) pp. 250–282.
23 Report of the Wirtschaftstab Ost 23 May, 1941, quoted in Bullock, *Hitler and Stalin*, p. 753; see Shirer, *Third Reich*, pp. 993–8.
24 Konrad Meyer, "Neues Landvolk: Verwirklichung im Neuen Osten" in *Neues Baurentum 33* (1941) No. 3, pp. 93–9, quoted in Aly and Heim , p.254.

that resistance was to be punished "not only by legal prosecution of the guilty, but by the spreading of such terror ... as is alone appropriate to eradicate every inclination to resist among the population".[25] In September 1941 a directive set reprisals at between fifty and one hundred Soviet citizens for the life of each German soldier.[26] At the same time it was "not obligatory" to prosecute crimes committed by members of the Wermacht against "enemy civilians".[27] Surely, though revolting, this is rational enough?

Terror works. If there is enough of it, terror can cow any population. Or, it can eliminate them. Terror is also a mystery. If an army needs information from a captured enemy, it could be argued that torture can extract information to save the lives of their comrades. While this is repulsive, it is utilitarian. Such instances happened during the Algerian war of independence; after some such interrogations tortured prisoners who had yielded secrets were given cigarettes. Terror is also a mystery: why do people enjoy making others suffer? That cannot happen because of necessity. Could it be that terror is an expression of hatred, the sign of a fractured mind?

Lenin was dismissive of anyone who could not stomach violence in support of his vision of world revolution. He demanded "the harshest revolutionary terror" in order, as he put it, "to come out the winner".[28] His recommended methods involved the use of "rifles, revolvers, bombs, knives, knuckle-dusters, sticks, paraffin-soaked rags ... guncotton, barbed wire, nails (to stop to cavalry) and so on and so forth".[29] If you did not like this, you were suffering from what he called a "flabby, impotent, parson's mode of thinking". He wanted "tougher leaders" to implement his orders, the "necessary measures",

---

25 Führer Order of 22/7/1941 quoted in Shirer, *Third Reich*, p. 995.

26 Bullock, *Hitler and Stalin*, p. 805.

27 Order of General Kietel 13/5/41 quoted in Shirer, *Third Reich*, p. 994.

28 Volkogonov, p. 181 quoting Trotsky, *O Lenine*, p. 104.

29 Volkogonov quoting Lenin, p. 70.

"without pity".[30] "Find some truly hard people", he wrote.[31] In short, he required the extinction of all the emotions that draw people together. His ostensible reason was necessity.

In 1917, during a short exile evading arrest by the Provisional Government, Lenin reasoned out the use of terror in his monograph "The State and Revolution". This became the dogmatic basis for the use of extreme violence against all opponents of the programme of the Communist Party.[32] In it he described his enemy as the class overlords. In his mind they were completely evil. They had kept power through "the greatest ferocity and savagery of suppression" involving "seas of blood" that had kept the proletariat "in a condition of slavery, serfdom and wage labour".[33] As far as he was concerned there was only one answer: "We must crush them in order to free humanity from wage-slavery; their resistance must be broken by force." His depth of hatred speaks through his words. His seriousness was apparent as soon as he took power. In 1918, faced with an uprising in five districts he ordered that it should be "crushed without pity". His justification was that "the interests of the whole revolution demand it". It was made explicit in his order to party members why terror was needed and how it was to be used:

> An example must be made. (1) Hang (and I mean hang so that the people can see) not less than 100 known kulaks, rich men, bloodsuckers. (2) Publish their names. (3) Take all their grain away from them. (4) Identify hostages as we described in our telegram yesterday. Do this so that for hundreds of miles around the people can see, tremble, know and cry: they are killing and will go on killing the bloodsucking kulaks.[34]

---

30 See R. Service, *Lenin: A Biography* (London, 2000) pp. 363–8.
31 Telegram of 11 August 1918 quoted in Service, p. 365.
32 Volkogonov, p. 146.
33 Quotes are taken from V.I. Lenin, *State and Revolution* (1917) Volume 33 of Complete Works.
34 Quoted in Volkogonov, pp. 69–70.

On a visit to the Soviet Union in 1987, Communist Party members told me that Lenin had had to use violence in order to support the revolution. When it came to the invasion of Czechoslovakia in 1967, this too was described as necessary "because, for us, the important matter was to save socialism". So, is anything all right provided you have good motives: saving/bringing Democracy; Christianity; Islam; Freedom? Was Lenin different? His motives were good. At least, you could argue that. In spite of all of the hate, he wanted to establish a literal paradise on earth. He did not call it that; he hated religion as a myth. He instead promised the greatest "moral and intellectual advance". What is the difference? Other leaders who promote destruction promise the same. It is always on their terms, if you agree with them or are of "their blood" or "their faith". Savage violence as the stairway to heaven. In *The State and Revolution*, Lenin promised no less than the transformation of society. All that was required was to implement his programme, absolutely and completely. Any lesser step was doomed to fail almost as a heresy. But if he could smash opposition, perfect harmony would reign, with no need for police or laws or courts:

> *Only in a Communist society ... where there are no longer any classes (... where there is no difference between the members of society in respect of their social means of production), only then "does the State disappear and one can speak of freedom". And then will democracy itself begin to wither away in virtue of the simple fact that, freed from capitalist slavery, from the innumerable horrors, savagery, absurdities and infamies of capitalist exploitation, people will gradually become accustomed to the observation of the elementary rules of social life ... without constraint, without subjection, without the special apparatus for compulsion which is called the State.*[35]

It is a myth to claim that a perfect answer has been found to the ills of human nature. A system that proclaims itself as the

---

35 Lenin, p. 172, quoting Engels.

custodian of perfection takes an inhumanly exalted view of itself. In consequence, it is likely to demonise every rival ideology. This is always a lie. It brings hatred because the mind is split. Instead of compassion, founded on an awareness of one's own failings, there is hatred.

We are repelled by, or pity, the demented murderer who claims to have killed on the orders of a voice of commanding authority inside his head, such as God or the devil. Yet, this insanity is the core drive of ideological systems. Both marshal the destruction of life in the pursuit of a higher aim. Like the person who cods himself into thinking that he is perfect, the ideological systems that are the most dangerous are those that claim to have all the answers. The myth is that there is a purpose beyond human rights to be obeyed unthinkingly. The unification of Ireland as a socialist republic; the revitalisation of the German people as the source of all human achievement; the dawn of world revolution; the purity of faith; the reunification of the Turkic peoples to the glory of the Turkish homeland; and the restoration of the fatherland to patriots are but examples of commands which have justified the ultimate forms of criminality. Are many of us likely to add in the aims of our own society to this obvious list?

In ideological possession, the greater towers over the lesser. Thoughts as to the unjustifiability of violent action, discrimination which recognises evil as the opposing force to good, must continue to be present in some way in minds of people who organise or execute the destruction of others. Reality may be made subject to myth, but can it ever be completely eradicated? We are equipped to separate the truth from the chaos of lies that descends upon societies that are being channelled towards acts of mass destruction. Ideological societies demand conformity. In that way, the lie goes, their superior promise will be fulfilled. Ideology justifies its actions through the proclamation of the promise of paradise. An idea, a mere creation of the human mind, is made the focus of all human effort from which no one may resile. Instead of knowledge, the mind has only belief. If people dissent, they are crushed. People who murder often engage in violence in order to protect their own inflated self-image from reality. An ideology that needs violence to protect itself fears the truth.[36]

It is a standard characteristic of an ideology that nothing merely human should stand in its way. The Nazi attitude, as expressed by Goebbels that "one cannot let sentimentality prevail", merely expresses the overarching nature of the ideological myth.[37] This is because destructive ideologies operate on an extra-human scale; the implementation of their programme is set on a parallel to a direct command from God. Thus, pity is to be excluded from the range of human emotions because, like scepticism, which probes for the truth, sympathy recognises the commonality of suffering, as friendship celebrates life.

The implication is that a set of ideas can be the most important aspect of a person's life. More important than friendship and the rights of other people; even one's own life?

In *Defying Hitler*, a memoir of life in Germany during the rise of the Nazis, Sebastian Haffner writes warmly about his friends from those times as well as describing the political situation. These matters are not always separate. He was studying to be a judge. The examinations were very tough. In consequence, he and a group of colleagues, who were all working as referendaires, legal researchers for judges sitting in Germany's superior courts, used to meet in order to debate legal points in preparation for their final examinations. In 1932, they were no more than an ambitious group of six young men on good terms with each other. A year later, hatred had split them up. They had disparate political sympathies that ranged from left to right. Their discussions moved naturally from law to politics, the discipline that usually makes law. As the Nazi party took power, it was announced that they would accept no new members after

---

36 For Carl Jung's explanation of fanaticism see C.W. 8.425.
37 Diary entry 27 March 1941 quoted in M. Burleigh, *The Third Reich: A New History* (London, 2000) p. 645.

a stated date. So, two of the group joined up. Their strong views were, up to that point, a focus for debate, not division. One evening, one of the friends, a party member, turned the discussion to a mass murder by the Nazis of Social Democrat party supporters in the Berlin district of Cöpernick the previous night. He described it as an act of state self-defence to break into people's homes and shoot them. Haffner spiked his anger by asking if he had in fact ever studied law: if this novel application of the principle of state self-defence could justify cold blooded murder, could it embrace similar measures against the members of their study group? The answer was, it could: against Haffner who, as a liberal, represented "a latent danger to the state". So, asked Haffner, did his friend intend to denounce him to the Gestapo? " I admit that for some time I have been wondering whether that is my duty", was the answer.[38] One imagines that scenes of this kind were replicated many times in societies that were moving towards madness. Things became so that one never knows whom to trust. Trust ceases to be on a human basis. Instead it is referable to a higher purpose.

At any time any of us might suddenly die of illness or from an accident. Equally, our society might be subjected to a terror attack that could kill us. Least likely is the idea that nasty people might take over the government and expropriate our homes and starve our families. As victims, we have little control over what happens to us. Those doing the expropriation have the power. It is easy enough to imagine people committing these criminal acts, as they are the subject of court cases every day. What is harder to understand is anyone doing such a thing with a good motive. How could anyone toss off their responsibilities by saying that although they killed so many individuals, they had a golden future in mind for any that might survive? Meanwhile how can they face the reality of the present?

Apparently good people can become caught up in a false myth and cling to it despite the suffering that is brings. Lev

---

38 S. Haffner, *Defying Hitler: A Memoir* (London, 2002) pp. 162–70.

Kopelev was a prisoner together with Alexander Solzhenitsyn, who made him the model for the erudite Lev Rubin in his novel *The First Circle*.[39] Kopelev was arrested because he had persistently spoken out, as an army officer, against the savagery of Soviet troops as they swept through East Prussia in 1945. Apart from the murder of women and children, he was particularly upset when Communist Party members were brutalised like other Germans. They were believers, like him.[40] But what did they believe in and what did it justify? In his two sets of memoirs he makes an honest self-appraisal. He believed in the transformative mission of communism. What the Party told him was right, he believed was right. This brought him to extremes of behaviour. In 1933 the message of his leaders in Moscow was that despite years of grain expropriation from farmers, they were still withholding food. The result was that the hoarding of the ignorant and greedy in the countryside was starving the "true workers" in the cities, in large state enterprises such as steel making. For hundreds of years, small farmers had traditionally left themselves short of food, if necessary, so that they would have seed corn to plant for the following spring. This way of life amounted to a universal folk instinct.[41] When the Soviet state promised that they would take every single thing and distribute seed corn according to a plan, the people were not inclined to trust them. So, it was decided, all of the grain had to be taken by force. Kopelev participated in the grim searches for every last vestige of grain that might have been hidden by Ukrainian farmers. The authorities encouraged denunciations, betrayal by family members and spying on neighbours. Years of these practices had exacerbated the natural shortages that occurred periodically so that millions were starving to death. Yet Kopelev admits that, even so, he went around with his

---

39 A. Solzhenitsyn, *The First Circle* (London, 1992) particularly see chapter 50.

40 L. Kopelev, *To Be Preserved Forever* (Philadelphia, 1977) pp. 59–104.

41 John Daly, personal communication.

detachment of enforcers, poking the earth for loose soil, to see if a hoard of seeds might be buried there, and probing people on the brink of death for information that would literally kill them: handing over their food. In what he describes as "the terrible Spring of 1933" he witnessed "women and children with distended bellies turning blue", their eyes lifeless of any hope. There were corpses everywhere, "in rugged sheepskin coats and cheap felt boots". He ordered the "barely walking, skeleton-thin or sickly-swollen people" out into the fields to make them "fulfil the Bolshevik sowing plan in shock-worker style".[42] Why did he do it? In his two sets of memoirs, I do not believe that he manages to explain it. Possibly because there could be no understandable, never mind rational, explanation. Really, all he says is that he believed:

> Our great goal was the universal triumph of Communism, and for the sake of that goal everything was possible – to lie, to steal, to destroy hundreds of thousands or even millions of people...everyone who stood in the way. And to hesitate or doubt about all of this was to give in to "intellectual squeamishness" and "stupid liberalism", the attributes of people who "could not see the forest for the trees".[43]

Kopelev claims that people can "become possessed". Not by the devil, but does it matter? Rather, by "a desire to serve values and powers above and beyond humanity".[44] Nor does he really say as to how he came to believe in, and to serve, these powers. He was brought up with no other belief and his belief in communism simply happened.[45]

The ultimate value for every person is his or her own life. If you loose it you have nothing, unless you believe in an afterlife. And that, let us face it, is only a belief. But sometimes it can be understandable that you might sacrifice your own life. You could

---

42 Kopelev, p. 12.
43 Kopelev, p. 11.
44 Kopelev, pp. 12–14.
45 L. Kopelev, *The Education of a True Believer* (London, 1981) pp. 42–142.

figure: yes, I have lived enough, but others deserve that chance too – my children, the people of my community. When a routine test caused a meltdown in the Chernobyl nuclear reactor in April 1986, many people gave their lives for others. Helicopter pilots bombed the burning reactor with sand and cement to put out the fire. They had no protection. When it was realised that the water under the reactor might form a critical mass with leaking uranium and graphite and cause a massive explosion, volunteers dived down repeatedly and eventually opened the safety valve to drain it off. These people got thanks and an unpleasant death. They were heroes; they did what had to be done.[46] Maybe they died with a sense of fulfilment. One hopes so.

In battle, the army that has indoctrinated its soldiers to risk death for the cause for which they believe that they are fighting has an advantage.[47] Even the most talented strategists can do nothing against enemy forces unless those under their command can be inspired with a commitment to face, and sometimes accept, death. American involvement in Vietnam pitted a well-trained army, equipped with the most efficient weaponry, against bands of committed guerrilla fighters. The support these guerrillas received from the villagers among whom they moved, like fish in water, to adopt Mao's phrase, was one critical factor. Divisiveness on the American side as to the justice of their cause weighed against them because criticism tends to undermine the commitment of a fighting force. Despite this, the forces were professional and well equipped. In contrast, the Vietcong forces were characterised by small fighting groups clustered around a communist official responsible for their continual reindoctrination. Daily reinforcement of the justice of their cause strengthened morale. Captured guerrillas were, on

---

46 S. Alexievich, *Voices from Chernobyl* (London, 2005) passim and see the *Guardian* "Buried Alive" 7 December 2000 and "Land of the Dead" 25 April 2005.

47 Religious belief can help the strength of a fighting force: M. Edwardes (ed.), *Ibn Ishaq: The Life of Muhammad, Apostle of Allah* (London, 2003) 51-103.

interrogation, found to be seized of a commitment superior to any other factor; their generation had been chosen to die for "the sacred cause" of the liberation of their homeland. The Vietcong were prepared to risk being killed, but the forces of South Vietnam put their own safety first, principally, it seems, because they lacked any ideological drive. Any key confrontation, which demanded that the South Vietnamese should risk death, was therefore shirked, building up Vietcong morale and safeguarding their strategic emplacement.[48]

A "cause worth dying for" is a clear advantage when two sides face each other in combat. As Stephen Holmes puts it "belief systems are military assets".[49] Again, the superior aim justifies destruction, in this case of the self. Even the use of battle-police, an almost universal feature of warfare, whereby soldiers are put in a situation where they must fight or be executed by their own side, is an insufficient substitute for heroism. Throughout the course of the war in Vietnam, very few Vietcong defected. The US bombing campaign against North Vietnam strengthened, rather than diminished, the population's fervour to win through.[50] General William Westmoreland, the commander of the US forces, could not believe that a military solution would not work. This, despite around two million Vietnamese deaths as against 78,000 of his own soldiers.[51] Warfare demands, if it is necessary, that core members of the fighting group must be prepared to put their lives on the line to advance the cause for which combat has been engaged.[52] This ability, to sacrifice oneself for a

---

48 N. Sheehan, A *Bright Shinning Lie: John Paul Vann and America in Vietnam* (London, 1988) pp. 203–65, see in particular the account of the battle of Ap Bac.

49 In D. Gambetta (ed.), *Making Sense of Suicide Missions* (Oxford, 2005) p. 160.

50 See S. Karnow, *Vietnam: A History* (London, 1994) pp. 412, 469, 473–9 and 645–7.

51 See the obituary of General Westmoreland in the *Guardian* 20 July 2005.

52 See J. Keegan, *The Face of Battle* (London, 1976) particularly pp. 72–8, 113–16 and 156–7.

"greater cause", implies that within the mind there is some value that potentially exceeds even that of self-preservation.

In Chernobyl, the aim was to preserve the community by irradiating oneself. In Vietnam, the aim was to free the homeland by dying in battle. Both of these are secular, and not religious, aims. When America was attacked on 11 September 2001, no armed warplanes were airborne that might, if ordered, attack the passenger planes that were being used as bombs. Several unarmed planes were in the air on training exercises, however. Colonel Robert Hasss of the Northeast Defence Sector explained that since "the only way to stop an aircraft is with your own aircraft if you do not have any weapons" that those on training exercises "would have been asked to give their lives themselves to prevent further attacks if needed".[53]

No matter how this is looked at, and despite the current offensiveness of the proposition, suicide missions can be undertaken for good motives: understandable ones and not just mythic intangibles. Perhaps, again, it is the quality of the myth that reveals whether the mind behind the action is fractured so that it pursues destruction for its own sake. In interviews with failed suicide bombers, conducted by BBC television in Israeli jails, one explained how they reconciled themselves to their mission: since fighting injustice was God's will, the suicide bomber does not need to account to his or her conscience for those killed, maimed or bereaved as Fate has decreed this to be their lot.[54] Osama bin Laden claimed that the attacks of 11 September "benefited Islam greatly", so that in Holland the number of people being received into Islam, in one particular centre, "during the days following the operations, were more than the people who accepted Islam in the last eleven years".[55] This is a myth. It cannot justify terror

---

53 Colonel Robert Hass in an interview with BBC television broadcast 1 September 2002 at 21.00 and quoted in Gambetta 274.
54 "Inside Israel's Jails" BBC 2 Television, 21 March 2005 at 21.00.
55 www.usatoday.com/news/attack/2001/12/13/transcript.htm, quoted in Gambetta, pp. 264–65.

and murder. Where do the myths end and where do they begin? Is it only the other side that are afflicted by insanity? Do we ever dare to think that our motivations for spreading Democracy or Christianity or Freedom may not possibly be tinged by some myth?

The heroes of Chernobyl had no such illusions. Professor Diego Gambetta speculates that suicide bombers may experience a dissociative state, in control of their actions while living outside themselves; "forgetting the self" as he puts it.[56] All of the impersonal things that people are prepared to die for are absolutes: my country, my religion, my party, democracy, communism, freedom. You could argue that since many of these reflect the importance of the continuity of the community, over the life of the individual, that there may be a dormant trait put in us by evolution that enables us to sacrifice our lives so that our group can continue. That is possible. But I do not see it as a complete answer. It is what people define themselves as that determines what they will die for. They may pretend to be Christians, but be unconverted as the Archbishop of Rwanda pointed out immediately before the genocide, when their nominal religion hides the concept of superiority that really matters to them: their ethnic group, their nationality, their dominant beliefs. In any society, the sense of self may be defined by nationalism, liberalism or some other quality apart from faith. In Islam, the sense of Islamic law that respects the immunity of non-combatants in warfare may be displaced by a victim mania that has turned to pure hatred of outsiders. Whether it is flags, revolution, religion, victimism or uniform, those who are dying, or killing while dying, are all driven by their own self-definition. People sacrificing themselves are less "forgetting the self" than "offering up" the self. The sense of what is absolute as a value within them is what governs their decision to die.

It would be easy to say that this is all the expression of religion, or some other set of absolute values as a substitute for reli-

---

56 Gambetta, p. 275.

gion. That would explain little.[57] Yet, there does seem to be a connection that is difficult to ignore. In January 1937, Carl Jung wrote that before the First World War people were convinced that every problem could be put right by rational means. That illusion was shattered. As the Second World War approached, he saw it as an "amazing spectacle" that states had taken on "the age-old totalitarian claims of theocracy" so that people were again ready to cut each other's throats "in support of childish theories as to how to create paradise on Earth".[58] Writing in 1942, another Swiss philosopher, Denis de Rougemont, defined a totalitarian regime as one which set out "to centralise, radically, all temporal power and all spiritual authority". When this happened a government became a "political religion", what he called "a regressive community based on the past".[59] Both agreed that these absolutist claims would suppress any dissent. A century before, Alexis de Tocqueville had described the French Revolution as a "species of religion", one that had "overrun the entire world with its apostles, militants and martyrs".[60]

I do not know if a religious instinct is part of the fundamental inheritance of the human mind. It is not even easy to define a religion beyond the concept of submitting one's will to a set of precepts apparently based on a divine revelation. The divine principle would appear to out rule ideologies. Or does it? It is much easier to recognise the practice of religion, with its sacred books, temples and rituals. Ideologies may appear to be outside a religious concept. In their mildest manifestation, many states take on at least some rituals such as national hymns, flags, ceremonies for opening parliament, exaggerated regard paid to royal personages,

---

57 Gambetta points out that between 1981 and 2003, more than half of suicide missions were carried out by secular groups: Gambetta, pp. 261, and see 279–88.

58 C.W. 11.47; see also 11.778; C.G. Jung, *C.G. Jung Speaking: Interviews and Encounters*, edited by W. McGuire and R.F.C. Hull (London, 1980) p. 1036.

59 D. de Rougemont, *Talk of the Devil* (London, 1945) pp. 50–1, originally *La Part du Diable* (Paris, 1942).

60 Quoted in Burleigh, p. 6.

founding fathers, the heroic dead, their precepts and pledges of allegiance. None of these prove the power to captivate the populace in a secular religion, much less explain merciless cruelty. De Rougemont presciently wrote that a state religion would not ask "What do you believe?" but rather "Who are your dead?" He predicted that political religions would claim, "more blood, more dead, more funeral rites, ceremonial imprecations, sacrifices of propitiation [and] the beat of gruesome drums". All of these affirm a sense of self-definition. At the same time, the possibility of a person centring himself or herself on a faith, whether transcendent or secular, has to already exist as a function of the mind before they can be seduced by ritual. Jung believed that it was through religion that people relate to whatever they hold to be the highest value. Hence, all absolute values were in fact religious.[61] According to him, the power of religious values alone had the power to transform people.

It is characteristic of religious experience that it seizes the core of our being and that this is felt as being independent of any act of willing on our part.[62] Religious teaching explains this as the coming into an individual of a vast external power that so reorients a person as to amount to them being born anew. When sane mythology expresses an absolute value it appears in the form of a prince, a priest or a great man, when personified, or as reflected in symbols of the infinite when in abstract; the stars, the sun, light, a pearl, a precious stone.[63] Leaders have notions of transcendence beamed onto them. Instead of being ordinary, they become part of the absolute answer. As regards notions of perfection, ideology is just that. Jung claimed that the mind has a centre that reflects our need to worship some form of divinity and that this, when evoked, is greater than any other value. One of Jung's patients described the feeling evoked by a dream of this psychic centre-point as "an impression of the

---

61 C.W. 11.137.
62 C.W. 11.6; Aion C.W. 9 II.216.
63 Aion C.W. 9 II.346, 354, 358.

most sublime harmony".[64] Jung claimed that this power within the mind was not to be denied: its suppression is answered by materialism, atheism, communism, militarism, nationalism and by every form of doctrinaire thinking that seeks to rule over society in making its own forms of magical appeasement a substitute for religious observance.[65] If this is right, then it follows that anything that is absolute ought to be expressed by people in a ritualised form, like a religion. Would that mean that weird mythic elements would also intrude into secular practice?

The merciless Lenin promoted the logic of atheism as the foundation of his new society. Yet, the manner in which his godless movement behaved reflected an easy slip into the external signs of religion. Lenin himself believed the ideas of communism to be "sacred".[66] His person became inviolable and his body, preserved after his death as a relic, became the central object of veneration of the Soviet State. Even before he died, any questioning of the correctness of his ideas, or of any measure sanctioned by him, had become a grave wrong within party circles.[67] All through the Soviet era, the party cadres described themselves as working "in the spirit of Lenin's commandments",[68] making it their life's work to defend Leninism "from any attack, any assault".[69] This they did in fulfilment of the promise that his ideology would, in effect, reveal paradise on Earth.[70]

Lenin had declared only one way for the party to proceed. Party membership became, like a religious ministry, the highest form of commitment to communist ideology: "There is no loftier title than that of a member of the party, of which Comrade Lenin has been founder and leader", Stalin said.[71] The central

---

64 C.W. 11.110.
65 Aion C.W. 9II.170, 141–2.
66 Volkoganov, p. 219.
67 I. Deutscher, *Stalin: A Political Biography* (London, 1982) p. 267.
68 Volkogonov, p. 451.
69 Volkogonov, p. 450.
70 Volkogonov, p. 477; generally see pp. 408–76.
71 Stalin's Speech to the second congress of the Soviet, quoted in Deutscher 272.

core of this quasi-priesthood never wavered from his ideas until the late 1980s, when the opening up of Soviet society to debate dissolved the entire edifice. In keeping with this mood of the times, two months after Lenin's death, another central committee member declared to a group of engineers that by carrying out the dead leader's "revolutionary proletarian commandments precisely and rigorously" Leninism would conquer the world. When that moment of total conquest arrived, he said, Communists would not simply rejoice, but they would take "the glad tidings" to Lenin's mausoleum on Red Square.[72] Who would hear this good news, since the afterlife had officially ceased to exist? Why announce it to a corpse and why the need of pilgrimages? Lenin's thought, and the Soviet system that was built on it, was the "holiest of holies".[73] For anyone to undermine it by expressing contrary thoughts remained a crime so long as the Soviet regime existed. In reality, such a crime is that of blasphemy.[74] Lenin remained ever-present. Even though he was dead, it was possible for party believers to express the emotion-filled thought that at high ceremonial gatherings he was there "among us".[75] At the second congress of the Soviets, Stalin read out an oath to the dead leader, vowing to keep faith with his precepts, as if he were a saint.[76] Even party buildings became like a church, a place of reverence for ideological morality, where even men's speech must be tempered by respect for that system of thought which represented the core drive of their being.[77]

---

72 Volkogonov, p. 477.
73 Volkogonov, p. 323.
74 *C. G. Jung Speaking*, p. 102-104.
75 "For where two or three come together in my name, I am there with them" Matthew 18:20.
76 "In leaving us, Comrade Lenin ordained us to keep faith with the principles of the Communist International. We vow to thee, Comrade Lenin, that we shall not spare our lives in the endeavour to strengthen and broaden the alliance of the workers of the whole-world the Communist International" is a sample; quoted in Deutscher, pp. 272–3.
77 Volkogonov, pp. 317–319.

This is but an example. Secular forms of worship characterise societies built on an ideology. The blasphemous and mes-
sianic claims of the Nazi leadership are another expression of
the invasion of ritual into the secular world of ideology: as is the
manner in which Japanese society expressed its wartime imperialism in a mass consciousness centred on the sacredness of the
State and its ambitions.[78] The Germans had their parades, the
touching of all flags of battle against the bloodstained banner
from the legendary Munich putsch and the revival of medieval
communities of supposed "knights". During the Second World
War, the Japanese were bombarded with tales of heroism by
their warriors, their mission as the saviour of Asia and militaris-
tic ceremonies dedicating aircraft carriers, regiments and army
bases. None of this caused people to rebel or to laugh, certainly not out loud. There has to be some sense of receptivity to this
nonsense within us. As an ideology takes over a community,
false symbols of religion come more and more to dominate
how it expresses itself. Religion, as such, can also fuse itself with
secular aims, as in medieval Europe, with the same result of the
myth of higher values justifying savagery. The Crusades and the
Inquisition are but examples of the consequences.

Even if a theory based on human susceptibility to religion
might answer, in part, the mystery of ideology, it could not be
a complete answer. People join ideological groups because it
makes them feel part of a great movement; Fromm's theory of
narcissism again. The ideology tells them what to do, provides
them with comrades and teaches them what to think. Some
higher purpose is then in charge of their very selves. Ideologies
teach hatred and do so successfully. This must partly be a reflection of the fact that their membership is full of hate. It is also an

---

78 As to Nazi Germany, see the examples in Burleigh, pp. 75, 100–17,
152–5, 194, 196, 212, 258–77; as to Japan, see the examples in L.
Young, *Japan's Total Empire: Manchuria and the Culture of Wartime
Imperialism* (Berkley, 1999) pp. 39, 67, 72–144, 148, 165, 176–8,
251, 271, 361, 364, 367–9, 375, 384.

expression of a basic human failing that is simply amplified by weight of numbers and self-righteousness. It seems to me that this is a question of imbalance. When a person's self-regard is inflated, the hidden evil in them is projected on to anyone who appears as an enemy. Legal practice shows the potential in this for violence. When a community defines itself in terms of its glorious history, its nobility of purpose and the injustices done to it, you equally have the potential for violence. On a much bigger scale.

Ideology falsely weighs the balance of ordinary human life towards the divine. It claims to seek justice, while dealing out violence in huge measures. It always seeks vast and unattainable results; perfection on earth. It claims not only that paradise is attainable but also that some other party, the Unionists, the Nationalists, the Jews, the Tutsi, the Armenians, are what stand in its way. Ideology is a false promise. It does not just offer a guide as to how to reconcile oneself with one's inherent evil to the benefit of one's community. True faith does this by drawing people into an uncomfortable examination of their faults. Ideology, instead, promises a childish and painless transformation. It has not just some of the answers to the problems of human life, but all of the answers. By joining an ideology, people can continue to lie to themselves about their lives through becoming part of a movement that promotes their very beings to the stature of perfection. Ideology falsely lays claim to transformation on a divine, and therefore unattainable, scale. The result is that the real or imagined opponent is not just wrong. He is the wrecker, the heretic, and the apostate. However it is expressed, he is the one to be made to suffer, together with all those like him. So, if an ideological movement is determined to "deal with" their enemies, how can they possibly escape death?

CHAPTER 7

Spared by a Killer

I T IS NOT EASY TO KILL someone. It requires the application of serious force and, in many cases, making careful preparation. Even if a person plans a murder, they sometimes find that they cannot go through with it. Even if they start it, some find that they cannot finish it. Murder is a horrific business. It takes time, and time allows people to change their minds. Often they later regret that they ever went through with it at all, not just because they have been caught but because of their conscience.

In one of the first murder cases that I dealt with, two men beat an elderly man to death outside his isolated farmhouse. They were uncle and nephew. It was one of many instances of violence motivated by the expectation of "hidden riches" that have regularly cropped up in criminal practice in Ireland. Although I did not represent him, I wondered whether the nephew, JC, ever really intended to kill the victim. He claimed that he had accompanied his uncle, a much older man, on what he thought was only a robbery expedition. Threats and mild force were what he said he foresaw as being enough to get the deceased to "cooperate". They did not work. The farmer fled the farmhouse. According to their confession statements to the police, the nephew caught up with him and then his uncle, who had picked up a plank, brought him down with a blow to his back. The nephew withdrew as the victim pleaded for his life while the uncle struck him repeatedly.

From a short distance away, the nephew picked up a stone and threw it at the prostrate man. As a matter of law, that action was one of participation in serious violence. It later made possible the jury's verdict of guilty of murder.

I often wondered what would have happened if JC had had the strength of mind to withdraw from that enterprise. Certainly, he would have lived the rest of his life more happily. But he didn't. There was nothing to stop him. His uncle was a man of savage temper and there was no one to step in. JC had told the interviewing detectives "I wish now someone could have offered me a way out."

In our kind of society, where murder is a crime, killing is infrequent. People don't do it because they fear detection. Criminal gangs go about murder enterprises in secrecy. They usually choose the killer from within their own number. People are less likely to "rat" if they all share the responsibility. If the murder has been carefully planned by all of them, the gang members are far less likely to back away from it. But things go wrong. A gun can jamb. A police car may unexpectedly come on the scene. Or, the trouble can be internal. In more than one planned murder, the killer has come face to face with the intended victim and not "had the bottle", as they say, to go through with it. In one instance, the "target" simply slammed the door on the killer carrying a machine gun and fled through a back garden. The criminal went back and reported "an escape". After all, the chosen killer may not hate the person chosen to die. His commitment is to the crime boss, who has been double-crossed or insulted some other way, and is seething with rage. In many of these cases a professional killer, with a "good track record", is chosen for the job. Nothing will stop him.

Killing someone is shameful. When you remove all of the other barriers, such as police and bodyguards, shame is what makes it difficult. People are not introduced to the task of murder without some preparation. Gitta Sereny's view of Franz Stangl was that he was groomed for his task as a death camp commander during his years of working in euthanasia "clinics".

Even at the height of a campaign of mass murder, the perpetrators need to hide away their slaughter or to explain it as merely a deportation, a pre-emptive strike, a self-defensive act or whatever lie calms the conscience of the population. Stangl, after all, when commandant at Treblinka, had to explain away his work to his wife; as we shall see, a task that was not easy. In 1943, an instance of the power of shame occurred in Nazi-dominated Germany. About five thousand German Jews, married to non-Jewish women were first rounded up and then released on the orders of the government. Almost all of their wives had demonstrated for justice for an entire week outside the detention centre where they were being held. This led to an official announcement that the Jewish men were to be classified as "privileged persons" and "incorporated in the national community".[1]

To succeed in mass murder you have to have secrecy and exclusiveness. Tricked by lies out of defending themselves, people are brought away and slaughtered: outside towns in Turkey, to camps in Nazi-occupied Europe, or herded together and dispatched by trained militias in Rwanda. There are two objectives in all of this: that no one should escape and that no one should interfere by offering people "a way out". To conjure up how the victims feel, you need little imagination. Utter terror. They are looking death in the face. But how do the killers feel? I have often wondered how they go through with the task of murder after murder.

In war soldiers are legally entitled to attack the enemy, and be attacked themselves, at any time prior to capture. As Professor Michael Walzer points out, sometimes soldiers who have the enemy in the sights of their rifle are unable to pull the trigger. By asking why people cannot kill, you go some way to explaining why they can. Walzer discovered five instances in war memoirs where the writers were unwilling to kill the enemy. These all occurred during lulls in the fighting. During the

---

1   M. Gilbert, *The Righteous: The Unsung Heroes of the Holocaust* (London, 2002) p. 165.

Spanish Civil War, George Orwell found that he was unable to shoot at a nationalist soldier because, when he spotted him, he was running along between the lines holding up his trousers with both his hands. He had come to Spain to kill fascists. A man doing something silly, he wrote "is visibly a fellow-creature, similar to yourself, and you don't feel like shooting at him." Robert Graves, a sniper during the Second World War, was prevented by a similar feeling from personally killing a German whom he spotted having a bath: "I disliked the idea of killing a naked man, so I handed the rifle to the sergeant with me." He did not stay to watch the result. In another memoir, from the First World War, a group of soldiers did not respond to an enemy soldier running towards them because he had his arms stretched out in front of him in a ridiculous posture as if he were trying to dive through the earth: "Nobody offered to shoot him, he looked too funny …" The two other accounts focused on the shared evocation of human feeling as a barrier. At Anzio, a British soldier woke one morning to an amazing sunrise that made him feel "like Noah must have done when he saw his rainbow." When a German soldier appeared, wandering about "revelling in the promise of warmth and spring", he and a colleague decided to scare him away, rather than kill him. Similarly, Emilio Lassu, an Italian fighting the Austrians, explained that he regarded his enemy in inanimate terms as "mysterious and terrible beings." When previously he had led attacks on their positions, he had thought of himself as fighting against the trenches and buildings where these creatures lived. Then, one morning, from a vantage point above their lines, he saw the Austrians having morning coffee and chatting. When an officer appeared, he took aim. But then the "target" lit a cigarette. He reflected that it was better to wait and to lead his men in a military attack: that would be war; this would be murder. That thought came to him because "This cigarette formed an invisible link between us. No sooner did I see its smoke than I wanted a cigarette myself…"

This is how Walzer interprets these various hesitations:

For what does it mean to say that someone has a right to life? To say that is to recognise a fellow creature, who is not threatening me… whose person is as valuable as my own. An enemy has to be described differently and though the stereotypes through which he is seen are often grotesque, they have a certain truth. He alienates himself from me when he tries to kill me, and from our common humanity. But the alienation is temporary, the humanity imminent. It is restored, as it were, by the prosaic acts that break down the stereotypes in each of the five stories. Because he is funny, naked, and so on, my enemy is changed… into a man.[2]

Walzer was writing about ordinary warfare, where the rule of surrender applies. It is much harder to find instances of refraining from killing someone when the entire objective of an operation is not just war but mass murder. The intensity of the discipline applied to the killers determines, at least to some degree, whether human sympathy might break out. I have found no instances of Nazi killing squads deciding not to murder people in death camps. In the one instance that came close, that of a child who had been pulled out alive from a gas chamber and revived, the SS man in charge had someone else kill her. [3]

People who are to be murdered are not treated as human beings. This makes it less shameful to kill them. It seems to me that Walzer is right in saying that submerging the victim's humanity aids the killing process. Neither the killers nor the organisers want anything that might awaken their conscience. That can happen when victims confront the killers to their face. It may or may not help to save them.[4]

In December 1998, Eric Firkins was one of a group of tourists on an expedition to a remote part of Yemen. One day they were taken captive by a group of terrorists. Their demand was for the release of captives in Yemeni prisons. The next day

2 M. Walzer, *Just and Unjust Wars: A Moral Argument With Historical Illustrations* (London, 1992, second edition) pp. 138–42.

3 M. Nyiszli, *Auschwitz: A Doctor's Eye-Witness Account* (London, 1973) pp. 88–93.

4 E. Staub, *The Roots of Evil: The Origins of Genocide and Other Group Violence* (Cambridge, 1989) pp. 165–9.

a party of soldiers, attempting to secure their release, ambushed the kidnappers and their hostages. Fire was returned with machine guns and rocket launchers. They started killing the tourists. Eric Firkins saw a kidnapper pointing a rifle at a tourist's back. He shouted "No, No". The would-be killer, who had just murdered two of the group, came over to him and put a revolver to his temple and shouted something in Arabic to the Yemeni army. At this point, Firkins had had enough and did not care if he was killed or not. He pushed the gun away from his head and looked straight into the kidnapper's eyes. The man seemed surprised but did not shoot. Instead, he put a rifle to the back of a woman hostage and marched her towards the soldiers who managed to shoot him dead.[5] It goes without saying that Fiakins was lucky. Killers can overcome any sense of fellow feeling that might make them hesitate, especially against a strong ideological background that damns a particular group. But still, it may not be easy for them to kill when confronted. During the deportation of the Jewish population of Tarnow to the Belzec death camp in 1942, the Gestapo herded all of the victims barefoot into the market square and then made them kneel down. Then they separated the children from their parents. While this was happening, on an apparent whim, a Gestapo man went over to a man who was kneeling with his daughter and shot him. To his surprise, the daughter stood up and shouted at him: "You scoundrel! What did my father do to you that you shot him?" He then threatened to kill her too:

> *The girl looked at him with a penetrating gaze. When he turned away, avoiding her eyes, she insulted him again, called him a mere coward who shot defenceless people, and shouted that he dared not look her in the eyes: "Look straight into my eyes, you coward … and shoot! Those eyes will pursue you and haunt you all your life!" The Gestapo man winced, turned away from the girl, as if to muster his courage, and after a moment aimed his revolver at her and shot her.[6]*

---

5   *Observer Magazine*, 8 February 2004.
6   A. Eisenberg, *Witness to the Holocaust* (New York, 1981) p. 267.

In ordinary social encounters one searches, as in a mirror, for the reaction of people to oneself. These are responded to on a conscious and on a subliminal level. The degradation of captives through herding, extracting information and enforcing compliance with orders changes the nature of a human relationship radically. Having defenceless and humiliated people under your total control, I believe, brings out the worst in people. This is explored in Chapter 9. In systems of government where the stripping of rights from people is arbitrary and absolute, no protection is offered from destructive impulses. The murderous drive that comes as a result of a degradation ritual will not be impeded.[7]

Even in such instances, the reaction of the victim can sometimes amount to a sufficient reassertion of human dignity to demand the right to one to one interaction. In a situation of extreme torture, such as that experienced by Rezak Hukanovic, as a Muslim captive in Serbian hands in Bosnia in 1992, it would seem unlikely that the victim could have any impact upon his captors. His memoir makes it clear that the institutions of torture and degradation were all organised to demand compliance both from the guards and from the captives. Hukanovic describes a bus journey to a torture camp and his response on being viciously beaten by Mrdja, a notoriously sadistic guard. On being singled out for attack he tried to cover his head against the blows:

> *"You put your hand like that just one more time and I will kill you like a dog". Then he hit [me] even harder than before. [I] felt the kind of pain that knocks the sense out of a man. Blood was all over [my] hair, face and neck, flooding [my] filthy sweat soaked t-shirt. [I] raised [my] head. Looking straight into the eyes that had signalled [my] bloody end, [I] said: "Look what you're doing to me! What have I ever done*

---

7 For an instance see African Rights, *Rwanda: Death, Despair and Defiance* (London, 1995) the case of Gloriose Mukakanimba, p. 591.

to you?" [My] question took Mrdja by surprise. Glancing
away to his right Mrdja saw Muharem Nezirevic, the Radio
Prijedor producer. "Ah, my little birdie, you again!" He start-
ed clubbing Muharum on the head. "So you didn't want to put
any news of the war from the front on right?"[8]

Was it possible that the victim heroically confronting his captor
unmasked his conduct? Any reminder of human interaction, it
seems, makes murder more difficult. It upsets the expected victim–killer dynamic.

This is born out by the instances where the victim has been
spared because he or she previously knew the killer chosen by
the organisers of mass murder. During the Rwanda genocide
this happened more than once. The chaotic nature of the systems of death dealing allowed people to opt out more easily
than in Nazi-occupied Europe. Thomas Kamilindi took refuge
from the genocide, together with his wife and many others, in
the Hôtel des Milles Collines in the middle of Kigali. Paul
Rusesabagina, the heroic manager of the establishment, used a
fax line that had not been cut off to telephone and fax "the
whole world", as he put it, to implore their help. Thomas used
the line to give an interview to a French radio station. In it he
embarrassed the genocidal regime by undermining its lies. He
was told that the regime had decided to kill him for this. A soldier arrived at the hotel. He got his name and discovered that
he had been a friend from childhood. He called him on the
internal phone and said:

"OK, I'm coming," and I went. He explained that the military com-
mand wanted me dead. I asked him who decided this, their names, and
who had sent him. He hesitated. Then he said, in effect, "I don't know
who's going to kill you. I can't do it. But I'm leaving the hotel and
they'll send someone for sure to kill you." Nobody else came for me...

---

8   R. Hukanovic, *The Tenth Circle of Hell* (London, 1997) pp. 110–11.
The author in the original refers to himself in the third person.

The situation normalised. I went out in the corridor again after a while, and we stayed put.[9]

Any gesture of recognition, or any hint of sympathy that establishes a real relationship between people, as equals, seems to make killing more difficult. So, to be identified as the wife of a man who was known and liked by some members of a murder expedition could be enough to be spared death in the chaos of the Rwandan genocide.[10] In another example, a man asked the soldier who had captured him for time to pray before he was murdered. It seems that accepting this request made it too difficult for the soldier to proceed to kill him.[11] In another case, a twenty-year-old woman was discovered with her two brothers hiding in a roof. People who knew her and her family found them. The militia who, perhaps looking for an excuse, said that they were young, spared them. They also said that their mother was "a good woman who used to give us drinks". It is possible that the surprise of encountering a known person from a respected family calmed the murderous intent and allowed for an exchange on a person-to-person level.

A possible pattern seems to emerge of encounters on a human level operating as a truthful mirror to the actions of the assailant. The equality of these encounters, and those that follow in this text, seems to be a crucial factor. Self-elevation to a level of being beyond evil, being a member of some group with all of the answers (perhaps thought of as being given by God), and notions of pursuing the "holy mission" of some ideology, destroys the equality of human contact. The problem with ideological groups is that they often try to preserve their "purity" by preaching that a believer should have no contact with an unbeliever and that no compromise, especially with "unbeleif",

---

9   P. Gourevitch, *We wish to Inform you that Tomorrow we will be Killed with our Families: Stories from Rwanda* (New York, 1998) pp. 132–3.

10 A. Des Forges, *Leave None to Tell the Story: Genocide in Rwanda* (London, 1999) p. 384.

11 African Rights, *Rwanda*, p. 574.

is possible. Apart from any potential psychological explanation founded on the effect of sundering the personality, so that good resides in the self and evil is projected onto others, despising others accounts for much of the dynamic of killing. You do not respond to people who "are despicable" on either a human or an honest level. Where there is no equality is there any hope of truthful interaction?

Violence, humiliation and imprisonment are commonly used as blinding devices to facilitate killing. If you allow people time to reflect, it is possible for them to confront each other's behaviour on a basis of true interaction. When Warsaw was invaded by the Germans in September 1939, notices were put up guaranteeing the life and property rights of the Jewish population. These were, of course, lies. Some months later, the pianist and composer Wladyslav Szpilman was walking with his brother and father, shortly after curfew time, attempting to return to their home. They encountered a German police patrol and were pushed up against the wall of a building. The policemen stepped back and began to prepare their weapons:

> At the same time I heard loud weeping and convulsive sobbing. I turned my head, and in the harsh torchlight I saw my father kneeling on the wet tarmac, sobbing and begging the policemen for our lives ... Henryk was bending over my father, whispering to him, trying to raise him to his feet ... I turned to the wall again. The situation had not changed. Father was weeping, Henryk was trying to calm him, the police were still aiming their guns at us ... a few moments passed and a loud voice came through the wall of light. "What do you do for a living?" Henryk answered for all three of us ... "We're musicians". One of the policemen stationed himself in front of me, grabbed my coat collar and shook me in a final fit of temper, not that there was any reason for it now he had decided to let us live "Lucky for you I'm a musician too!" He gave me a shove, and I stumbled back against the wall. "Get out". We ran off into the dark, anxious to get out of range of their torches as fast as possible, before they could change their minds. We could hear their voices falling away behind us, engaged in violent argument. The other two were remonstrating with the one who had let us go. They thought we deserved

> *no sympathy, since we had started the war in which Germans were dying.*[12]

So, was it that being a musician was like the soldier wanting a cigarette: something that established the common nature of the human experience between one of the killers and their victims? It does not seem to be as simple as that. What stood the protagonists apart was the notion that an utterly defenceless people, the Jews, were required under the prevailing ideology to be thought of as the aggressors. Yet, a common human factor broke through. It is in order to ensure that those types of incidents do not multiply and result in victims being spared, that mass murder is systematically organised and the executioners made subject to peer pressure and discipline.

If ideology is, as seems to be the case, one of the foundations of pitiless killing, can you use ideology to stand the killer's motivations upside down? In theory, it should be possible. But, it is not easy, as an ideology can become the core of a person's being: something that needs almost a conversion experience to break down, or the chance to find out that killers and victims are closer than they think. An isolated example from Poland tends to show this. This incident happened in the aftermath of the Nazi occupation when propaganda had whipped up anti-Jewish feelings to a fever pitch. An unpublished manuscript by Ben Helfgott, a survivor of the Theresienstadt concentration camp is quoted by Martin Gilbert in his book on the Holocaust. It is a lonely illustration of a Jew being spared death, though outside the era and control of the Nazi organisation that permitted of no exceptions. Shortly after the Nazi occupation of Poland had been ended, waiting late at night at the train station in Czestochowa for a connection to their home village in Poland, Ben and his cousin, then aged twelve and fifteen years, were accosted by two Polish Army officers. They were ordered to accompany them to a police station to have their

---

12 W. Szpilman, *The Pianist* (London, 2002) pp. 52–3.

papers checked. Walking endlessly through deserted streets in the early morning, Ben made an enquiry as to where the police station was. It emerged, in the most derogatory fashion, that the officers intended to murder the boys because they were Jewish. In a house, their suitcases were emptied of their best clothes, given to them by the Red Cross. They were then marched off again through the deserted city. The narrative continues:

> As we walked ... I tried desperately to renew conversation so as to restore the personal and human touch, but it was to no avail. I endeavoured to conceal and ignore my true feelings and innermost thoughts, pretending to believe that they were acting in the name of the law, but they became strangely uncommunicative. After what seemed like an eternity we arrived at a place that looked fearfully foreboding. The buildings were derelict and abandoned; there was no sign of human habitation; all one could hear was the howling of the wind, the barking of the dogs and the mating calls of the cats. The two officers menacingly extracted the pistols from their holsters, and ordered us to walk to the nearest wall. Both my cousin and I felt rooted to the ground, unable to move. When, at last, I recovered my composure, I emitted a torrent of desperate pleas and entreaties. I pleaded with them "haven't we suffered enough? Haven't the Nazis caused enough destruction and devastation to all of us? Our common enemy is destroyed and the future is ours. We have survived against all the odds and why are you intent on promoting the heinous crimes that the Nazis have unleashed. Don't we speak the same language as you? Didn't we imbibe the same culture as you?" I went on in the same vein and speaking agitatedly for some time. Eventually one of the officers said "Let's leave them, they are after all still boys." As they put away their pistols, they made a remark which still rings loud in my ears. "You can consider yourselves lucky. We have killed many of your kind. You are the first ones we have left alive". With this comment they disappeared ...[13]

The lengthy passage of time and the orderly journey through the city streets perhaps allowed for reality to penetrate through

---

13 M. Gilbert, *The Holocaust: The Jewish Tragedy* (London, 1990) pp. 813–4.

the killers' self-deception. In their minds, were they going to kill something other than people? One wonders what their image of the boys was. Does Lieutenant Calley's "blob" description for the people that he killed help us here? Whatever image the kidnappers had, that image was not enforced through brutalisation. As an encounter, it became one almost on a level of one person to another. The outburst of Ben Helfgott had the effect of confronting the image being projected onto him and his cousin. Like the protest of Hukanovic, it was truth in confrontation with deception. The result was the unexpected creation of the image of normality which, it appears, was the opposite to whatever process was operating in the minds of the killers to make the victims worthy objects for death.

The construct of difference and of guilt was undermined. There is a similar incident from Rwanda. A woman called Josianne from Nyanza sought refuge from the genocide with her father and others in a group of three houses. Those were subjected to attack by burning, demolition and grenades. The militia blew a hole in the wall and came in. People escaping were murdered by machete. Then the killers came to her. She offered to pay the killers, but two other women who had made a similar offer were murdered:

> One of them hit me on the head. Before he continued another intera-hamwe said: "Don't let's kill her." Then they began to ask me a lot of questions which was strange because we knew each other very well. These people were from our sector. "Are you Tutsi?" I said yes. "What is your quarrel with Habyarimana?" I said that I did not have any quarrels with Habyarimana. I explained that I was actually born during his regime. "What is your relationship with the RPF?" I told them I did not have a relationship with the RPF.[14]

She was then allocated, under a Hutu ID card, as a "wife" to a member of the militia. She had moved outside possession by the symbols that marked her out as suitable only for destruction.

---

14 African Rights, *Rwanda*, p.783.

Driving the engine that sought the death of the intended victims in these instances were notions of justification that were essentially a product of an artificially created theory of enmity: Tutsis, or Jews or Muslims or whatever, must die because of some repellence which is seen as their very essence. The case from Poland tells us most. Ben Helfgott perhaps was spared because he had said enough of his own hopes for the future to evoke a pattern of thinking alien to that which allows such murder: the Nazis had not just been destroyed, both the killers and their intended victims had fought against them together. The basic ideal of a free Poland was common to them all. They shared fundamental hopes of wanting to construct a world that set up positive virtues in opposition to the evils of Nazism. Just as the image of the age in the past where a nation had attained the zenith of its culture is a universal image, it would seem that the golden era to come also inspires people to seek that ideal.[15] It can also operate as a justification for the means that will bring it about. Politics seems to be driven by what can be created by communal effort. Even in the age of economics as the determinant of politics, resort is made to archetypal language that seeks to evoke why a particular movement has a vision for the future. Although intangible and less than fully describable, this kind of rhetoric motivates people to march with its forces. As the victims and the murderers shared the ideal of restoring Poland from the ashes, that common vision counter-forced the alien myth of destructive Jewry. Finally, the young man was allowed to make his plea. When one officer relented, a mirror had been set up to the behaviour of the other that would shame him.

Then there are those who escape death because they are lucky; they never really encounter a killer. The person who confronts them is an unwilling member of a mass murder group. As the genocidal campaign in Rwanda had far less time to prepare thoroughly than that in Nazi-occupied Europe, it produced a good number of such instances. Here are a few.

---

15 C.G. Jung, *Mankind and His Symbols* (London, 1978) pp. 72–5.

Eugène was hidden from the Rwandan mass murder militia for several weeks after the killing of the President in April 1994.[16] The young domestic help of a friend of his assisted him to conceal himself above the ceiling of a house. Both his friend and the domestic help were Hutu. The Interahamwe militia visited the house many times. On the last occasion, they found that the ceiling had collapsed. Eugène had already escaped and had hidden outside in bushes. The state of the house occasioned the suspicion of the militia:

> One of them came out. I froze with terror as I heard footsteps approach me. He put a knife in my chest. I remember thinking that I had only a few seconds left to live. I denied I was the person they were looking for. He asked for my ID card. When he saw Butare marked as my place of origin, he said, "You are really lucky, you come from the same préfecture as me. For that reason I will not denounce you." He told me to stay where I was.[17]

What was the motivation of this single member of the militia? Probably he was one of the unwilling, but coerced, people who were looking for any kind of excuse not to kill. He was alone. So, it was possible for him not to call on others to share in the murder of Eugène, which can operate as a distancing factor. He did not call out to his colleagues, which he could so easily have done, in order to then proceed to beat and torture his victim. Killers are subjected to discipline to ensure they perform their task. The same process occurs in the organisation of soldiers in warfare. They are made part of the mob in order that the mob may move through them in the base collective possession of the myths shared out by deception.[18] Many are forced into battle, but carry a spear only; participation in murder is at the behest of others.[19]

---

16 First names are used as some names gathered by African Rights have been changed to protect the informants.

17 African Rights, *Rwanda*, p. 574.

18 C.W. 91.225.

19 For an example see D. Goldenhagen, *Hitler's Willing Executioners: Ordinary Germans and the Holocaust* (London, 1996) p. 300.

It might be possible to consider that a similar factor of non-involvement was at work in the case of Chantal, though in this instance her assailant boasted of having murdered many. There is no way to know whether this was true or not. Chantal had survived the massacre of some two thousand six hundred people at the parish centre at Hanika. She had hidden with her infant under corpses during the main attack, but her baby was macheted on the head and died the next day. Fleeing some distance away, she hid in a toilet trench for five days. Driven by hunger, she tried to return to the parish centre but on the way she ran into a soldier:

> *He stopped me and asked me for an ID card, or I should say my ethnic card. I told him I was not old enough to have an ethnic card, that is eighteen. With the situation I was in, it was impossible to discover my true age (thirty). I had become so small. He asked me where I lived. I offered to help him carry his load, things he had just looted. He hid me in an empty house and brought me bread and an avocado. He told me he could not hide me in his home because he was the chief of the killers. He had a gun. He left me some water and I spent the night there. I could not eat and drink all he had brought me because I could not understand why this man was being so kind to me.*[20]

Neither killer nor victim threatened the other and the soldier did not exercise the authority of violence to begin a dangerous slide towards interrogation and torture. The fact that help was offered to him by his intended victim might also be a disarming feature. Perhaps the fact that they talked on a one to one basis, and had travelled as equals over a short distance, made the summoning up of destructive impulses more difficult. Perhaps he was never a killer?

It seems to be very rare that a degraded individual chosen to be a victim can impact, save in the most extraordinary circumstances, on the mind of the killers so as to show him his own shame. People at the social level of the killer gangs, their

---

20 African Rights, *Rwanda*, p. 516.

comrades or people whom they respect, can hold up a mirror showing the true face of the killer's motivation. This can have the effect of repelling him, at least temporarily, from murder. In an instance from the Soviet labour camps, a prisoner, who dealt in icons before his "sentence" was about to attack a Jewish inmate. He was put off when an older prisoner shouted at him that a man "who bought and sold pictures of Christ" ought to be ashamed of himself.[21] Where people associated with a killer group make a stand in favour of sparing a particular individual, the mirror of social interaction more brightly reflects the real image of behaviour which self-deception dims.

The Jewish community in Iraq were, in the aftermath of the Israeli victory in the Six Day War of 1967, a convenient group to be scape-goated by the ruling Ba'ath party. The war resulted in ten Iraqi soldiers being killed, while thirty were left wounded. In December 1968 a further sixteen soldiers, from an Iraqi artillery battery stationed in Jordan, were killed and thirty were wounded in an Israeli air attack. The response of the regime was to promise to "strike mercilessly with a fist of steel at ... the handmaidens of imperialism and zionism". As a matter of fact, the Jewish community had been in Iraq for two thousand or more years. Even before the air strike on the artillery brigade "spies" were being arrested. These included seventeen Jews. After interrogation, no doubt leading to suitable "confessions", in a later show trial, thirteen of the prisoners were executed as "traitors". The government, as a policy to "purify" the nation from "Imperialism and its control", announced measures for crushing phantom "spy networks". During this period, Max Sawdayee, a member of the Jewish community, was returning with his daughter from an ordinary domestic shopping trip through the streets of Baghdad in October 1969. A truck carrying a tank approached at speed as they crossed the road. They ran to avoid it. In the process he dropped two glass phials of orange juice powder. The truck stopped and Max was accosted by two

---

21 A. Applebaum, *Gulag: A History of the Soviet Camps* (London, 2004).

armed and angry soldiers who accused him of deliberately spraying a sinister powder in the path of their military vehicle. An ordinary household incident had taken on a mythical character. A sergeant ordered him to produce his identity card. When it was shown, the sergeant required him to accompany them to Rashid Army Camp "for questioning". Sawdayee's daughter, hearing this, then began to cry, instinctively aware that questioning a prisoner in the society where they lived was not an instrument in the search for truth:

> *I say nothing but look at the driver for a moment. What bothers me most is that the other soldier continues aiming his gun at my daughter's head ... Many people gather around by now and begin to ask silly questions. The scene lasts for about a quarter of an hour, when someone among the crowd, a decent man, approaches and asks both soldiers to get into their truck and make away, as no harm has been done and nothing of importance has occurred. A woman brings a broom from a nearby shop and starts to clean the pavement in a hurry, pushing glass and powder aside. The driver, simply feeling ashamed of himself, his anger stilled, takes his companion up to the truck. Turning back to me, he shouts: "Hey Jew, you are wise and lucky to stop just where you were and not move! That saved you."*[22]

Killing entire groups of people happen, for "reasons" that are not the product of rational argument. Max was saved by the sudden appearance of the mirror of equal interaction that showed the soldiers how ugly their proposed behaviour was. This was despite the victim's membership of a hated group. Members of an intending murderer's own group have at least a chance of overcoming the impulse to murder.

In a similar incident from the Armenian genocide, a leading Turkish businessman in Harpoot took in and sheltered his former business partner, an Armenian. He was ordered to surrender

---

22 M. Sawdayee, *All Waiting To Be Hanged: Iraq Post Six Day War Diary* (Tel Aviv, 1974) pp. 145–6, quoted in S. Al-Khalil, *Republic of Fear* (London, 1991) pp. 46–7. For some family history see www.sawdayee.com.

him, but refused. When the local governor threatened to have him hanged, the Turk replied: "If it is my allotted time to die, I shall consider it an honour to die in defence of such a man. His father showed me every kindness in my youth, and this young man has been a faithful friend. [I have never seen] any wrong in him, and I will not betray him now. If you must execute the order, I am ready to be hanged". Both were spared.[23] Accounts from the Rwanda genocide also show how a social equal can shame a killer out of his intent to murder.

Marie Christine was captured about two weeks after the killings began in Rwanda. Forced to report to the authorities, she was discovered to be a Tutsi:

> The councillor ... handed me over to some men to be killed. They said it was important to make sure that they were not being asked to kill an innocent person. They tried to find people who knew me, saying that if nobody vouched for me then I could not be an innocent person. There was so much fear about what an association with a Tutsi could mean that everybody denied ever having known me, even the old lady who had hidden me. But when it came to killing me some of them wanted to carry it out. One of the men told me to go. When the others started to follow me, he told them to lay off.[24]

One notes that her treatment was humane and did not slip into what appears to be a preparatory pattern of degradation. Another man, Jean, who was captured in a military ambush, again found an advocate among the killer group. This was enough to save him:

> They took my money. They were deciding how to kill me when a Hutu doctor who knew me pleaded my case. He made such a fuss about me that they finally let me go. The doctor put me in his car and drove me to the health centre. I stayed there the whole time.[25]

---

23 H. Riggs, *Days of Tragedy in Armenia: Personal Experiences in Harpoot, 1915–1917* (Ann Arbor, 1997) p. 97.
24 African Rights, *Rwanda*, p. 768.
25 African Rights, *Rwanda*, p. 1045.

The case of Sedata is similar. She had tried to work normally as a cleaner in a hospital, but had witnessed a Tutsi doctor being beaten to death a week after the President's murder. Frightened, she turned to a Hutu neighbour for help. His daughter escorted her on a route that led through a Burundi refugee camp. In Burundi the ethnic mix was the opposite of Rwanda and those in the camp were Hutu:

> *The refugees arrested me. One of them was a former policeman in Burundi. He told me to sit down while he went to fetch Rwandese soldiers to deal with me. But the women and children among the Burundi refugees crowded around me and pleaded for my release. They knew I was an employee at the hospital. Finally, the policeman agreed to let me go, saying "After all, she is there for the picking whenever we want her."*[26]

Mass killings are made possible by the application to whole populations of symbols that empower aggression. The ideology that drives mass murder can be turned against the killers. In Rwanda, people could use the argument: why kill this harmless person, why not go away and fight like a soldier? There are no instances of this in Nazi-occupied Europe. There, every member of the victim groups were portrayed as evil, not just their fighters.

Marie Munyekazi lost most of her extended family and her three small daughters in the genocide in Rwanda. About a week after President Habyarimana's death the Presidential Guards arrested her in a house-to-house search in Kigali. One of them said that she had to be killed and took her outside with another woman to murder them. It just so happened that a soldier whom she knew from Butare then passed by. He spoke to her, asking her what the trouble was. Her captor replied: "These women are rebels and must be killed". Her friend, the soldier, confronted him by asking: "How can these women be a threat to you? If you want rebels go and fight the Rwanda

---

26 African Rights, *Rwanda*, p. 1025.

Patriotic Front. They are in Gikondo and Rebero".[27] This saved her and her companion. In another case a woman called Marthe was captured at a barrier and put down into a hole. When a member of the militia raised his rifle to kill her, another militia man who knew her intervened. He said: "Why are you killing this girl instead of going to find the Inkotanyi and fighting them? You shouldn't kill this girl. There's no point in that." He then gave the killer a sum of money to make him leave.[28] Could it be said, in these instances, that the killers were forced to see their own nature? It might be said that shame would hardly stop them, but that appears to be at least a factor. One that can be exploited by a social equal.

Could it be that people intent on mass murder, participants in an organisation that dispatched hundreds of thousands of lives, could not stand to have innocent blood on their hands? These cases seem to support Solzhenitsyn's optimistic prognosis that a glimmer of conscience always remains alive, hidden somewhere in the human mind.[29] No person who was actually killed in the situations from which any of these people were spared was guilty of anything. They were simply members of a targeted victim group. Yet, if people were saved for not being rebels, or for not approving of the assassination of President Habyarimana, it would seem that it was the opposite side of that equation which drove the murders, or at least made killing acceptable. The existence of circumstances that allowed a genuine enquiry to be made, and the making of an enquiry in a spirit that sought information, as opposed to engaging in interrogation for the purpose of terror and degradation, allowed a myth to be undermined. By this process, the feeling of superiority, which seems the concomitant positive of the negative image of enmity, weakened. It was not driven to come to fulfilment by crushing "the cockroach" underfoot.

---

27 African Rights, *Rwanda*, p. 676.
28 Des Forges, pp. 588–91.
29 A. Solzhenitsyn, *The Gulag Archipelago* (London, 1974) p. 172.

But what about the interveners, as the law might call them? The organisers of mass murder must loath them, their notions of humanity standing in the way of inhuman plans. In fact, like Lenin, you could accuse them of a flabby, parson's mode of thinking. This kind of person can always pop up to prevent completion of the plan of mass murder down to the last enemy. They are always there.

Many people in Nazi occupied Europe helped their Jewish compatriots when to do so, under the Nazi occupation, meant certain death if caught.[30] Equally, Armenians were helped by being hidden or otherwise aided by Turks during the massacres of 1915 to 1917. As well as the depressing stories from the Rwanda genocide of Hutus turning on their Tutsi neighbours, there are many examples of help being offered despite the risk that this involved.[31] A genuinely good person can be the saviour of a person from the designated victim group. Because of the structured polarisation of society that destructive leadership imposes, the victim can only be helped in secret. Otherwise, as we shall see in the next chapter, the saviour will be regarded as being as bad as the victim. The good help the imperilled in secret in order not to jeopardise the position of either. Such examples will occur in any instance where fate leads the victim onto the path of encountering a selfless person. The task of destructive leadership is to make such examples as rare as possible, by denying people the freedom to act individually. Decent people will want to help members of the "enemy group" despite these obstacles. Examples are easily found, people who felt that it would be better for their children to have "dead parents rather than cowards as parents".[32]

Sometimes a succession of private saviours will be needed over a period of peril lasting years. The Polish musician Wladyslav Szpilman, whose father persuaded the German

---

30 Gilbert, *The Righteous*, passim.
31 For an example see African Rights, *Rwanda*, p. 470–473 and the example of Eugène at p. 574.
32 Gilbert, *The Righteous*, p. 379.

patrol not to kill him and his sons, was assisted in escaping from the Jewish Ghetto in Warsaw before its final liquidation, and was then hidden by a succession of friends who provided him with food and lodging. To be found helping him meant certain death at the hands of the Nazis, merely because he was a Jew. When eventually an officer of the German army discovered him it so happened that this officer was Captain Wilhelm Hosenfeld, a Christian who had come to hate the leadership of his country.[33] He helped Szpilman by advising him on a more secure hiding place and by bringing him food. There are other instances of this phenomenon from Rwanda. One is that of two women who were fortunate enough to be captured by two soldiers who seem to have been carrying out the genocide under compulsion. When captors and prisoners were away from the sight of anyone who might report on them, they swiftly fired their guns into the air and released their prisoners. Later, one of those soldiers escorted one of the women out of the hands of the militia to safety.[34] It seems that these soldiers had, wherever possible, used a position of power under a regime devoted to murder to quietly defy the objective of killing.

It is easier, but only because we think so highly of ourselves, to understand the saviours in these situations. It is more difficult to imagine oneself as a person engaged in mindless slaughter. Having some idea of what stops people from killing their hated enemy only helps our understanding of the problem to some degree. But how can one understand what really drove the killers, not just what stopped a tiny minority of them? It is best, perhaps to take one instance of mass murder. The prime example in the chapter which follows is the mass murder in Rwanda. The deceptive constructions placed upon the Tutsi population of Rwanda seem to me to be central to any understanding of the process of murder to which they were subjected. These mass killings were myth-driven. The justifications were invented, as plain lies, by the leaders of the mass murder.

33 Szpilman, pp. 177–88.
34 Des Forges, pp. 480–4.

This was done in order to construct in the minds of the population an image of an incorrigible and rampant enemy.[35] Once that image is a living presence in the mind, it drives those possessed of it towards the satisfaction of the underlying instinct it reflects. At its worst, the only response to that image that seems possible is the eradication of the enemy.

There is nothing to be learned from the examples in this chapter of people who met members of the apparent killer group and who were not killed. Those they encountered were never driven by any desire to kill. In effect, they were never spared death because the people they met never hated them and never intended to kill them. All of the people spared from death that are mentioned in this chapter escaped because they were transformed in the eyes of their intending killers. Some, like Hukanovic, because he reasserted himself as a real personality despite being degraded through torture. Some, like the Helfgotts, found a point of ideological connection with their captors that made murder more troubling. It became almost as if the kidnappers were going to have to kill one of their own. Is this a key? Well, it may be. The other spared individuals had little chance of being listened to by those who confronted them. Max Sawdayee would have stood no chance but for the intervention of the decent-minded people who shamed the soldiers out of arresting him. It is legitimate to wonder where he would have found an advocate in a torture camp dedicated to extracting "confessions". Marie Munyekazi, and a few others, found a saviour in the aggressor group. Without them, they would have been certainly lost.

Is there a connection, therefore, between the Rashid detention centre, to which Mr Sawdayee was to be brought, and any wider situation? I think there may be. The organisers of mass murder do not want any interference. The point of ideological indoctrination, believers shying away from "impure contact" and dominating society with an infection of mad ideas is to

---

35 Al-Khalil, p. 58.

ensure that the killers will never be deferred from their "duty". For the purposes of the execution of mass murder, an armed camp must be made of the whole of society. There must be no dissent. De Rougemont's intuition of all temporal power and all spiritual authority being concentrated into one must be brought to pass. That is the essence of totalitarianism: no dissent, no saviours, no imperfection in the execution of evil.

The point of corralling society into hatred, and characterising those who oppose murderous schemes as being "with the enemy", is to create a situation where no one dares to question any individual instance of murder. That gets rid of the interveners. The mirror of equal social interaction is covered for fear of what it will reveal. The nuisance of dissent is silenced. No one will offer a way out.

But how is that done? How can that be possible?

CHAPTER 8

Closing the Circle of Hatred

ONE OF THE EARLIEST VICTIMS of the genocidal regime in Rwanda was lady called Rosalie Gicanda. She lived in a modest house in Butare with her bed-bound mother and the women who cared for both of them. Acting on orders, on 20 April 1994 a detachment of soldiers seized her and six of her domestic helpers, drove them away and shot them. The soldiers then returned and pillaged her home. Two days later they murdered her mother. Back in 1959, Rosalie Gicanda had been the Queen of Rwanda. For over thirty years she had been a private citizen and her dignified withdrawal from public life, and her quiet practice of her Christian faith, had attracted wide respect.[1] She was no threat to anyone. But she was represented as a threat. She symbolised the myth that underpinned the mass murder of a million people.

Is hatred an accident, like where two friends fall out over a business deal, or can people be made to hate? It you want to get people to kill, then you must first of all make them hate. Perhaps you can manipulate people into hatred? On more than one occasion in criminal practice, I came across cases where what was holding someone back from an attack was fear of what their associates might think. A lie can get people to change their minds. It opens up the way to destroy someone. Hatred does not just drop out of the sky. It can be built up by cunning: step-by-step and lie-by-lie.

---

1   A. Des Forges, *Leave None to Tell the Story: Genocide in Rwanda* (New York, 1999) pp. 470, 471.

This is a process where logic and blind emotion work together. You can tell people the lie that will make them hate other people so that they see them as an enemy. They will then be inclined to destroy them, or at least be indifferent to their fate. Hatred is an emotion that is not divorced from thought. People can reason out why they hate someone. They can infect others with their hatred if their emotion is strong enough and their reasons are convincing. It may be that the closer that our minds get to pure hatred, the easier it becomes for us to draw others into sharing our loathing. Like an artist, we become inspired and hate speaks through us. The best of reasons for destroying people come to us.[2]

How do you find a reason for killing innocent people? There can be no reason. So, you must create a myth. One that makes people hate. What that myth is, and what makes it suitable to inspire hatred depends on how people see themselves.

Rwanda had been firstly a German and then a Belgian colony. The masters of the country had used the Tutsi population to rule on their behalf. In their bizarre colonial way of thinking, thrown up by European notions of superiority, the inhabitants of Africa were widely regarded as the descendants of Ham, son of Noah and accursed by him so that he was reduced to being a slave for his brother.[3] But there were mild exceptions to the idea of the African sub-human. These included the Watutsi. The Europeans choose them to be the masters of Rwanda because they were imagined to show in their features, "fine oval faces, large eyes, and high noses", that they were lost Coptic Christians from Ethiopia: "men who were as unalike as they could be from the common order of the natives".[4] This

---

2   C.W. 10.455.
3   G. Prunier, *The Rwanda Crisis: History of a Genocide* (New York, 1995) pp. 5–16.
4   P. Gourevitch, *We Wish to Inform you that Tomorrow we will be Killed with our Families: Stories from Rwanda* (New York, 1998) p. 52, quoting John Hanning Speke, *Journal of the Discovery of the South of the Nile* (1863).

justified the traditional colonial methodology of dividing a nation by privilege and then ruling it through a favoured oligarchy. When in the aftermath of the First World War, the Belgians took over from the Germans, these divisions were continued and enforced; much to the resentment of the 85 per cent majority Hutu population. In 1933–34, Belgian administrators conducted a census of Rwanda that officially divided the population into Tutsis and Hutus. All had to carry ethnic identity cards. By law, no one could change that identity. Under the Europeans, armies of Hutus were dragooned into forced labour on public schemes and private plantations under Tutsi taskmasters. "You whip the Hutu or we will whip you", was the European attitude.[5] It led to mass migration, the neglect of farms and famine. It enforced division and inequality. Naturally, it inspired hatred. Rwandans, who had a strong sense of national identity, began to see themselves as they were described. The King of Rwanda, previously the father of the nation, became regarded as the head Tutsi. As independence approached, in 1957 a group of Hutus published a document calling for what they claimed was democracy; the Hutu Manifesto. Built on the tribal divisions of colonialism, it demanded that the country should be handed over to them. Ethnic cards were to be retained so that a Hutu majority should always remain identifiably in power. European support changed sides. In a bloody revolution in 1959, the Hutu Manifesto group seized power. Rwanda became what was supposed to be a democratic republic. Thousands of Tutsis were killed in the turmoil and many thousands more fled into exile, particularly to Burundi where they were a majority.

Society in Rwanda became dominated by Hutu rule. The Tutsi were excluded from power. They were never to be allowed to rule again. Across Rwanda's borders, first and second-generation exiles demanded to return and to reclaim a share in governing their country. Their army, the Rwanda

---

5   Prunier, pp. 47–62.

Patriotic Front, or RPF, invaded Rwanda several times in support of this objective. One encroachment by the exiles in 1963
led to about ten thousand deaths. Twenty prominent Tutsis in
Rwanda were executed in its aftermath by the government, following on the "discovery" on the body of an invader of a list of
future ministers in a minority government.[6] Twice in the 1990s
the Rwanda Patriotic Front again attempted a forcible return.
A 1990 incursion managed to cross the border without making
serious gains. It was not a real threat to the government but it
was presented as such. Under the pretext of an attack on the
capital Kigali, in fact faked by the Rwandan Army[7], several
thousand opponents of the regime were arrested by the government and many were tortured.[8] A ceasefire in March 1991
did not end either the dispute or the power monopoly of
President Habyarimana's leadership group. A further attack in
February 1993 in reality brought the RPF close to Kigali and
threatened to overthrow the Rwandan government. Later that
year, in Arusha in Tanzania, the Hutu supremacists were forced
to reach an accord with the enemy RPF. They never wanted
peace with the exiles and they never wanted to share power. It
suited the government to present the exiled RPF as a deadly
threat by Tutsi supremacists. Historical reasons facilitated the
government in presenting RPF aims as genocidal. In 1972,
between one and two hundred thousand Hutus had been massacred by the Tutsi-dominated government in Burundi.[9]
Further mass murders of Hutus there in 1988 and October
1993 were presented, in the official propaganda of the
Rwandan government, as presages of what was to come should
the Tutsi-dominated RPF succeed in an invasion.[10] There could

---

6   African Rights, *Rwanda: Death Despair and Defiance* (London, 1995)
    pp. 12–13.
7   African Rights, *Rwanda*, p. 50.
8   African Rights, *Rwanda*, p. 29.
9   F. Chalk and K. Jonassohn, *The History and Sociology of Genocide:
    Analyses and Case Studies* (Yale, 1990) pp. 384–93.
10 African Rights, *Rwanda*, p. 40.

be no compromise with the RPF. That exiled force was never spoken of save in terms of it being in the grip of supremacist aims.

The 1959 Revolution was the psychological pivot of the new State. It was the event that overthrew colonial domination and the overlordship of their Tutsi "allies". According to the Hutu "Ten Commandments':

> *The social revolution of 1959, the Referendum of 1961, and the Hutu ideology, must be taught to every Mohutu at every level. Every Hutu must spread this ideology widely. Any Mohutu who persecutes his brother for having read, spread and taught this ideology is a traitor.*[11]

In the years leading up to 1994, mass distortion of fact was used to prepare the population for the eventual massacre of the Tutsi minority. This was done by drawing together the currents of historical resentment in order to inspire feelings of bottomless panic at the prospect of a return to a Tutsi-ruled oligarchy.[12] In the aftermath of the 1990 incursions by the RPF, the editor of the "Kangura" newspaper was released from jail. Kangura means "wake up". The publication announced itself as "the voice that seeks to awake and guide the majority people".[13] It projected a stream of vituperation onto the minority population. Documents were published, purporting to have their origin outside Rwanda in the RPF outlining, like a latter-day Protocols of the Elders of Zion[14], a master plan to smash the Rwandan State and to return it to Tutsi feudal overlordship. The government secretly funded "Kangura". Inside Rwanda, accomplices were already stated to be working to betray the

---

11 Extracts from The Hutu Ten Commandments, quoted in African Rights, *Rwanda*, p. 42–3, published in *Kangura* 10 December 1990.
12 African Rights, *Rwanda*, p. 37–8.
13 J.–P. Chrétien, *Rwanda: Les Médias du Génocide* (Paris, 1995) pp. 33–42; Gourevitch. Pp. 85–8.
14 As to which see N. Cohn, *Warrant for Genocide: The Myth of the Jewish World Conspiracy and the Protocols of the Elders of Zion* (London, 1996) pp. 214–37.

1959 revolution. The line that "Kangura" had taken from 1990 was that the Tutsi were plotting the domination of all of central Africa.[15] In 1991 the government openly published a document entitled: "The Whole Truth Of The October 1990 War Imposed Upon Rwanda By The Aggressors From Uganda Armed Forces". What was this "truth"? It was supposedly to expose the motives of the enemy inside Rwanda, allied to the RPF outside the country. Their aim was to:

> ... set up an extended Hima-Tutsi kingdom in the Bantu area of the Great Lakes region. It should be recalled that in identification with the Aryan race, both ethnic groups consider themselves as being superior to other ethnic groups and used the swastika of Hitler as their symbol.[16]

A Ministry of Defence publication of September 1992 further identified "the enemy" as those who had never accepted "the realities of the Social Revolution of 1959 and who want to take power in Rwanda by any means including force".[17] The deeply divided nature of society was never acknowledged, much less the role of the Hutu supremacists in splitting the country into two rigid groups. They had no sins. Instead, oppression and exclusion were called democracy.

Four days after the signing of the Arusha Accords in September 1993 a new television and radio station, "Radio Télévision Milles Collines", Radio RTLMC as it was called, was set up with secret government funding. Its object, like "Kangura", was to be an instrument of hate.[18] In advocating the feudalist designs and incorrigibility of the minority population it centred its rhetoric on the idea that the RPF threatened the undoing of the 1959 Revolution. No mention was made of the

---

15 Chrétien, pp. 163–6.
16 Quoted in African Rights, *Rwanda*, p. 41, and see Gourevitch, pp. 96–7.
17 Ministière de la Defence National – Definition et identification de l'ennemi, quoted in African Rights, *Rwanda*, p. 39.
18 Chrétien, pp. 63–82.

duplicity of the Hutu-power clique that ruled the country. Speeches by Dr Léon Mugesera, a leading Hutu supremacy ideologue, were broadcast. These exulted in the idea of slaughter. A "permanent solution" to the Tutsi "problem" was proposed. It was not power sharing and dialogue, the basis of the Arusha Accords, but extermination. That was the only answer possible, it was asserted, to the ambitions of those who, for this purpose, were described as being in the grip of an irreversible power lust. Such creatures, it was said, should be dumped in the Nyarbarango River, a tributary of the Nile. Their murder would reverse the root cause of all of Rwanda's trouble by sending the Tutsi back, dead, to Ethiopia, their mythical place of origin. The greed and power-hunger of the country's ruling elite was not even hinted at as contributing to Rwanda's turmoil. Instead, it was the legend of invasion and conquest, according to the self-serving European myth, by the grasping and exploitative Tutsis that was to blame.[19]

With the murder of President Habyarimana the official and unofficial lines of hate-evocation no longer needed to keep up the pretence of distance from each other. All the Tutsis in Rwanda were painted as accomplices of "the murderers" and of the "wrecking plans" of the RPF. Radio Rwanda broadcast such statements as:

> *The enemy – we know him. We have only one enemy; it is he who has never accepted the fact of the Republic and his allies. The enemy is he who operates from outside the country and who wants to put the country under foreign domination. The majority of the population, who have benefited from the 1959 Revolution, rise up and make sure that the enemy and his accomplices are not around you.*[20]

On Radio RTLMC, the broadcasts gave voice to the seizure of the mind by a pure hate. In their daily lives most people disguise their hatred. Here, it boiled over:

---

19 African Rights, *Rwanda*, p. 78–79: Gourevitch, pp. 96–7.
20 Recollections of Gaspard Karemara as to the Broadcasts of Radio Rwanda in April, 1994, quoted in African Rights, *Rwanda*, p. 85.

Fight the Inyezni, pound them. Stand up. Keep away from lies and rumours. If they pound you with heavy artillery, bombs, go into bunkers. Then after that you take your spears, clubs, guns, swords, stones, everything, sharpen them, hack them, these enemies, these cockroaches, these enemies of democracy, show that you can defend yourself – support your soldiers.[21]

After about a million deaths, the radio urged:" Exterminate them... so that neither our children, our grandchildren or our great grandchildren need ever hear again of the thing called the Inkotanyi!"[22] Even in these insane statements, the broadcaster is inspired by now familiar and universal patterns of lies: genocide is "self-defence"; destroy the line down to the last child; and killing civilians is a "military necessity".

It was precisely the smashing and hacking to pieces of the refugees, created by exploiting the crisis of President Habyarimana's murder, that was achieved by the Rwandan government. The population was set upon the refugees. All Hutus had to treat the Tutsi like "a mad dog". The radio said: "You have to beat it up and up and up; otherwise it bites you." The radio broadcaster was not simply issuing a cold propaganda message calculatedly designed to evoke hatred. Logic and emotion coincided. Could one think, as many killers claim when being tried for murder, that some force had taken hold of people?

Where the perpetrators gave vent to their murder motivation in words, half-disguised lies were voiced: the killings are a measure against "anti-democratic forces"; the measures are "necessary" and so the massacres are justified.[23] Those who were digging the graves of the Tutsis projected onto their victims the same motivation that they themselves were acting out.[24] Mass murder was "self-defence".[25] The Tutsis were killed

---

21 RTLMC Broadcast: April–May, 1994, quoted in African Rights – Rwanda 80.
22 Chrétien 81.
23 African Rights, *Rwanda*, pp. 164, 165, 115, 92, 81, 72, 79.
24 African Rights, *Rwanda*, pp. 115, 997, 915, 69.
25 African Rights, *Rwanda*, pp. 1092, 436.

because they were bent on the "genocide of the majority".[26] Tutsis were described by those who killed them, as in the government documents, as "accomplices of the RPF" and of their anti-democratic plans. Lies were spread that particular victims were RPF supporters,[27] through giving money to them, for example. They were identified and dealt with as vicious conspirators with plans that struck at the heart of Rwandan society.[28] In the hate-rhetoric, Tutsis were described as hiding the RPF in their houses;[29] as concealing guns for the RPF;[30] as keeping grenades for the RPF;[31] as having poison to use against the Hutus;[32] as having poisoned a soldier;[33] as transmitting messages to the rebels or receiving them on a fax machine; or as holding a dialogue with them.[34] Hatred could also be whipped up by alleging that a victim had incriminating documents.[35]

It did not matter how real or unreal in terms of fact any euphemism was. A fourteen-year-old girl could be an accomplice,[36] as could any child, or even a baby.[37] Those being dispatched by the forces of mass murder were themselves "murderers"; in fact, they were described as being "originally bad". The massacres became justified to eliminate the "root cause" of the trouble.[38] The radio would call out "don't let the accomplices pass ... burn them ... kill them".[39] The victims, tarred as

---

26 Des Forges, pp. 544, 542,509, 376.
27 Des Forges, pp. 387.
28 African Rights, *Rwanda*, pp. 607, 714, 780.
29 African Rights, *Rwanda*, pp. 506, 169, 205, 245, 1043.
30 African Rights, *Rwanda*, pp. 636, 591, 460.
31 African Rights, *Rwanda*, p. 186.
32 African Rights, *Rwanda*, p. 313.
33 Des Forges, p. 293.
34 African Rights, *Rwanda*, pp. 679, 636, 590.
35 Des Forges, p. 569.
36 African Rights, *Rwanda*, p. 811.
37 African Rights, *Rwanda*, pp. 626, 614, 559–60.
38 Interview by Jane Perlez with François Karera, International Herald Tribune 16/8/1994 "A Hutu Justifies Genocide", quoted in African Rights, *Rwanda*, pp. 124–5.
39 African Rights, *Rwanda*, p. 606.

the internal allies of an external demonic force, were rounded up by deception, tricked of their means of self-defence and then dispatched by knives, machetes, hammers, grenades and arson by those who chose to believe that all the wrongs in their world were to be ascribed to their neighbours.

Does any of this does answer the question as to whether there is an identifiable pattern to hatred? Not of itself. However, what happened in Rwanda may suggest four possible patterns, all of them centred on deceit. Firstly, there is the pattern of deliberation: taking the fundamental fears of people and saying – that is what the enemy are planning. Secondly, the references to the enemy within a country being aided by conspirators outside it is also replicated elsewhere. Thirdly, hatred is not logical; it is mythical and that seems to be typical of it, that it changes reality. Finally, the documents already quoted offer a hint at possibly the most important task that the organisers of mass murder undertake – that of isolating the enemy completely.

The first possible pattern focuses on the horrible and unchangeable nature of the enemy. What is being promoted is death. Is murder the only outcome of hatred? That cannot be correct but perhaps it is the ultimate outcome for extreme forms of hatred. To get there you have to show the enemy as striking at the essence of the aggressor's being. This is about the nature of the self. If you find out how people really define themselves, in terms of the absolutes of nationality or political doctrine or religion, whatever is their innermost being, an attack on that evokes serious anger. Possibly, that might sometimes be forgiven but for the pattern in mass murder of presenting the enemy as incorrigible. You are persuaded that no matter what you do they will be the same. So, break off negotiations; it is pointless. The pattern of eradicating a people right down to the last child makes some perverse sense when you are led to think of the enemy as irremediable; he will never change because it is in his disposition to be evil. In Rwanda there were constant references to two or three generations of exiles, never mind what they were like when they were "running the country", being driven by the same aims of domination and exploitation.

You see the same pattern at work in other mass murders. In Nazi occupied Europe, the focus of official lies was on allegedly hereditary nature of "the criminal aims" of the Jewish people. A criminal lawyer can understand the dynamic of calling someone a criminal. It is part disgust and part attraction. When you experience crime vicariously, do you enjoy the glow of savagery that is in all of us? A lawyer sees this in some of the people who come to court only to observe the worst cases of rape or murder and in the widespread, and very profitable, obsession with brutality in all forms of mass media. The idea that a criminal nature is hereditary is an old and dangerous nonsense. Many people believe it. One suspects that Lombroso merely gave expression to it. The Nazis exploited it. A 1942 textbook of criminology, on the supposedly "criminal nature" of the Jews, argued that were an evil character to be accepted as part of a person's genetic disposition, the State would be justified in murder:

> *If the hereditary criminal nature of Jews can be demonstrated, then not only is each people morally justified in exterminating the hereditary criminals – but any people that still keeps and protects Jews is just as guilty of an offence against public safety as someone who cultivates cholera germs without observing the proper precautions.*[40]

The Jewish people were presented as arising "from criminal roots" and being welded together by their "hereditary criminality".[41] The physical aspect of this dynamic was exploited in the repulsive lies that the Nazi leadership was able to make attractive through the abuse of drawings, literature and films.

40 Von Leers, *Verbrechternatur der Juden* (Berlin, 1942) quoted in Cohn, p. 228.
41 Deutscher Wochendienst, 2 April, 1944, quoted in Marrus, *The Holocaust in History* (London, 1993) p. 25.

The Nazis harped on this theme of the inherent nature of the Jewish people as destroyers.[42] They were presented as showing physically, in their very body, their inner evil. Stalin, it will be recalled, gave expression to this myth about Trotsky. In 1935 the Nazis claimed that a statistical study had shown a pre-eminence of Jewish participants in all categories of crime. Three years later, the press section of the Ministry of Justice instructed pros-ecutors that it was no longer necessary to forward all copies of indictments against Jews. The controlled press of Nazi Germany was already so full of stories of Jewish criminality that now it was only necessary to forward dispatch on:

> ... cases that raised new legal points; those in which the perpetrator had demonstrated a particularly evil intention; those in which the crime had been perpetrated on an especially large scale or had caused particular damage or aroused uncommon interest among the public; finally, cases of race defilement in which the perpetrator was a recurrent offender or had abused a position of power.[43]

The malice that hatred inspires is almost beyond belief. Himmler saw ritual murder as a lie that supported the bigger lie of the myth of Jewish determination to enslave other nations. He suggested that the Nazi State should employ investigators in other countries to "investigate" instances of children disappear-ing. Then, in planned broadcasts they would announce that Jews had stolen the child so that it could be ritually slaughtered and eaten. Of course, in a demented and enclosed society, this lie might be effective: "I am of the opinion that we could give anti-Semitism an incredible virulence by means of anti-Semitic propaganda in English, perhaps even in Russian, giving special

---

42 Bauer, *A History of the Holocaust*, pp. 83–109, quoted in F. Chalk andK. Jonassohn, *The History and Sociology of Genocide: Analyses and Case Studies* (Yale, 1990) p. 339.

43 Minister of Justice to State Prosecutors 24.2.1938, quoted in S. Friedlander, *Nazi Germany and the Jews: The Years of Persecution 1933–1939* (London, 1998) p. 254.

publicity to ritual murders."[44] Apart from an allegedly unchangeable disposition, the Jews were presented as the agents of Marxism. This was the antithesis of official Nazi doctrines. Constant references to disease, germs and viruses reflected some mad notion that, by their irremediable nature, in their contact with others the Jewish people could not fail to infect them.[45] They were presented as "contagious" both as to genetic contact and as to the transmission of the "deadly idea" of Bolshevism.[46] The prominence of people of Jewish origins in the revolutionary movements in Russia, and in the communist party leadership up to the purges of the 1930s, provided an expedient by which the terror of a communist revolution and the fight against what was presented to be the ideological adversary of Nazism could be focused on an imperative to destroy the root cause. Before the war, the deportation of the Jewish people could be presented as part of a programme to eliminate an internal threat. After the invasion of Russia, this was explicitly presented as the aim of "the elimination of all Bolshevik leaders and commissars, the Bolshevik-Jewish intelligentsia".[47]

Cultural norms determine, to some extent, the different symbols that represent the core values of what a society holds most sacred. In the centuries before the Reformation, stealing the Host or otherwise blaspheming the sacraments of the Church, constituted the most profound abominations. These actions cut off the perpetrators from human considerations and

---

44 Quoted in Poliakov and Wolf, *Das Dritte Reich und die Juden* (Berlin – Grunvald, 1955) p. 360 and quoted, in turn, in Cohn, p. 227.

45 For examples of references to disease as justifying murder see for M. Gilbert, *The Holocaust: The Jewish Tragedy* (London, 1990) pp. 119, 319; R. Gellateley, *Backing Hitler: Consent and Coercion in Nazi Germany* (London, 2001) p. 141.

46 Cohn, pp. 189, 199, 203, 206, 227.

47 A. Bullock, *Hitler and Stalin: Parallel Lives* (London, 1993) p. 817. See further pp. 812–26. On the prominence of people of Jewish origin in the Russian Revolution see R. Pipes, *Russia under the Bolshevik Regime 1919–1924* (London, 1994) pp. 112–14 and Cohn, p. 133.

inflated them into demonic others that must be violently flushed out by torture and then eradicated.[48] During the Russian civil war, the idea that the Jewish community supported the Bolsheviks could unleash a violent pogrom by those supporting the White Army.[49] An idea can become, in the mind of any human person, "a passion, a real obsession of addicts which can go as far as crime".[50] In ordinary circumstances, those proclaiming fantastic ideas will be shunned. Panic, however, undermines the foundation of reason in any society, enabling scapegoating ideas to become generally accepted. War, civil turmoil and perhaps natural disasters leave us open to the scheming of the planners of hate.

In justifying the mass murder of the Armenian people, the Committee of Union and Progress also exploited the deepest fears of the Turkish people. The period from 1911 to 1915 was characterised by the disintegration of the Ottoman Empire. Over one third of its land area had been redeemed by nationalist movements and over one-fifth of its population was lost.[51] In the aftermath of these losses, the Young Turk movement planned revenge on its Russian enemy through a plan, in reality no more than a fantasy, of seizing the Caucuses region and uniting all Turkic-speaking peoples in a new empire. The Great War provided a ready-made justification for an attack on Russia; a great opportunity to fulfil a mythic ideal.[52] Both sides used the war as a cloak for other schemes. Russia, if victorious

---

48 J. Trachtenberg, *The Devil and the Jews: The Medieval Conception of the Jew and Its Relation to Modern Anti-Semitism* (Philadelphia, 1983) pp. 205–16.

49 Cohn, pp. 135–6.

50 Beraud. "Ce que J'ai vu à Berlin", *Le Journal*, October 1926, quoted in Friedlander, p. 106.

51 This account draws on R. Hovannisian, *The Armenian Genocide in Perspective* (New Brunswick, 1998) the chapter by Melson, "Provocation or Nationalism: A Critical Enquiry into the Armenian Genocide of 1915", pp. 61–85.

52 Walker, *Armenia: The Survival of a Nation* (London, 1980) pp. 197–99.

over the Central Powers, was to receive both Armenia and Constantinople in fulfilment of a long-standing promise from its British and French allies.[53] Searching for allies, the Tsar visited the Russia-Turkey front in the Caucuses and promised the Head of the Armenian Church that "a most brilliant future awaits the Armenians".[54] Inspired by this, and by the memory of past massacres, four corps of Armenian volunteers enrolled in the Russian Army. Most were from the Russian part of Armenia, but some also undoubtedly came from the former Ottoman Empire.[55] At the end of 1914 the Turkish Minister for War, Enver Pasha, then launched a massive offensive using the 75,000 troops of the Third Army against the Russian military based at Sarikamish. Within weeks the Turks had been routed, the courage of their fighting force undermined in large part by their poor equipment and the bitter cold. They lost nearly four fifths of their fighting men. Defeated, Enver returned to the capital where he relinquished his personal command. Despite making a show of thanking the Armenian population for their loyalty, he sought a scapegoat.[56] He described the Armenians as spies, thus placing responsibility for the defeat onto them.[57]

From February 1915, the exclusion of the Armenian population was commenced. All Armenian government officials were dismissed.[58] All of the serving Armenian troops were disarmed, demobilised and then grouped into penal labour-battalions. At the same time, a bizarre search for arms commenced in order to "prove" an internal conspiracy, linked to the Russian enemy, to overthrow what was left of the former empire. This operated as a

---

53 M. Gilbert, *The First World War* (London, 1994) p. 135.

54 Quoted in Gilbert, *First World War*, p. 108.

55 G.S. Graber, *Caravans To Oblivion: The Armenian Genocide 1915* (New York, 1996) pp. 59–62.

56 J. Bryce and A. Toynbee, *The Treatment of the Armenians in the Ottoman Empire 1915–1916: Documents Presented to Viscount Grey of Culloden* (Princeton, 2000) pp. 109, 117.

57 C. Walker, *Armenia: The Survival of a Nation* (London, 1980) p. 199.

58 Walker, p. 200.

pretext for imprisoning leading members of Armenian communities all over Turkey. Ideologically, the Turkish population, which lived side by side with the Armenians, was prepared for what followed through labelling the intended victims as traitors.[59] Armenians were made to seem as if they were concealing weapons. This replaced ordinary neighbourly confidence with suspicion that government claims were true that all Armenians were involved in a conspiracy to overthrow and defeat Turkey.[60] Through torture, widely publicised "confessions" to that effect were also obtained.[61] A typical example of how this process was executed comes from the city of Harpoot. The authorities let it be known that if the Armenians would voluntarily surrender their weapons, which they were officially supposed to possess, that all further persecutions would cease. Because of distrust, the Armenians would not accept this. But, when the Governor swore a solemn oath to protect them, they decided to present a collection of weapons. Their action became distorted into a measure for demonising all Armenians into the view that suited those intent on their destruction. The Reverend Henry Riggs, a clergyman from the USA, was a witness to those events:

> *There were only a few weapons left, and the owners of those decided that there was no use in further clinging to the hope of self-defense. So the weapons were surrendered, and to make the more complete show of surrender, some few Armenians who had no weapons, actually brought some and surrendered them to the police. Instead of bringing relief, however, this action seemed to further inflame the Turks. It became known that the Vali, Sabit Bey, who had persuaded the Armenians by his solemn oaths to trust him, had – to his eternal damnation be it said – sent a photograph of those weapons to Constantinople, with a report that he had uncovered a plot to overthrow the government.[62]*

---

59 For examples see Boyce and Toynbee, pp. 43, 64, 76, 95, 102.
60 H. Riggs, *Days of Tragedy in Armenia: Personal Experiences of Harpoot 1915* (Ann Arbour, Michigan, 1997) pp. 48–9, 66, 76–7; Boyce and Toynbee, p. 64.
61 Riggs, p. 48; Boyce and Toynbee, p. 126.
62 Riggs, p. 77.

All were "guilty". The "arms conspirators", meaning all Armenians, were brought into the countryside, roped together in groups, told they were being deported to a faraway city and then murdered.[63]

What about the myth of the enemy within and the enemy without? In these three examples, the Holocaust and the Rwandan and Armenian genocides, the enemy was supposed to be both inside and outside the country. The Jews were alleged by the Nazis to be part of a world-wide conspiracy; the Armenians were portrayed as being in league with the Russians; and the Tutsis were eliminated on the basis that they could never be loyal to Rwanda, but to the invading RPF. In Stalin's Russia, one finds the same kind of pattern: the search for internal enemies plotting with outsiders in diabolical schemes. Possibly this sometimes has a rational explanation, since many plotters in history have sought outside help. On this, I can only offer a speculation. At the furthest extremes of hatred, the mind finds enemies everywhere. Those who are kept within the circle as allies are, as in a criminal gang, defined according to rigid criteria, which become more extreme with pressure. Those outside are hated with unremitting anger. Both constructs of the deadly enemy and the noble self are unreal. They are liable to break down at any time. Hatred is always deepened by the repulsive side of human nature that is within us, through projection. Instead of dealing with why we hate, we cope by hating our enemies with even greater intensity. What is inside us colours the external enemy. Projection must, like a beam of light, come from somewhere. Since hatred contorts facts, making our enemies revolting, that distortion must have come from inside us. Despite what we choose to see as the scheming, irremediable enemy with plans to strike us to the core of our beings, we must have some awareness of the blackness within ourselves that at least colours our view of that enemy. So, we are not only seeking to destroy the enemy on the outside, we are

---

63 A. Toynbee, *A Summary of Armenian History* (London, 1916) chapter 25.

also driven to seek out the internal disturbance that we push outside ourselves. The enemy is both within and without.

Hatred is unreal. This third possible pattern is shown in the bizarre expressions of speech with which people mouth on about those they describe as despicable. To the nineteenth century German settlers of East Africa the original population were "baboons".[64] As they applied this description, the settlers operated a policy to control the tribes "by unmitigated terrorism and even cruelty". When they rebelled they were to be destroyed "by shedding rivers of blood and money". In that way the seeds would be sown of "something new that will endure"; a vision of a golden age to come.[65] Is this one of the fantasies of empire that are the shiny upside of destruction? During the 1994 genocide, the Tutsi minority in Rwanda were described as "cockroaches from cockroaches who speak for cockroaches". The radio constantly hammered out untrue or grossly exaggerated stories that in every district occupied by the RPF advance terrible mass killings had taken place. Even some Tutsi, influenced by this rhetoric, fled the advance of the RPF, fearing for their own safety.[66] It was constantly repeated that the RPF were out to kill "innocent people", after which they would return to their "lairs and animal holes".[67] They were "vipers", "blood drinkers",[68] "scum",[69] "mad dogs",[70] "dirt"[71] and "snakes"[72] that

---

64 Chalk and Jonassohn, p. 235.

65 Statements by General Von Trotha quoted in H. Drechsler, *Let Us Die Fighting: The Struggle of the Herero and the Nema Against German Imperialism (1884–1915)* (London, 1981). p. 241.

66 Des Forges, p. 587.

67 Article in Kangura by Hassan Ngeze, January, 1994, quoted in African Rights, *Rwanda*, p. 72–3.

68 African Rights, *Rwanda*, p. 64.

69 Speech by Leon Muggasara, November 1992, quoted in Gourevitch, p. 96.

70 RTLMC Broadcast, April–May, 1994, quoted in African Rights, *Rwanda*, p. 81.

71 African Rights, *Rwanda*, p. 342.

72 African Rights, *Rwanda*, pp. 42, 307, 641, 756, 787.

"sneaked in like snakes".[73] Lest they "bite and kill you"[74], they were to be killed; "wiped out".[75] As in Cambodia from 1975 to 1978, what was "infected must be cut out" and that which was "rotten must be removed".[76] The "savage ones who cannot be re-educated" had to be dealt with: "if you want to tear out the weed you must go for the roots".[77] In Rwanda people were told: "in killing a snake wrapped around a gourd, you break the gourd if you want to kill him".[78] When eventually the RPF took over the whole of Rwanda, two million people fled either to the French-controlled zone of safety or, when the French withdrew, across the border. For the colonial settlers of New England, the native Americans, whom ultimately they destroyed, were "lice ... flies, rats and mice" sent by God to punish his people because of their sinful ways.[79] They were "Satan's agents". Again, the enemy was both within and without. Satan, in the guise of the "savage and pagan" natives, was allied to the sin within their own community. The "believers" were in continual danger from the "savage people, who are cruel, barbarous and most dangerous".[80] Under the Nazi leadership, the Jewish people were described as a parasitic force; terms derived from the insect world. [81]

Solzhenitsyn traces the vicious attitude towards ideological enemies of the Soviet State, inconvenient obstacles to its power,

73 Des Forges, p. 419.
74 African Rights, *Rwanda*, p. 42.
75 African Rights, *Rwanda*, p. 76.
76 Chalk and Jonassohn, p. 404.
77 "Revolutionary Flags" No. 3, March 1978, pp. 37–53, quoted in K.D. Jackson, *Cambodia 1975–1978: Rendezvous With Death* (Princeton, 1989) pp. 297, 273, 200.
78 Des Forges, p. 468.
79 Poem by Captain Waite Winthrop, quoted in Leach, *Flintlock and Tomahawke: New England in King Philip's War* (New York, 1966) p. 192 quoted in Chalk and Jonassohn, pp. 193–4.
80 Nash, *Red, White and Blue: The Peoples of Early America* (New Jersey, Second Edition, 1982) pp. 74–86 quoted in Chalk and Jonassohn, p. 191.
81 Bauer, *A History of the Holocaust* (London, 1982) p. 83–109.

back to Lenin's declaration in a letter to Maxim Gorky in September 1922 that the intellectuals were not the brains of the nation "they're its shit". He applied the same term to anyone who opposed him.[82] Thus, "insects", "parasites" and "malingerers" would be cleared out[83]: "dogs" would be shot[84], and "leeches on the capitalist structure", such as lawyers, gendarmes, priests and notaries, would be removed.[85]

This is not just dehumanising people. Despite the wide resort to zoological appellations, as well as images of disease, spiritual decay and infestation, the hate-rhetoric phenomenon goes beyond any human attribute. It becomes mythical. Emotion speaks in terms so powerful that it lapses into the fantastical. It displays the unreal, fact altering, nature of hatred and, paradoxically, the perverse cleverness of those that exploit it. They can evoke what is within all of us. They create an attitude of regarding those to be "pushed into a corner" as a demonic force. Where that description evokes the response that correlates to the aggression within us, is it possibly the instinct that is drawn up that seeks to smash an image of a treacherous, murderous and incorrigible enemy?

But the circle of hatred is not yet closed. People can still see sense, despite turmoil all around them and lies echoing in their ears. This is demonstrated by all of the interveners who saved the lives of those damned by hatred that were mentioned in the last chapter. They must be excluded. This is the fourth pattern that makes hatred effective.

"Whoever collaborates with the enemy, works for him, or gives him information, is also the enemy. We will systematically eliminate them", warned a notice in Rwanda.[86] In order to

---

82 Lenin, *Collected Works* (Moscow, Fifth Edition) Volume 51, p. 48, quoted in D. Volkogonov, *Lenin: Life and Legacy* (London, 1995); and see A. Solzhenitsyn, *The Gulag Archipelago* (London, 1974) p. 328.
83 Solzhenitsyn, p 27.
84 Solzhenitsyn, p. 101.
85 Solzhenitsyn, p. 313.
86 Quoted in Gourevitch.

give effect to the plan of genocide, members of the Interahamwe militia were given orders that every Hutu who cooperated with the enemy group should be reported to the brigade leader: the death squad would then come and kill him in the night.[87] When the President of Rwanda was murdered, and the plans of genocide began to be put into effect, people looked to the administrative authorities to help them. The "interim government" saw the administration as the means to effect the mass murder. Anyone who stood in the way was cleared out. The former Queen of Rwanda looked to her local chief of administration, the Préfet of Butare, to protect her; and he did. But he could help her and the other victims only for a time. Since the killing of the President, the Butare Préfet, Jean-Baptiste Habyalimana, had enforced an order announced by the Ministry of Defence to keep people at home.[88] On 10 April 1994, he called an urgent meeting of his security committee in response to attacks, in his own district and in neighbouring areas, which had displaced refugees into the zone for which he was responsible. He listened to accounts of growing violence in sub-districts under his control and, in response, told his administrators that they alone had the function of keeping order: not the army and not the militia of the Hutu-supremacists. He made it clear to the military that they had no function in dealing with the problem of refugees. The job of administration, he stressed, was to feed the refugees and to keep order: civil law remained in force and should be used to identify and hold troublemakers. He offered to confront the military himself. At subsequent public meetings, he ordered his subordinates to calm people and to prevent disorder. He disobeyed an order from the central authorities not to issue travel permits to people seeking to flee Rwanda. This was an open defiance of the self-justifying government ideology that all the troubles of Rwanda came from allowing Tutsis to leave the country in the aftermath of

---

87 African Rights, *Rwanda*, pp. 65, 592, 599, 473, 338, 591.
88 This account is mainly taken from Des Forges, pp. 353–594.

the 1959 revolution.[89] He then refused to leave his area in order to attend a meeting of all Préfets in Kigali with the self-proclaimed interim government. On 12 April he was left isolated in Butare by the cutting of long-distance telephone services. He personally visited the thousands of refugees gathered at Cyanhinda and Nkomero and assured them they would be safe and that supplies of aid would be provided.[90] Those bourgmestres opposed to the killings, and the preliminary intimidation and corralling of the Tutsi population, constantly turned to him for help. On 11 April, the radio prepared the ground for his departure by implying that he had neglected his duty in not attending the government meeting of Préfets to which he had been invited. Six days later, his successful opposition of the slaughter was neutralised when the government announced over the radio that he had been removed from office.

On 19 April a new Préfet was installed in a ceremony attended by an assemblage of interim government leaders, including the President, the Prime Minister and the Minister of Justice. Normally, at such a meeting, the outgoing Préfet would be formally thanked and would remain an honoured guest of the assembly. Instead, Habyalimana was dismissed and told to leave. The message was clear: anyone who opposed the plan of extermination from within the administration would face, at the very least, such a humiliation. It was on the next day that the former Queen of Rwanda was taken away and murdered.

Another leading opponent of the genocide, Major Habyarabatuma, who as local police commander had used his power to face down thugs imported into his area for the purpose of murder, was on the same day sent to the war front against the invading RPF in Kigali.[91] Two bourgmestres in Butare province who actively opposed the killings were

---

89 Des Forges, p. 204.
90 Des Forges, pp. 444, 446.
91 Des Forges, p 462.

denounced by their officials, hunted down, and killed.[92] Those bourgmestres who did not embrace the plan of annihilation were warned that their attitude placed their lives in danger.[93] The security committee of Butare was then turned to the business of "pacification'; hunting down escaped and undetected Tutsi through the concentrated use of local administration in support of genocide. At its meeting on 6 May, this committee discussed the catching of "persons who have disappeared without our knowledge".[94] One such was Mr. Habyalimana the former Préfet: "no one knows where he is". A week later he was captured, humiliated by being imprisoned in a lock up next to what used to be his seat of power, and then sent to the seat of the interim-government in Gitarama where he was murdered[95]. Within ten days of his removal, the majority of the Tutsi population in his préfecture were herded into convenient pockets of apparent refuge. There, they were easily murdered by the now dominant forces of genocide.[96] A bourgmestre from another area then took up the leadership role. He proposed that the refugees should quietly return home. They were first required to surrender their "weapons", the existence of which was part of the myth justifying their slaughter. Before there was a chance to answer, an attack began, "a strictly military operation" according to an eyewitness.[97] Huge numbers of troops were transported in to effect the slaughter.[98] The result was the death of around twenty thousand people shortly after the murder of the person who had tried to save them. At the level of local administration, officials who showed any humane consideration towards the thousands of refugees massed under their protection were replaced. In Gitarama the bourgmestre tried from the

---

92 Des Forges, pp. 495–99.
93 De Forges, p. 466.
94 Des Forges, p. 531.
95 Des Forges, p. 533, Gourevitch, pp. 261–2.
96 Des Forges, pp. 592, 470–514.
97 African Rights, *Rwanda*, p. 339; Des Forges, pp. 592, 470–514.
98 Gourevitch, p. 262.

beginning to stop the killings: then he too was forced to flee.[99] In Musebeya the bourgmestre was ousted for protecting threatened Tutsi. The militia made it clear that they were in control. They publicly referred to him as "an accomplice".[100] The departures of such protecting figures, and the removal and murder of protecting figures such as the Préfet of Butare, cleared the way for the massacres.

In other places and at all levels, the same pattern was repeated. "Whoever hides and does not show up to carry out the plans decided upon by the administration is also an enemy", was the attitude.[101] Three soldiers who genuinely guarded refugees in the Adventist Church at Ngoma were replaced by three others: these soldiers did not interfere when the militia then attacked with grenades and guns.[102] At Nyamashake, four gendarmes refused to leave their posts even when told that a nearby town was under attack by the RPF. They were then accused of being "RPF accomplices" and taken away to Cyangugu where reportedly two of them were murdered.[103] Areas untouched by anything other than sporadic excesses were whipped into participating in mass murder by those who came from outside.[104] Leaders in death-dealing visited the less enthused areas. These encouragers included the Minister for Youth[105] and the new President of Rwanda.[106] If locals could not face killing other locals, then a notorious band of killers, or an infamous murderer, could be imported.[107] The attitude expressed was "we will not kill you but others will".[108] In many areas, groups of Burundian exiles, embittered and revengeful over earlier massacres of Hutus

---

99 African Rights, *Rwanda*, p. 624; and see Des Forges, p. 282.
100 Des Forges, pp. 351–2.
101 Des Forges, p. 547.
102 African Rights, *Rwanda*, p. 442.
103 African Rights, *Rwanda*, pp. 458–60.
104 African Rights, *Rwanda*, pp. 468, 777, 995, 1013–16, 648.
105 African Rights, *Rwanda*, p. 361.
106 Gourevitch, p. 261–2.
107 African Rights, *Rwanda*, pp. 615, 523, 535, 488, 742.
108 African Rights, *Rwanda*, p. 301.

in their country, were marshalled into efficient killing squads and sent from place to place in aid of the extermination campaign. This pattern repeats itself in the roving groups of SS militias employed in the Holocaust and in the army and militia groups used in the Armenian genocide.[109]

The vicious taboo against associating with a declared enemy recurs as a pattern within aggressor groups because such association threatens the purpose of isolating dissent. A complete state of polarisation will be achieved in society when merely being with a member of the victim group casts those in his company as part of that group.[110] The attitude of the Albigensian crusade was that any word or sign that showed that a Catholic considered heretics to be "good men" evidenced guilt of the crime of heresy. This pattern echoes through eras and places far removed from thirteenth century France. This was and is, a strategy designed to cut off one group of the population from another. The myth is that of the heretic, or the enemy of the people. He is a creation of the mind so powerful that even knowing him will infect you. The idea in the logic of executing mass murder is enclosing your enemy in a circle of hatred. The objective is that simple human interaction should be made criminal.[111] When, in June 1937, Stalin's administration announced a plot by the Red Army high command, under Marshal Tukhachevsky to destroy the government in league with the Germans, anyone who was his friend was arrested and sent to the camps.[112] Tukhachevsky was one of many "plotters" and "wreckers" and "capitalist allies". It became impossible to hold even photo-

---

109 For example, see Walker, pp. 139, 159, 161. See also L. Young, *Japan's Total Empire: Manchuria and the Culture of Wartime Imperialism* (Berkeley, 1999) pp. 119–23; L. Dawidowicz, *The War Against the Jews 1933–1945* (London, 1983) passim; Gilbert, *The Holocaust*, passim.

110 For example, see Walker, pp. 139, 159, 161; see also Young, pp. 119–23; Dawidowicz, passim; Gilbert, *The Holocaust*, passim.

111 M. Ruthven, *Torture: The Grand Conspiracy* (London, 1978) pp. 90–7, quoted in Chalk and Jonassohn, p. 130.

112 For an account see Bullock, *Hitler and Stalin*, pp. 526–30.

graphs or letters of what eventually became millions of enemies of the people. [113] In the territories occupied by the Nazis it was proclaimed that anyone "who tries to hide a Jew, or to assist him in hiding will be shot dead".[114] To defy the drive towards extermination required "boundless self-sacrifice".[115] The policy of the Nazi government was to break all social ties between neighbours. The worst "crime" in their eyes, was being Jewish. An all-encompassing offence of being "friendly to the Jews" was a primary and widely used instrument of isolation. It became unwise even to salute a Jewish neighbour in the public street.[116] When Jewish-owned businesses still functioned in Germany, those patronising them ran the risk of being officially photographed. The Jewish community was also subjected to a barrage of loathsome hate-rhetoric, deliberately orchestrated by the government, to the extent that it became impossible to express any view in support of them.[117] At a lower stage of hatred, those merely sympathetic to persons incarcerated in concentration camps put themselves at risk of being regarded as enemies of the regime.[118] In Nazi Germany, anti-association laws were described as being "not measures intended to breed and perpetuate race hatred, but measures which mean the beginning of an easing in the relations between the German and the Jewish peoples".[119] Of course, this was a lie. In the

---

113 D. Shostakovich, related to S. Volkov, *Testimony: The Memoirs of Dimitri Shostakovich* (London, 1979) p. 91. For a similar experience see D.M. Thomas, *Solzhenitsyn: A Century of His Life* (London, 1998) p. 64.

114 Proclamation of 27 July 1942, quoted in D. Goldenhagen, *Hitler's Willing Executioners: Ordinary Germans and the Holocaust* (London, 1996) p. 23. For examples see Gilbert. pp. 451, 409, 504, 188. For a personal account see C. Bielenberg, *The Past is Myself* (London, 1997) p. 114.

115 Quoted in Gilbert, *The Holocaust*, p. 661.

116 Gellately, pp. 134–50.

117 Gellately, p. 129.

118 Gellately, p. 217.

119 Loesner and Knost, *Die Nurmberger Gesetze* (Berlin, 1936) pp. 16–17 quoted in Friedlander, p. 367.

massacres of the Armenian people, the same determination to exclude human sympathy, which after all arises from human contact, was applied so that the murder plan would proceed uninterrupted. By orders of the central government, the polarisation of the Turkish population in hostility to their Armenian neighbours, already pushed forward by lies, was made a matter of law:

> *Any official or a special individual who opposes this sacred and patriotic work and fails to discharge the duties imposed on him or protects or hides this or that Armenian in any way, shall be branded as an enemy of the country and religion and punished accordingly.*[120]

Typical of the administration of these deadly prejudice was a proclamation issued by the Governor of Van: "The Armenians must be exterminated. If any Moslem protects a Christian, first, his house shall be burnt; then the Christian killed before his eyes, then his family [the protector's] and himself".[121] It became impossible even for an American missionary to shield an Armenian.[122] In the province of Erzerum, during the same month, a public meeting was told that the Armenians were traitors: Moslems who shielded Armenian friends would be liable to suffer as Armenians.[123] Greeks who came to the aid of Armenians also suffered retribution.[124]

I do not argue that there is no good in human nature. Nor do I suggest that our simple humanity is so frail that we are all

---

120 Order addressed to the governors, mayors and town authorities where the Armenians lived, by Talaat (Minister of the Interior), Enver (Minister of War) and Nazim (Executive Secretary of the Union and Progress Committee) dated 5 April 1915 and reproduced in D. Boyajain, *Armenia: The Case for a Forgotten Genocide* (New Jersey, 1972) pp. 319, 320.
121 Ussher, *An American Physician in Turkey* (Boston, 1917) p. 224, quoted in Walker, p. 207.
122 Riggs, pp. 67, 96–7.
123 Great Britain, *Parliamentary Papers Miscellaneous No. 31* (1916) 231, quoted in Walker 214.
124 Walker, p. 221.

liable to be made into murderers just because of the cunning of evil people. Look at the lies that are necessary to make evil prevail. Look at the ingenuity, the sheer low criminal cunning, that must be cranked into gear to get people to hate. It is a measure of the power of human sympathy that huge effort is needed to enclose any society in hatred. It seems that real social turmoil is also needed. That, as we have seen, can also be engineered. And when it is, the peddlers of hate still have hard work to do. The examples in this chapter demonstrate this.

In Rwanda, the population did not rise spontaneously against the refugees. The crowd of machete-wielding murderers that ultimately dispatched most of the victims were usually not neighbours but killers imported from other areas.[125] People lived in peace, apart from a few settling of grudges, until the organisers of the genocide came into their area to start their dirty work.[126] The worst of the actual killing occurred from 15 April 1994, nine days after the murder of President Habyarimana. By then, the period of "maximum anguish" at his death should have passed, accepting for a moment the untenable theory of a population rising up in "spontaneous slaughter". In order to murder the Armenians, the group in power in Turkey had to systematically terrorise and mislead their own people. The entire thing was organised from the central leadership.[127] Their systems were well tried. It had worked before: provoke people into defending themselves and call it a "rebellion".[128] Take away people's rights and then make them a derisory offer; when they do not accept it, scandalise them. If this hatred had not been engineered, people would have lived together; at least in relative peace. That was not what was wanted. First the lies are put

---

125 For other examples see Des Forges, pp. 247–8, 271, 320, 339, 393, 412, 465–6, 472, 506, 509.

126 See the examples of how people were turned on their neighbors in African Rights, *Rwanda*, pp. 454 and 518.

127 H. Morgenthau, *Ambassador Morgenthau's Story* (Ann Arbour, 2000) p. 233.

128 Dadrian, p. 120.

about. Then the schemers can move in and murder who ever they like.[129] They have their "proof".

Any reasonable person would say that if people are about to be attacked they are entitled to defend themselves and have weapons to do it with. In many parts of the world we see not only revenge killings, but also attacks on population centres dressed up as the imposition of law. And if they attack back, do the aggressors have their justification? That is how they would like to see it because that is precisely what they have planned. On a domestic level, the law says that the defence of provocation is not available to a defendant who goads someone with the intention that he will respond, thereby giving his assailant the chance to kill him. All over the world this pattern replicates itself: attack a centre of population, or a group that you want to victimise, and when they defend themselves proclaim that you are restoring order. Or say that the government is putting down a rebellion. Where those bent on aggression take over society, lies replace law. Unfortunately, lies work their mischief over time. The genocide in Rwanda was planned over a period of years. The government, like the Nazis, used every instrument of mass disinformation to turn the population to hatred. Does this kind of saturation by demonising lies work?

It seems that it might, eventually, at least in combination with measures that destroy anyone of independent thought. Possibly there is a critical number of the population that the murderers need to get on their side in order to "succeed". If they have a period of years in which no opposing voice can be heard, then any plan of aggression might succeed.[130] There is no proof of this, it is only a suggestion. But what is certain is that people can be made to hate. Even among the members of the National Socialist party it would appear that virulent anti-Semites did not make up the majority. But, when all is said and

---

129 Walker, p. 171; and see V. Dadrian, *A History of the Armenian Genocide* (Providence, 1997) pp. 147–57.

130 Gilbert, *The Holocaust* quoting "Contra Komintern", 2 November 1939.

done, every one of them was a member of a criminal gang. Even in such company, can Solzhenitsyn's theory, that some humanity always remains somewhere in everyone, be demonstrated? I do not know. But what seems to be demonstrable is that human sympathy is a quality in flux.

Can you lose even the little bit that you have not destroyed? In the aftermath of Krystalnacht in November 1938 a German sociologist conducted a survey among party members. In response to an apparently casual comment, "Well – so a start is being made at last with carrying out the programme against the Jews?": 41 party members responded. Of these, 26 were indignant at the outrages; 13 were non-committal in response; and 2 approved because of the stated reason that "terror must be met with terror". In 1942, the same sociologist put questions to 61 party members in order to discover their attitude to the roundup and deportation, to an unexplained destination in the East, of the Jewish community of Germany. Of these, 16 were concerned for the deportees, 3 expressed the belief that they were responsible for the war and must be exterminated. Those who were indifferent amounted to 42 out of the sample. In other words, the percentage of those who could not care as to what happened to the Jews, and chose to look the other way, had climbed from 32 per cent to 69 per cent over the further four years of unrelenting exposure to lies.[131]

Hatred is debasing. It imprisons the mind. And then there is the business of killing. It brings up the paradox of those who like to kill and those who pretend that they have nothing to do with it.

131 M. Müller-Claudius, *Der Antisemitismus und das Deutsche Verhängnis* (Frankfurt, 1948) pp. 162–6; cited in Cohn, pp. 231–7.

CHAPTER 9

I Was Not Responsible

ROBBERIES AGAINST isolated old people follow a discernible pattern. They start with a prospect that must terrify anyone. Unknown to the victims, and over a period of days or weeks, people of evil intent begin to spy on them.[1] Strangers might start calling: offering something for sale or pretending an interest in their welfare, all the while trying to find their vulnerability. In many cases, elderly isolated people, through fear or reclusiveness, will not open their door. So, those who appear offenceless are sent to bring down their guard; a woman or two, soft spoken and sympathetic. Once the door is opened, the men burst through.

Several of these crimes saw an elderly man first rendered defenceless by being tied up and then, the surprising thing, beaten to death. In most of these cases, only the bare details emerged upon the arrest of the suspects. In a very few, the less hardened gang members went further and described what had happened inside the house; how an intended robbery became a murder.

Why do people kill? There is nothing less threatening or offensive than an elderly stranger. If hatred is the driving force of violence, then how could you hate such a person? Yet, in several of these cases, the post mortem examination showed that multiple blows had been inflicted on the deceased. Generally,

---

1   Possibly this is what gave rise to superstitions about the evil eye.

the attackers had not come armed with any weapons. There was no need to. Strength of numbers and intimidation would be enough. But they were upset: fear of detection and the anticipation of criminal activity had made them jittery. Whatever demon is inside us can, it seems, more easily break out in panic. When the victim had tried to defend himself, his weapon was immediately turned back on him. Whatever state the burglars were in was easily notched up by any challenge. In one case, a shotgun was broken over an elderly man, in another his walking stick. It would be too facile to say that some kind of inner legend of hidden treasure spurred on the burglars' determination to beat its whereabouts out of their victims. While that motivated the enterprise in the first place, I never came across a case where the victims under interrogation told anything other than the truth; they had nothing much. The criminals who took part in these robberies all testified that their victims had pleaded for mercy. That was not enough. In several cases, the attackers went further than rough interrogation. Even where there had been no resistance, gang members began to beat their captive. He was tied up, on the surface so that the house could be ransacked. But that was not an easing of the situation. Nor does it seem to have been the point. There was a continuity in what began as a degradation ritual and ended in death. Shouting became roughness became violence. As this progressed, the victims lost all physical and mental control. This is not pleasant. It is what happens in extreme fear. It assaults the senses: sight, hearing and smell.

There is an inner and an outer pattern to things that happen again and again. The outer pattern is not so hard to describe. If you find the outer pattern, it may open up some degree of understanding of what drives human nature.

In criminal practice your job is to defend your client against accusations by his accomplices that it was he who planned the heist, that he was the leader, that it was he who was the killer. It lessens the guilt of their confederates to claim that, maybe also their burden. They will assert that another member of the gang lost "his cool". All of them can plead this, so that there is no prime culprit, the person who killed the victim. In reality someone must have. In the case of AM, where one gang member asserted that another had done the murder, he described him as "mad, acting like an animal." That claim recurred in almost all of these cases. Where, in a few cases, there were admissions to killing, through police statements or in court, the defence of the killers almost always was the familiar one that they were on "automatic pilot." Where a criminal claimed that he did not participate, to use a nice legal word, in the killing, he squarely placed all the responsibility on Tom or Willie, or whoever. Those keeping watch outside deflected any of their culpability for violence and death by saying that they "never expected it to happen." Perhaps that could be said, as to right at the start, or as to the tense journey to the crime scene, but they invariably claimed that the murder had "nothing to do with them" even as they heard the screams of the victim from inside his own house.

All of these victims had inherent dignity. Putting together evidence on a homicide involves detectives interviewing people as to when the dead man was last seen. Invariably, other details emerged as well: the deceased was well liked; their eccentricities were a feature of local life. No one spoke of them other than with the greatest respect. But where was that respect once their house was invaded? It was the first thing that was taken from them.

And then there were the handful of cases where two elderly people lived together but only one of them was killed. The other was locked away in a bathroom, or shied back as the madness erupted, hoping that he or she would be left alone. If it were ever credible that the killers had, as they claimed, totally lost control, that excuse seems to evaporate where only one vulnerable person is murdered while another one is left be. Does it just so happen that it is the person who is humiliated and beaten that is killed while the one who escapes degradation also escapes death? I met with a few of these survivors over the years. After all the legal proceedings had finished, I remember talking to one of them, KH, who told me that he had only managed to retain something of his dignity because it was his companion, and not he, who was chosen for the "interrogation". It was pure luck, perhaps aided by his composure, that he was not, first, humiliated and, then, killed. That seems to be the order in which these things happen. As we have seen in Chapter 7, it emerges in other survivor stories.

These cases present the paradox in human violence: they do not solve it. Why does "merely helping" enable some people to kill while others revel in destruction?[2] Do both approaches make killing palatable?

If you could say how killing began, you might answer many questions. The ethologist Professor Irenäus Eibl-Eibsfeldt, an expert on the connections between human and animal behaviour, thought that human murder began almost as an accident. In the animal world, members of the same species almost always are able to ward off a fatal attack by fleeing from, or submitting to, their stronger rival. A classic example is the wolf that rolls on its back and exposes its throat to be ripped out by the dominant male of its group. Evolution has made submission enough, so both wolves live. When man began to use weapons in conflict, stones and then hand axes, the theory goes that the opponent would be dead "… before he has a chance of appealing to our sympathy by an appropriate gesture of submission."[3] When a weapon of distance was used, like a bow and arrow, the same feature was exacerbated. More so, when people become part of inanimate weapons, tanks and war planes. Fighting them, you can think of your opponent as a machine. Eibl-Eibsfeldt also asserts that it is thanks to "our highly developed intellect" that

---

2   The contradictory descriptions of the killing processes in Auschwitz and Birkenau by Dr Miklos Nyiszli are worth noting; M. Nyiszli, *Auschwitz: A Doctor's Eye-witness Account* (London, 1973) pp. 48 and 71–72.

3   I. Eibl-Eibsfeldt, *The Biology of Peace and War: Men Animals and Aggression* (New York, 1979) p. 123.

people can convince themselves that "their opponents are not men, but are at best beasts or highly dangerous monsters" and that "such 'vermin' not only may, but must be killed".[4]

In 1991 during the First Gulf War, press conferences in Allied Headquarters were shown video recordings from cameras attached to the nose cones of cruise missiles. These showed targets inside Baghdad from the point of view of the destroying weapon. In one clip that was widely broadcast, a deathly grey picture from the missile displayed, first, a streetscape, next, the top of a building and then a plunge into its heart before the picture liquidised as the high explosive detonated. "That is, that was, my counterpart's command centre", announced a general to a titter of laughter from journalists. What was not shown was the effect of high explosive on the human body. In the Second Gulf War, soldiers are now going into battle with headsets blasting rock music into their brain. They look and sound less human, their shape distorted by the equipment they carry and their minds desensitised to the effects of violence. By mechanising the means of delivering death, we make of it a profession that most people can pursue, if they need to. It becomes less and less the preserve of those who hate.

You can be mentally and physically removed from slaughter even as you cause people to die. A pilot who took part in the saturation bombing of German cities in 1944 described himself as "totally isolated from the conflagration." To him, floating thousands of meters high in the sky, the "flames and all sorts of coloured lights" from the bombs reminded him of a "fine fireworks display at Battersea Park." [5] In an interview fifty years later, he looked back on the policy of destroying entire cities as "morally wrong." A psychologist would say that his lack of affective realisation of death blunted his moral revulsion and so helped him to kill. That cannot be a complete answer. Yet, it is

---

4 I. Eibl-Eibsfeldt, *Love and Hate: The Natural History of Behaviour Patterns* (London, 1972) p. 97.

5 Sandra Berwick, "Bombers who Still Fan the Flames", the *Independent*, 6 August 1994.

curious how sudden closeness to an enemy blunts the killing edge: the examples of the soldiers put off firing on seeing their target enjoying a bath or holding up their trousers come to mind. This suggests that distance artificially enables our aggressive potential. If you were to construct a killing machine from scratch, for maximum efficiency, experience suggests that deniability is an even bigger factor than distancing. Especially deniability to oneself.

Many instances of mass murder are effected through systems that kill while "not meaning to kill". Attrition camps, where people are brought to die over time of starvation and ill treatment, have been a feature of the twentieth century. Of those "sentenced" to Stalin's gulags, some sources have up to a third of the prisoners dying in their first year.[6] Overall, the death rate is inestimable. Ann Applebaum reluctantly records annual official death records showing a low of less than 1 per cent in 1953 and a high of 24.9 per cent in 1942.[7] Robert Conquest estimates that the collectivisation campaign in the Ukraine cost about fourteen and a half million deaths between 1930 and 1937.[8] To this misery, you could add the thousands of German prisoners of war in Soviet camps who never returned, the victims of the famine that followed on Mao's "great leap forward" and many other instances of "unintentional killing". In the genocide of the Armenian people, the leaders were shot first of all and then the rest of the population was marched into the Anatolian desert. The setting up of camps where no one could survive attests to a centralised plan of murder.[9] When the Armenians who had survived the forced marches, including murder and rape by soldiers and bandits, arrived at such places,

6   A. Antonov Ovseyenko, *The Time of Stalin: Portrait of a Tyranny* (New York, 1981) p. 253.

7   A. Applebaum, *The Gulag: A History* (London, 2004) pp. 515–522.

8   R. Conquest, *Harvest of Sorrow* (New York, 1987), quoted in F. Chalk and K. Jonassohn, *The History and Sociology of Genocide: Analyses and Case Studies* (Yale, 1990) p. 300.

9   See the account of Auguste Bernau, quoted in C. Walker, *Armenia: The Survival of a Nation* (London, 1980) pp. 227–229.

they died. At Deir-ez-Zor the Turkish governor tried to alleviate the suffering of the remnants of the deportees. A person "well known for his cruelty and barbarity" replaced him.[10] Clearly, it was a lie to suggest that the establishment of which he took charge had any other purpose than death. We do not know if this kind of activity, starving people to death or treating them so badly in captivity that they die of disease, is a strategy devised so as to deny any later responsibility. That answer would be consistent with the excuses typical of those accused of gang crimes. The very widespread use of methods that kill, but not by direct violence, suggests that an intention to kill may be oblique or may even be missing in the attrition cases. But when you have control of a system that causes people to drop dead time after time, reality must break through soon enough that those responsible for the conditions are actually doing the killing. Can they, these kinds of killers, have any excuse left? Such as, that they are killing while pretending not to kill?

In 1904, General Lothar von Trotha was sent to Namibia from Berlin in order to quell a revolt by the Herero people. "Tensions" with the four thousand German settlers had boiled over when a forty-kilometre strip of land along the path of a railway line had been taken. All native peoples were to be excluded and all water sources occupied. Years of injustice compounded a sense that the Herero had little to lose. Their supreme chief, Samuel Maherero, declared that death "had lost much of its horror". His orders for insurrection were restrictive: non-Germans, missionaries, women and children were not to be killed. About one hundred settlers lost their lives and the rest retreated into fortified areas. General von Trotha's plans for quelling the rebellion were of a different order of honesty, and

---

10 Lepsius, *Deutschland und Armenia 1914–1918* (Potsdam, 1919) p. 493, quoted in Walker, p. 229. For other cases of replacing unwilling officials see J. Boyce and A. Toynbee, *The Treatment of Armenians in the Ottoman Empire 1915–1916: Documents Presented to Viscount Grey of Culloden* (Princeton, 2000) pp. 75, 95; G.S. Graber, *Caravans To Oblivion: The Armenian Genocide 1915* (New York, 1996) p. 109.

of destructiveness. Six German detachments were deployed around the rebel area in a formation that Horst Drechsler, the historian of these events, judges was designed to achieve genocide.[11] That is not how it was presented. The General reminded his troops that, in fulfilling his orders, they should "always bear in mind the good reputation that the German soldier has acquired."[12] His men were ordered to fire shots over the heads of the tribespeople so as to drive them away, not randomly but into the Omaheke desert. No male prisoners were to be taken but neither, it might appear, was a mass slaughter to take place. The plan would not "give rise to atrocities committed on women and children". Why? Because, according to the written orders for the operation, "these will surely run away". In reality, this was a plan of extermination. It was made impossible for the Herero to escape. Then the German forces moved on them. Casualties in fighting were slight. The Herero were barred from a breakout and then driven by artillery and machinegun fire to the edge of the Omaheke. Von Trotha then forced the entire people into the desert. He put up a cordon of over 250 kilometres, sealing the Herero people off from any real possibility of escaping into a landscape where they might survive. The cordon was maintained for nearly a year from August 1904. Of about 80,000 Herero people alive in that year, only around 16,000 remained in 1911. Around a thousand of these had escaped to British-held colonies. Of those placed in prisoner of war camps, between October 1904 and March 1907, about 45 per cent died. Although few were actually killed, they were contrived to die as surely as if those in the desert had been executed and those in the camps randomly shot. This method enabled the colonists to bring the entire area under European control.

We do not know how these soldiers felt standing and firing shots over the heads of a shattered people retreating into the

---

11 H. Drechsler, *Let Us Die Fighting: The Struggle of the Herero and the Nama Against German Imperialism (1884–1915)* (London, 1981) pp. 150–159.
12 For an incident of driving victims into a swamp, see M. Burleigh, *The Third Reich: A New History* (London, 2000) p. 566.

desert. Probably, they felt that they retained that "good reputation" which was so important to their commander. Clearly, Von Trotha's idea was to put a distance between his soldiers and their unpleasant duty, and, bizarrely enough, to protect his own good name. What kind of conscience could he have had?

This kind of self-delusion probably does not subsist in isolation from other patterns. Just as the mass murder of, among others, the Armenians and the Jews was buoyed up on the lie of the superiority of the killers, the genocide of the Herero was also justified by General von Trotha as a "racial struggle". The Herero he wrote, from his "infinite knowledge of many African tribes", would yield only to "brute force": negotiations were "quite pointless." The myth of the irremediable enemy was also supported by the myth of service to the great leader: "Since I neither can nor will come to terms with these people without express orders from His Majesty the Emperor and King, it is essential that all sections of the nation be subjected to rather stern treatment." With that "principle" in mind, he had ordered that all captured warriors should be "court-martialled and hanged", while any women and children who, no doubt in desperation, had sought his aid were to be "driven back into the sandveld". There could be no question of a balance of lives and interests in a matter such as this. General von Trotha's mode of thinking emerges in this report that he made back to his superiors in Europe:

> To accept women and children who are for the most part sick, poses a grave risk to the force, and to feed them is out of the question. For this reason, I deem it wiser for the entire nation to perish than to infect our soldiers into the bargain and to make inroads into our water and food supplies. Over and above this, any gesture of leniency on my part would be regarded as a sign of weakness by the Herero.

Can the mind can be divided by lies? Is it possible that one part of the human mind can lie to another part so as to make intentional killing palatable? The plea "I was not involved", has surfaced as incongruously in multiple murder cases as it has in the robbery murder cases that I have mentioned. The notion that violence, in all its ugliness, has to be made palatable is connected to it.

In Nazi-occupied Poland of 1941, as the Einsatzgruppen went about their job of murdering Polish Jews and Polish leaders, the SS leader Heinrich Himmler asked to see a "shooting operation" as part of a tour of inspection. A hundred prisoners were selected for a demonstration. They had to jump into their own mass graves. Then they were shot and the next batch of victims were made to lie on their bodies. As Himmler stood peering at this, a splash of brains hit him in the face. He turned green. An SS General had to hold him steady and lead him away from the grave.[13] After the demonstration, he made a little speech to his men about the hard nature of their duties. We have already seen the kind of thing he came out with.[14] What troubled him, he later claimed, was the strain on the executioners. Returning to Berlin, he ordered research on killing methods. This led first to the gas van, where the exhaust was redirected to a sealed passenger area, and ultimately to the gas chamber.[15] Many, many people could then be killed well away from most peoples' senses. Physical distancing introduces great possibilities for self-deceit.

Rudolf Höss chose denial right up to his execution. He claimed in his prison memoir to have given "no reflection" to Himmler's order to him, in the summer of 1941, to build a centre for mass killings at Auschwitz.[16] In his last letter to his wife he claimed this: "without realising it, I had become a cog in the terrible German extermination machine." Most of "the horrible things" that had been carried out under his command, he said, he had only learned about during the legal process in

---

13 For a contemporary account see M. Gilbert, *The Holocaust: The Jewish Tragedy* (London, 1987) p. 191.

14 Chapter 4.

15 A. Bullock, *Hitler and Stalin: Parallel Lives* (London, 1993) p. 818.

16 S. Paskuly (ed.), *Rudolf Höss Death Dealer: Memoirs of the SS Kommandant of Auschwitz* (New York, 1996) p. 153.

Poland that ended in his execution. "I cannot describe how I was deceived," he wrote about the horrors of Auschwitz. But, he had his excuse: "I did not do it personally".[17] Franz Stangl attempted to follow the same path right up to the point where the probing by Gitta Sereny left him having to acknowledge that he was up a blind alley. His method of maintaining the lie of non-involvement opens up a possible window for understanding one aspect of the conscience that allows us to live with violence.

Stangl was a professional policeman; an individual versed in the criminal law. German law, as he understood it, required every crime to have "a subject, an object, an action and an intent." In other words, in a robbery there has to be a robber, the victim from whom something is taken, an act of stealing with violence and that has to be the robber's purpose. There are your four elements, and it is tidy to separate them, but usually unreal. In a crime, the actor and the victim are, for all practical purposes, always present. Law defines the action: robbery is stealing with violence; murder is intentional killing; manslaughter is unintentional killing, or killing under provocation. A serious crime cannot occur by accident: the robber has to have a purpose of stealing through violence; the murderer has to deal with the victim with the purpose of that they should die or be seriously injured; the manslaughterer has to act with such culpable negligence that any reasonable person would realise that his neglect of proper standards was putting lives unnecessarily at risk. Why bother with all of this? Why not say, as the robbers and murderers of elderly farmers have so often said: "I was only watching out"; "I was only searching the house"; "I could do nothing to stop the killer, and anyway I was afraid of him"; "What happened was not what I wanted, I am a kind person"? Well, you can say this.

The Hartheim Institute, at which Franz Stangl began his

---

17 Letter of 11 April 1947, quoted in Paskuly, pp. 89–193, and see p. 186.

career in murder, killed infirm and mentally ill persons. He concealed the nature of this occupation from his wife. According to himself, he was not "involved ... in the operational sense". He was "merely doing police work". This was in the early days of the Nazi regime, and their plan of "purifying" their "race". His later assignment to the death camp at Sobibor he ascribed to coercion. He explained that a remark had been made by his superior officer: "if any of you don't like that you can leave...under the earth ...not over it".[18] His promotion to Kommandant of the Treblinka camp was accepted because, he claimed, of his fears of a sadistic superior officer. He told Sereny that he feared for the safety of his family, who were then in Poland.[19]

When Franz Stangl's wife found out what was happening in the death camp at Sobibor he told her that the work was secret, which to a degree was true. He pushed away her questions. Again, the mirror: he must have feared what he would see in his wife's reaction to his life. He pleaded with her to back off: "... I can't discuss it. All I can tell you, and you must believe me: whatever is wrong – I have nothing to do with it".[20] When he became Kommandant at Treblinka which, it was tacitly accepted, was "the same sort of place as Sobibor", he concealed his position of ultimate responsibility from her.[21] He told her, on a visit home to Austria in 1942 that "he was only responsible for the valuables, construction and discipline". To us, these are naked attempts to change the unchangeable. To him, his leading role in the process of murder seems to have been made easier by him convincing himself that he was not actually involved. He looked to petty and meaningless acts of kindness to paint himself as a caring person. For instance, he claimed to have intervened on behalf of a prisoner defrauded of a watch on his arrival by a guard. Ordinarily, death camp guards carried the

18 G. Sereny, *Into that Darkness: From Mercy Killing to Mass Murder* (London, 1974) pp. 110–113, 131.
19 Sereny, p. 134.
20 Sereny, p. 133.
21 Sereny, p. 210.

power of summary murder.[22] He then returned to work in his office at "a great deal of paper work". By the time he met the next transport of victims, those involved in the hands–on killing "were already well ahead with the work". He ignored the fact that the prisoner who had received the benefit of his attempt at rectifying a petty theft was already swallowed up by death at the hands of men under his command. Notwithstanding the fact that all the prisoners under his charge died, except for a very few who escaped towards the end of the war, Stangl indignant-ly denied an allegation by a surviving prisoner that he had, on one occasion, shot into a crowd.[23]

This denial of responsibility seems insane. Was Stangl living in a phantom world, immune to the viciousness all around him? Stangl claimed to Sereny that the only way he could live with his own conscience "was by compartmentalising" his thinking. She asked him what he would have done had it been he who was assigned to actually carry out the gassings. His answer was: "I wasn't. That was done by two Russians - Ivan and Nicolau, under the command of ... [Gustav Münzberger]."[24] What dif-ference, in any rational sense, could that distinction between actual duties make? All of them were part of a murder machine, and not unwittingly in any sense.

According to Stangl and to Otto Horn, an SS guard subse-quently acquitted in the Treblinka trial, the actual gassings at the death–camp were indeed carried out by two Russians, "Ivan and Nicolau", who performed their task under Gustav Münzberger. Horn, assigned by Stangl to incineration duties after the gassings, described Münzberger's job as being to stand at the doors of the gas chambers and to drive the victims in with a whip. Surely, he could not possibly disavow his part in these thousands of mur-ders? Münzberger, who had served a prison sentence for his part in these murders denied, on his wife's prompting, any direct

---

22 Sereny, p. , p. 139.
23 Sereny, p. 164, 122-124.
24 Sereny, p. 164.

hand in them. According to him, the Jewish prisoners were organised by their own Jewish police. He left out that prisoners organised themselves at the command of the Nazis, and did so in the hope that some of them might survive. It was only the actual executioners, "the Ukrainians" according to him, that bore any of the guilt for the mass murders. He shunned any responsibility: " We didn't have to do anything. There wasn't really anything for us to do. Yes, we just had to be there; that's right, that's all".[25]

Anything can be twisted. Whether you are the person supplying the weapon, the person using it or the leader of the operation, you can always plead that you are not responsible. In an interview with a man accused of up to seventy killings in Rwanda, the American writer Philip Gourevitch recorded his admission of participation as involving him having no responsibility at all. He also rationalised his role by compartmentalising his function. He was actually the leader of a roadblock brigade that stopped and identified Tutsis, who were then murdered. His excuses were that he had been "called upon by the State to kill." He was told that he had a duty to do this, "otherwise you'd be imprisoned or killed." Anyway, his role at the roadblock massacres was minimal: "We were just pawns in this. We were just tools."[26]

You can always claim, it seems, not to be involved. And, if you are placed squarely in the picture, you can say that you were there because of coercion; killing other people because you feared for your own life or that of your family. How can there be any reality in this? Well, in some remote sense there is. A man can join an army engaged in a war but have a pretty clear conscience that, because he is involved in logistics and not killing, that he has no moral responsibility.[27] A man can say: "My role

---

25 Sereny, p. 224.
26 P. Gourevitch, *We Wish To Inform You That Tomorrow We Will Be Killed With Our Families: Stories From Rwanda* (London, 1999) p. 307.
27 E. Staub, *The Roots of Evil: The Origins of Genocide and Other Group Violence* (Cambridge, 1989) pp. 28–29.

is meals", or "maintaining an electric fence to keep in the prisoners", or "transporting deportees". All these statements say: "what happens after that has nothing to do with me." At some point this distancing is real enough and at another point, the Höss and Stangl examples, it breaks down as an affront to reality. That is what a lie is. What causes people to be killed at roadblocks, in camps or on death marches is that their death is intended. When you become part of that, the responsibility for their death extends to you. Distancing by method of death dealing, and distancing by compartmentalising your mind can help to make this palatable. Distancing by replacing real words with euphemisms about the process of death dealing is probably a symptom of how a killer's mind is working.[28]

But what about the other side to this, that represented by the corpse with multiple wounds? The pursuit of death is a savage business. Why go into it at all? Why describe what happens? Lawyers see it and they know that distancing and mental compartmentalisation are only a part of the issue. People want, some of them at least, to get their hands really bloody. While Rudolf Höss, his cohorts and his kind, plead their separation from murder, there are always those who do the deed and who apparently revel in it. These are the people who will choose the methods of killing that will bring them closest to the agony of their victims. You can take instances from any mass murder. This account comes from a survivor of the massacre at Nyanza-Rebero in Rwanda:

The soldiers told the Interahamwe to wait. Clearly they wanted to begin the massacre themselves. Then the soldiers began by throwing grenades … There was blood everywhere and people moaning in agony. As people were hit, the blood spread out, spraying from their bodies. There were people asking to be shot instead of being ripped apart by grenades. The soil was reddened with blood. But they also had guns and they shot, shot and shot … After some hours they realised they had killed an awful

---

28 J. Waller, *Becoming Evil: How Ordinary People Commit Genocide and Mass Murder* (Oxford, 2002) pp. 188–189, 246–247; Staub, p. 29.

lot of people. I heard one of the soldiers say to a group of Interahamwe, "Go and see if there is still anyone alive". They had machetes, knives, spears and bows and arrows. They used these weapons to finish off the wounded. They did not even spare children and old people who were wounded. Then they came to me. A huge machete landed on my neck and my right hand. As if this was not enough they cut me up with a knife all over. Finally, they left in the evening.[29]

Similar methodology was used elsewhere.[30] In a large massacre at a convent in Byumba, refugees who had come to seek refuge there were corralled, and then marched one at a time into a house. They were then brought out the back door of the house. As they came out, they were each felled by a blow to the head with a hammer or machete and then shot by a soldier. A survivor, who watched this process, until the killers brought out his wife, described the activity as "very systematic".[31] So, why not just shoot the people? In Mibilizi, boys as young as ten were used to murder children of their own age, beating them, stripping and then torturing them before dispatching them with sticks and clubs. In many other instances, weapons of participation were chosen over weapons of distance to dispatch Tutsi victims.[32] A survivor of the massacre at Bugarama, where "people were hunted like animals", describes knives and machetes being used in preference to guns.[33] Similarly, throughout the days of the slaughter, instances occurred of people being forced to kill their own children;[34] forcing a man to kill his brother;[35] killing a daughter, but leaving the mother alive;[36] spearing

---

29 African Rights, *Rwanda: Death Despair and Defiance* (London, 1995) pp. 567–568.
30 See the example of Kicukiro, African Rights, *Rwanda*, p. 836.
31 African Rights, *Rwanda*, p. 607.
32 For example see African Rights, *Rwanda*, p. 629, 651.
33 African Rights, *Rwanda*, p. 1028. For another instance of hunting see Gilbert, *The Holocaust*, p. 493.
34 African Rights, *Rwanda*, p. 625, 638.
35 African Rights, *Rwanda*, p. 639, 641.
36 African Rights, *Rwanda*, p. 702.

infants;[37] and putting a baby to the breast of its murdered mother.[38] The literature of the Holocaust of the Jewish people is replete with similar instances. Those include: beating women prisoners to death with clubs and axes and throwing them down stairs;[39] forcing a woman into labour and killing her by stepping on her;[40] smashing children's heads against walls or burying them alive;[41] forcing a prisoner to dance to music while beating him;[42] tearing people to pieces with dogs;[43] and kicking a prisoner to death by rupturing his hernia.[44] Similar instances of immersion in the suffering of the chosen victim occurred during the attempts to eradicate the Armenians.[45] This pattern also emerges in massacres in every culture and age where immersion killing has been deliberately chosen in preference to methods of death by distancing.[46]

One may wonder if the assailants could find such methods of murder enjoyable. Those who witnessed at least some of such incidents saw the functionaries laugh or smile.[47] The

---

37 African Rights, *Rwanda*, p. 541.

38 African Rights, *Rwanda*, p. 673.

39 Incident at Budy, quoted in Paskuly 333–335.

40 Gilbert, *The Holocaust*, p. 796.

41 Gilbert, *The Holocaust*, numerous examples occur through the text at e.g. pp. 203, 305, 320, 330, 347, 359, 365, 388, 392, 399, 403, 411, 424, 434, 437, 439, 443, 455, 457, 481, 494, 479, 549, 665, 687.

42 Gilbert, *The Holocaust*, p. 501.

43 Gilbert, *The Holocaust*, p. 457.

44 Gilbert, *The Holocaust*, p. 571.

45 For instance see D. Boyajian, *Armenia: The Case for a Forgotten Genocide* (New Jersey, 1972) pp. 353–354, 386–414, 422; Bryce and Toynbee, pp. 66–68, 79, 121–122, 189.

46 For instances on Japanese behaviour towards the Chinese during the Nanking massacre see I. Chang, *The Rape of Nanking* (London, 1998) pp. 81–104.

47 Gilbert, *The Holocaust*, for example see pp. 699, 269, 524, 64, 267, 315, 326, 571, 457, 442, 271; D. Goldenhagen, *Hitler's Willing Executioners: Ordinary Germans and the Holocaust* (London, 1996) p. 452; Similarly see the accounts of Japanese behaviour in China quoted in Chang, pp. 83, 4, 145, 246. See further Chalk and Jonassohn, pp. 90, 103, 150, 198, 212, 381.

photographic record of the meeting out of the basest brutality shows evidence that people can revel in their closeness to the act of murder.[48] Is such conduct accidental in terms of its parallels from one era and place to another? Is it perhaps innate; awaiting the signals that awake viciousness from its slumber? And then: what about human sympathy, that quality that is supposed to stop us murdering each other?

The idea of making a person a quarry, hunting them down, puts the victim in a position where cries of panic, pleas for mercy, total submission and complete lack of ability to threaten are unequivocally displayed. Yet, it would seem, these have no inhibiting effect on the instincts of those intent on such forms of murder. Instead, humiliation seems to evoke the exact opposite of the intra-specific killing bar. Because hunting is such a deliberate activity, it may tell us something. The weapons must be prepared and the quarry directed into a position to be killed. All those activities are organised and directed. At the remove of at least some hours from such activities, there is ample time for reality to be engaged. There is time for emotions to cool. Yet, in Rwanda they were preparing their scythes for people hunting in the same way as they set up roadblocks and sharpened their spears and machetes for the day's "work".[49] Neighbours would participate in such hunts, crying out "here they are" as the exhausted victims fled by.[50] The huntsmen would explain to

---

48 For instance see Callahan, Kornely and Cohen, *Margaret Bourke White: Photographer* (London, 1998) p. 152; O. Figes, *A People's Tragedy: The Russian Revolution 1891–1924* (London, 1996) p. 577, Chang, p. 163; Boyajian, p. 114; J. Rabe, *The Good Man of Nanking: The Diaries of John Rabe* (London, 1998) passim; Robert Fisk, "Cleansing Bosnia at a Camp Called Jasenovac", the *Independent*, Weekend, 15 August, 1992; the *Irish Times*, page 1 photo, 22 February, 2002. The drawings of Colonel Danzig Baldayev, who served in the Gulag system, also put across the nature of the victim - oppressor relationship; see Angus MacQueen, "Art of Darkness", *Sunday Times Magazine*, 20 June 1999.

49 African Rights, *Rwanda*, p. 859.

50 African Rights, *Rwanda*, p. 678.

those interested: "We are looking for Inyenzi".[51] Trees were cut down and swamps were scoured in the search.[52] Children were used in these searches.[53] People were smoked out of their places of refuge.[54] Victims cowered in forests, listening to the sounds of such search parties. Hunters went about from place to place offering their services to communities outside their own areas.[55] Those who embarked on these hunts are likely to have individually encountered and to have killed some people on a one to one basis. Gilbert, in his study of the Holocaust, records instances of Jews who had escaped to the Polish forests being hunted down by Germans, or by fellow-Poles, in the expectation of the receipt of a bounty. Mere money is surely insufficient to promote such activity. In any peaceful society, the contract-murderer commands a huge price. There is a quality to these accounts of hunting down people which indicates that, for those involved, it must have been a pleasurable communal event. Nor is there, apparently, a complete remove from the moral order. Once again, the participants can feel a degree of self-revulsion, provided the true nature of their actions can be reflected back upon them through the reaction of a social equal. This does not always stop them, especially if they have group support. The historian records the diary of a schoolteacher travelling through Siedliska and going into the local co-operative shop. Local farmers were buying scythes "for the round-up ... of the Jews". The schoolteacher asked the price that they would receive on capturing a Jew. When he received no answer he suggested that more should be paid than the thirty pieces of silver with which Christ had been bought. The embarrassed silence did not stop "the round-up" proceeding later that day.[56]

---

51 African Rights, *Rwanda*, p. 591.
52 African Rights, *Rwanda*, p. 584/651.
53 African Rights, *Rwanda*, p. 851.
54 African Rights, *Rwanda*, p. 865.
55 African Rights, *Rwanda*, p. 595.
56 Gilbert, *The Holocaust*, p. 493.

These examples defy the explanation of Professor Irenäus Eibl-Eibsfeldt that weapons overcome the sympathy of the assailant for his victim through swift or distant dispatch. Cultural competition, he also claimed, accelerated difference between various peoples and assisted in "the rapid development of the brain." In this way people became distant from each other, a process that he calls "cultural pseudo-speciation". This perceived difference, the argument goes, allowed us to kill each other in the same way that we might kill animals.[57] In other words, the "them and us" explanation.[58] Is this consistent with the evidence?

What ethologists would describe as signals to evoke intra-specific sympathy must have been present in abundance in all of the instances of brutality that have been traversed in this chapter. The suffering of the Armenian people, as they were marched to their deaths through starvation and exhaustion over many weeks, must also have evoked sympathy.[59] What all of these horrors have in common with the robbery murders is the deliberate and systematic degradation of the victims. In the context of mass murder, degraded conditions do not occur accidentally. No matter how hard you try to distance yourself from them, they are deliberately created. Are they a part of the process that enables murder?

Human killing of fellow persons is not like the process of killing meat, or hunting wild animals for food or because they are verminous.[60] People kill because of their emotions, and killing is an emotional activity. Some of those who have participated in the mayhem of human slaughter later described their

---

57 *Peace and War*, pp. 122–123; see also by the same author, *Love and Hate*, p. 220.
58 Staub 58-62.
59 See, for instance, the description in V. Dadrian, *The History of the Armenian Genocide* (Providence, 1995) pp. 219–234. In a strange mirroring of these marches, the survivors of the Nazi death camps were marched aimlessly around by their captors at the end of the Second Word War, dying on the way.
60 Robert Butler, personal communication.

actions as being trance-like or automatic.[61] You could view this as just another disavowal of responsibility. But, it seems, people do become different in order to kill. A survivor of the slaughter in Rwanda recalled that her house had been invaded by strangers and by people whom she knew. However, she said: "Even the ones I knew I couldn't recognise them. They had transformed themselves into animals. They were like lions".[62] Rezak Hukanovic, in his memoir of the Bosnian camps where Muslims were murdered, describes throat slitting as a favoured form of destroying the enemy. This seems to have been chosen for pleasure. He describes the murderers as emitting "the cackles and screeches of wild animals aroused by the smell of fresh blood", their eyes permeated by "brutal lust".[63] In his pastoral letter warning the Ukrainians against the Nazi campaign of murder against the Jewish people, Metropolitan Andrei Shepetytsky told his people that killing the innocent evokes a bloodthirstiness that becomes a physical lust.[64] Whether these statements are universally accurate or not, it is inescapable that the emotions that can erupt from within us are terrifying. From the era of the Abdul Hamit massacres of the Armenians under the Ottoman Empire, a witness recorded how his church had been turned into a killing-ground:

> The mob had plundered the Georgian church, desecrated it, murdered all who had sought shelter there, and as a sacrifice, beheaded the sexton on the stone threshold. Now it filled our yard. The blows of an axe crashed into the church door. The attackers rushed in, tore the Bibles and hymn books to pieces, broke and shattered whatever they could, blasphemed the cross…We could see and hear all these things from the room in which

---

61 M. Bilton and K. Sim, *Four Hours in Mai Lai: A War Crime and its Aftermath* (London, 1993) p. 368.
62 A. Des Forges, *Leave None to Tell the Story: Genocide in Rwanda* (London, 1999) p. 478, and see p. 583 African Rights, *Rwanda*, p. 514.
63 R. Hukanovic, *The Tenth Circle of Hell: A Memoir of the Death Camps of Bosnia* (London, 1993) p. 109.
64 For the exact quotation, see Chapter 2.

we were huddled ... They were coming up the stairs ... now butchers and victims were face to face. The leader of the mob cried: "Muhammede salavat" (Believe in Mohammed and deny your religion). [Disregarding our suprications to be spared] squinting horribly, he repeated his words in a terrifying voice. [When no one responded] the leader repeated again and gave orders to massacre. The first attack was on our pastor. The blow of an axe decapitated him. His blood, spurting in all directions, spattered the walls and ceiling with red ...[65]

Could this experience be, for the killers and for their victims, an encounter with a vast destructive power rising up from within their unconscious? That is why, I suppose, killers often describe themselves as acting "on automatic pilot". Perhaps, on occasion, it is true. But can it be said that murder is an accident of nature? That is doubtful. Responsibility continues to exist in the killers because, through deception, they have summoned up those forces. This is not about "the rapid development of the brain" and it is not about "our highly developed intellects". If anything, it is about instinct. With instinct, there is a way of activating it; as in smell, sight and hearing. Humiliation helps to make this happen. It is an experience of all of the senses. Like an instinct, it is within us and, like an instinct, we do precisely what is necessary to activate it. Unlike an animal, it is not random circumstances that seem to evoke the drive to destroy within us, but conscious choice.

Is that the point of fear, of humiliation and of torture? Do we cause people to become as our instinct wants us to experience them through our senses?. Is that the solution to the paradox of human division between distancing from death and immersion in death dealing? Deliberation is central to the methodology of mass murder. In his eyewitness account of the Armenian genocide, the Reverend Henry Riggs reasoned that deliberate humiliation was the point of the savage arms-searches by the Turkish authorities. He wrote that it reduced the

---

65 Hartunian, *Neither to Laugh nor to Weep: A History of the Armenian Genocide* (Boston, 1968) pp. 12–14, quoted in Dadrian, p. 151.

Armenian people "to a state of terror that was pitiable to behold and which was evidently one of the purposes of the campaign that was being waged against them".[66] In the mass murders in Rwanda, it is noticeable that in virtually every documented case a particular preparation occurred before the killings. An example from an area where Tutsi were heavily outnumbered is perhaps useful as, in those circumstances, they could not easily be seen as a threat. In the President's home area of Gisenyi, there were, by reason of the war of 1990, relatively few Tutsi people remaining there. Hiding places had been sought out by the targeted people as soon as the nature of the response to the President's murder became apparent. This response was one of merciless and organised terror. It involved hacking people to death after tricking them into revealing themselves by plain lies, or dragging them from their hiding places or invading places of refuge with murderous intent. According to a group of priests from the area who survived, the terror of what was happening drove people to seek refuge in communal places, such as churches, or to hide in their own houses. The unsanitary nature of the conditions of mass refuge, the lack of food for the refugees and their terror degraded them. It was then that the militias moved in and killed them. Was that the point? One would wonder if it were not enough for the murderers simply to take such people out and then execute them in as dignified a way as is possible? If that were so, the treatment might indeed be capable of being argued as being akin, at least in cultural terms, to the dispatch of animals. One vainly scours the record of the literature of mass murder for any such examples.

Daniel Goldenhagen, in his work on the Holocaust, asks why the Nazi policy of murder included that of putting Jewish people to work.[67] In his view, the answer derives from the incompatible aims of the elimination and, after June 1941, the extermination of the Jewish communities in Nazi-occupied

---

66 H. Riggs, *Days of Tragedy in Armenia: Personal Experiences in Harpoot, 1915–1917* (Ann Arbor, 1997) p. 62.
67 Goldenhagen, p. 283.

Europe with the need to use slave labour in war works. He argues that camps generally thought of as slave labour barracks were really attrition institutions where prisoners were worked to death. He points to the constant brutalisation, which characterised these institutions, as being contrary to any economic rationality.[68] Deliberate and severe malnourishment was coupled with sadistic policies of "discipline". Such could not and, he argues, did not aid production but only sated the perpetrator's desire to indulge in humiliation, torture and murder.[69] Goldenhagen writes of the induction process of Jewish prisoners into becoming inmates of camps as being: "reminiscent of the rituals performed upon free people being transformed into slaves, into socially dead beings."[70] Solzhenitsyn also makes the same point in his novel *The First Circle*, where a diplomat is arrested and is made into a prisoner by a process of delousing and inhuman treatment that includes taking all of his clothes and returning them to him without any buttons or a belt after disinfecting them unnecessarily.[71] Is this why the victims of murder are so often tortured out of their dignity?

When, during the Rwandan genocide, Bishop Nyundo of Kalibushi was seized by the Rwandan army he was, prior to his murder, stripped of his dignity. This was effected by insults and by taking from him the symbols of his status "his watch, his glasses, his shoes, his ring, his identity card and his driver's licence." He was also brought to a place of death which, of itself, effects a transformation of fear upon a victim.[72] In the same way, during the Armenian genocide, the Bishop of Diarbekir was tortured prior to being killed, by being stabbed,

---

68 Goldenhagen, pp. 294–311.

69 Goldenhagen, pp. 308–309.

70 Goldenhagen, p. 298. He instances the behaviour of Christian Wirth, Kommandant of the Clothing Works Camp at Lublin Airport, in perverting a small boy. This boy rode on his own pony after Wirth, shooting and killing perhaps fifty to sixty prisoners, possibly including his own mother.

71 A. Solzhenitsyn, *The First Circle* (London, 1992).

72 African Rights, *Rwanda*, p. 545.

by having his teeth knocked out and by being set alight.[73] When you do these kinds of things to a person you remove essential components of the attributes of their humanity. [74] It is therefore not surprising that those who wish to engage in both murder and mass murder also wish to first strip their victims of all that belongs to them.[75] Fear degrades people. So does hate rhetoric. That is why it emerges in this context.

Those who organise the mass murder seem always to plan that the victims should be treated so that they are degraded. Terrifying people, crowding them together, starving them and making them look and smell filthy transforms them into beings of an appearance and behaviour that may make some mental connection with an inner image of what is capable of being killed. If the organisers of these systems give people work, it does not accord with work of dignity, but it appears to be designed to humiliate, or to be performed under conditions of barbarity where no vestige of apparent humanity might re-appear.[76] Forms of captivity that are characterised by constant terror and a policy that prisoners should live in filth set the stage for savagery. Such conditions prevent any return, by a victimised person, from his or her degraded state to one where killing became less easy. Aggression seems to draw energy from the process of degradation.[77]

Is it possible that the murderer first creates the image of enmity, or the image of degradation, and then moves to destroy it? The activity of mutilating a corpse after death is among the most puzzling issues that can confront someone in criminal practice. How can the dead bother the living? But, in some individual murders, and regularly throughout the literature dealing with mass murder, at least isolated instances occur. The

---

73 Riggs, pp.. 53–54.
74 Waller, pp. 244–255.
75 Goldenhagen, p. 298; Riggs, pp. 49, 62, 80, 84, 95, 170; Gilbert, passim; African Rights, *Rwanda*, passim.
76 See Goldenhagen, pp. 311–316.
77 Staub, pp. 58–62.

Prophet of Islam was so horrified at the practice that he forbade it.[78] I can only speculate that hatred drives on the killer to utterly destroy not just the life of the victim but that his focus is also on his image. As his body represents this, the killer also wishes to tear it apart. Then it ceases to exist. Here is an instance. On 9 January 1905 a huge march was organised by a priest to present a petition to the Czar in St Petersburg. The petition was moderate in tone, asking the Emperor to use his position to ameliorate the lives of his people. The demonstrators were unarmed and their mood was peaceful. As the crowd moved towards the Winter Palace, Cossack cavalry attacked them. Maxim Gorky witnessed the death of one protester:

> The dragoon circled around him and, shrieking like a woman, waved his sabre in the air … Swooping down from his dancing horse … he slashed him across the face, cutting him open from the eyes to the chin. I remember the strangely enlarged eyes of the worker and … the murderer's face, the hairs of his moustache standing up on his elevated lip. Brandishing his tarnished shaft of steel he let out another shriek and, with a wheeze, spat at the dead man through his teeth.[79]

Mutilation of the dead is an activity common to all cultures and to all ages.[80] Mutilation of the dead may be a continuation of the drive of hate against the enemy. Possibly by cutting up a body, an image of dismembered power is put in place that gives satisfaction to the internal image that drives on hate. It seems possible that the action of cursing a corpse, or cutting it up, continues the process of reducing the enemy which humiliation begins.

---

78 M. Edwardes (ed.), *Ibn Ishaq: The Life of Muhammad, Apostle of Allah* (London, 2003) pp. 110–115.

79 A.M. Gorky, *Gor'kii v Epokhu Revoliutsii, 1905–1907 Materialy, Vospominaniia, Issledovaniia* (Moscow, 1957), quoted in Figes, p. 177.

80 See Walker, pp. 155, 217; Gilbert, *The Holocaust*, pp. 630, 648; Des Forges, pp. 191, 215; African Rights, *Rwanda*, p. 80; Chalk and Jonassohn, p. 200; Figes, pp. 96, 440, 322; Bilton and Sim, pp. 364–368.

Is it really easier to kill when people are degraded, fearful and humiliated? Rudolf Höss, when occupying the villa assigned to him as Kommandant of Auschwitz, had occasion to have his brother-in-law stay with him over a four-week period. They walked on a number of occasions through the death camp. On one occasion they came upon a truckload of dead bodies. The two men had a brief discussion about the legal and moral implications of the death camp. Höss said that an outsider could not understand the task he was engaged in. "Here we look at things differently", he said. Later, explaining the term "Untermenschen", used by the controllers of the camp in referring to the inmates, Höss said: "They are not like you and me. You saw them yourself; they are different. They look different. They do not behave like human beings."[81] His statement is a marked departure from reality: Höss had created the conditions that reduced the prisoners to the state he used to justify his conduct towards them. The system he was part of was engaged in the process that degraded people; thus the participants engaged in a deception to facilitate their ultimate purpose.

One might wonder whether reducing people to the lowest state of dignity that being alive allows, is in itself enough to allow them to be seen differently, as Höss claimed to see them. Such a notion might particularly be tested from the perspective of another prisoner. In the course of her study of Franz Stangl, Gitta Sereny interviewed many survivors of the Treblinka and Sobibor death-camps. One of these was Richard Glazar. A Czech national, he was arrested when he was twenty-two for the "crime of being Jewish" and was transported, after a time in Theresienstadt, to Treblinka. The police officer in charge of the passenger train referred to the two thousand passengers, among whom Glazar was transported, as being "pieces".[82] On arrival, Stangl referred to these prisoners as "cargo". During the "peak

---

81 Tom Segev, unpublished thesis, *The Commanders of Nazi Concentration Camps*, quoted in Paskuly, p. 198.
82 See the observations of Waller, pp. 188–189.

period" of slaughter, from October 1942 to January 1943, up to 20,000 people a day arrived at the death-camp. Glazar had developed strategies for survival in the camp. He had amazing luck in avoiding death. He told Sereny that he was possessed of an overriding will to live.[83] His survival strategies included care to his appearance so that he appeared clean, well groomed and shaved on roll call. This helped him to survive, he believed, even creating a "kind of respect" in the guards; provided his good deportment was not overdone. At the beginning of a particular "busy" period, the transports came from the Jewish communities in Warsaw and the West. It is not to be doubted that their fate was a cause of grief to the original prisoners who, for one reason or another, still survived. Richard Glazar said, however, that his sense of identification waned when the transports of unfortunate captives from Eastern Europe began to enter the camp. They were the remnants of Jewish communities from Byelorussia and from the extreme east of Poland. He looked on them as "people from a different world." What they were like, their image, affected his response to them. I quote his words: "They were filthy. They knew nothing. It was impossible to feel any compassion, any solidarity with them. Of course, I am not talking about the Warsaw or Krakow intellectuals; they were no different from us."[84]

Franz Stangl, as Kommandant of the death-camp, backed up the opinion of the Reverend Henry Riggs as to the purpose of terror on a victim population. The intention of the policy of cruelty and humiliation was "to make it possible" for the mass murder to be carried out. This was also, he said, the reason for the hate propaganda that drove the ideological engine of these activities.[85] Sereny refers to the incidents of the death-camp system as being "organised systematically" for that purpose, thus

---

83 Of course, the outcome of such strategies also involved extreme good luck, as well as these, among other factors; see Sereny, pp. 183, 186.

84 Sereny, pp. 198–199; and see pp. 100–101.

85 Sereny, p. 232.

achieving, as Goldenhagen also argues, "not only physical, but spiritual murder." Stangl, in keeping with his attitude of distancing himself, both from responsibility and from the process of murder, claimed to have absented himself from the area where the killing was actually carried out.[86] He echoed Rudolf Höss by saying that seeing people filing along to their death without resistance opened up a gulf of contempt.[87] Whatever image the prisoners presented, they could not help it. In terms of how the people who hated them might react to them, they had been transformed for the purposes of murder. Deliberately.

If there is, as Jung would say, an archetypal shadow then, in seeking out its fullest expression, it is likely to seek that state in the victim which charges the killer's mind with the potential to fulfil his chosen task. It may also be that the killer can be driven by the power-drive of the shadow to proceed to a particular kind or degree of humiliation to make his task possible. Stangl claimed not to see these people, "naked, packed together, being driven with whips", as individuals. Beyond the process of unloading the prisoners, and driving them towards the death-apparatus, there was a further moment of transformation in the undressing rooms. Stangl claims: "I avoided it from my innermost being; I couldn't confront them; I couldn't lie to them; I avoided at any price talking to those who were about to die: I couldn't stand it".[88] How does a person intent on killing get over the job of transforming a person into a victim? I do not know. Experience, however, suggests that in murder cases it can either be a case of degradingly toying with your victim or of treating him immediately with unremitting brutality. Either way, his dignity is gone.

This is a matter not of intellect, but of emotion taking over a person. These are among the internal dangers that our own lies make us prone to. But can we really live out a myth?

---

86 Sereny, p. 101.
87 Sereny, p. 232.
88 Sereny, p. 203.

CHAPTER 10

The Trap of Deceit

I N T H E F O L K T A L E "The Woodcutter's Son', recorded by the brothers Grimm, a boy goes one day with his father to work deep in the forest. The boy wanders off and comes upon an ancient tree. In among its roots he finds a bottle from which a voice cries out to be released. Without thinking, the child unstops the bottle. A spirit emerges that towers over him, telling him that now it has been set free it must break his neck. Cleverly appealing to the vanity of the spirit, the boy suggests that its powers could not be so great as to have allowed it to shrink itself down into a bottle: the proof of that would be for it to re-enter the bottle. "Of course, I can do that", says the spirit and goes back in. The boy traps it. Now that he has it under his control, he will only let the spirit emerge again if it will promise not to harm him. The spirit agrees and the boy frees it. In gratitude, the spirit gifts him a cloth that heals wounds and turns base metals into silver. In the result, he becomes happy and rich.

This folk tale never mentions deceit. It is about the powers that lurk within all of us, how they can enhance our lives or else destroy us; the dual nature of unconscious forces. Generations of parents and grandparents would have told children tales like this to warn them that there are forces in the world that are beyond our control. Experience has repeatedly confirmed that the greatest destroyer of human life is within the human mind. If these forces are to be let out, it must only be when we are using our wits to guard ourselves against them. When we do not exercise that control, will those powers destroy us? We are entitled to wonder why the forces of the mind should not be completely benign; why what nature has put within us should not enhance our existence? This is not life. That kind of naïve assumption ignores the machines and structures of torture, hatred and deceit that are the product of human intelligence. Someone thought these things up. The recurring patterns of how those thoughts express themselves suggests that the means of expressing hatred are inspired by a common source.

In May 1942, Carl Jung wrote a letter to a friend in which he warned her against trusting the promptings coming from her unconscious mind as if it were guiding her like a loving parent. He cautioned that the unconscious mind was an aspect of nature, and was to be treated as warily as any other natural force:

> It is inhuman and needs the human mind to function usefully for man's purposes. Nature is an incomparable guide if you know how to follow her. She is like the needle of the compass pointing North, which is most useful when you have a good man-made ship and know how to navigate ... The unconscious is useless without the human mind. It always seeks its collective purposes and never your individual destiny.[1]

Jung was saying no more than the folk tale: you must be suspicious of following the impulses that your mind seems to find attractive. Instead, you have to think. You must, in every circumstance, exercise control over your mind. Does thinking, of itself, guard against hatred? There are many kinds of thought; including cunning calculation and deceit. It might reasonably be said that when you lie, you think. That is correct, as far as it goes. But no aspect of apparently conscious thought is divorced from whatever unconscious motive prompted it. It is the positive or the negative aspect within the unconscious to which

---

1. C.G. Jung, *Letters I* (Princeton, 1973, edited by Gerhard Adler and Aniela Jaffé).

your mind is allied that moves through your thoughts and suggests where it may next take you. Fundamentally, the process of human behaviour, long-term or short-term, seems to depend on which aspect of the mind to which consciousness allies itself. You can choose the world, because reality is reflected only in truth, or you can choose fantasy. Deceit perhaps affronts nature, but so why should it lead to disastrous consequences? More particularly, any argument for a link with violence, on a mass or individual scale, needs to be demonstrated as the core danger of the deceitful aspect of myth.

In so far as the chapters of this book have argued for the integration of lying into the process of destruction that, however, does not necessarily prove that deceit is the engine of destruction: that when you lie the effect is to risk a volcanic eruption of savagery. Why would the consequences of deceit not turn out well? Possibly, you could argue, because lies distort reality and that reality is nothing more or less than the reflection of the truth in our minds. You could argue that nature is only served by being reflected through the conscious acceptance of reality. Such an argument seems to personify nature. To say that nature becomes like an offended beast when lies distort the world into myth, that it will strike back against unreality, is undemonstrated: in itself no more than a myth. Surely, deceit merely reduces our understanding, makes us blunder around in the collision between myth and reality, and that that is its only consequence? The limit of any rational argument on deceit should be that those who distort their understanding with unreality cannot understand the world as well as those who have a clear vision. I can only offer a personal view that deceit risks opening up our natural impulses to hatred and destruction. My suspicion is that there is some natural consequence at work in the choice of deceit over truth; that enhancement and destruction are aspects of how we relate to our unconscious minds through reality or through myth.

When the composer Wladyslav Szpilman was spared from a Nazi police patrol in Warsaw by the pleading of his father, an incident touched on in Chapter 7 of this book, he had many more trials to survive before the Nazi occupation of Poland ended. After being helped to escape from the Warsaw ghetto, he hid for months in an unoccupied flat. Eventually, Captain Wilhelm Hosenfeld, a member of the German army, discovered him. Instead of killing him, the officer helped him to survive until the Russian army captured the city. Captain Hosenfeld was a man who had seen human destructiveness in many of its forms. His opinion on the genesis of evil is worth considering. Two years before rescuing Szpilman, he had confided this observation to his diary:

> *Lying is the worst of all evils. Everything else that is diabolical comes from it. And we have been lied to; public opinion is constantly deceived. Not a page of a newspaper is free of lies, whether it deals with political, economic, historical, social or cultural affairs. Truth is under pressure everywhere; the facts are distorted, twisted and made into their opposite. Can this turn out well?*[2]

I think that when lies dominate a person or a society that the consequences cannot turn out well. It is not just that experience teaches us that lies are the basic weapon of crime and that criminals are liars. It is because lies deform people, reducing them to less than their full selves. When you meet people who have subjected themselves to a process of self-deceit over years, and certainly the criminal courts are just one of a number of good places to meet them, it strikes you that they have been diminished by their lies. A lie is an attack on reality. It affronts creation. It undermines the clarity of our perception, the very basis of consciousness, and leaves us vulnerable to unpredictable consequences. Lies weaken us in our personality while supposedly enhancing our lives. If you create a life that is built on a lie you can never trust the impulses that emerge from your mind. Whatever your mind prompts you to do, through emotion and

---

2   Diary of Wilhelm Hosenfeld, 21 August 1942, quoted in W. Szpilman, *The Pianist* (London, 1999) p. 200.

suggestion, will sift through the filter of deceit that you have imposed on yourself. Your impulses will be to seek empty leaders; to join ideologies with all the answers; and to hate all that is despicable in your own thinking but which you deny to yourself. It seems to me that when you weaken yourself down to what Solzhenitsyn might call a threshold state, the danger emerges that in a crisis when you need the help of your unconscious mind, it is more likely that you will get the demonic side.

Even among the Vikings, it marked out a person as having gone to the bad that they would try to ruin someone else by telling lies about them.[3] Those who habitually lie to their advantage ignore the power of deceit. Lies follow their own channel within the mind and open up consequences that consciousness, as the genuine attempt to reflect truth, would normally check. Instead of being wary of lying, people think of the benefits that deception will bring them. Rationally, perhaps one might think that the worst thing about deceit is that it leaves those who use it open to the consequences of being found out in a lie. But perhaps it goes further. Deceit causes injustices, big and small, to those with whom we interact. Probably, we do not really care about that. However, we should care about weakening our very selves. Deceits that touch on our nature, what we are and how we define ourselves, leave us open to negative eruptions of the potential of our minds. Lying leaves us less strong mentally. Consistently, those who have observed evil people, whether false leaders encountered in the grand circumstances in which they surround themselves, or criminals on the lesser stage of life, refer to their insignificance, their lack of colour or warmth, their banality.

When Sabine Dardenne came to describe Marc Dutroux, the man who had abducted her and held her as a twelve-year-old sex slave, she spoke about her abuser in terms of his smallness. In her memoir *I Choose to Live*, she characterises him as a

---

3   T.M. Andersson, *The Sagas of the Icelanders* (London, 2000) pp. 20–33.

"calculating, manipulative and plausible liar".[4] Dutroux spun a web of fantasy about his criminal perversion by claiming that he was merely an intermediary; capturing children for a vicious criminal network that served the sexual gratification of important public figures in Belgium. He told Sabine that he was terrified of "his bosses". Explicitly, he said he was their "victim". In reality, this network of controlling demons was a self-serving myth. It took the police years to sort out the fact from the fiction in his account before the case could come to trial. In the end, the reality that emerged was that he had acted solely for his own gratification, assisted by his wife and another accomplice. His allegations threw Europe into a frenzy of speculation about corruption in public life. The truth was that he was not the puppet of a criminal gang, only of his own perversion. The only fear he had was of being caught. He was not affected as to how his actions would destroy other people. He let two small girls, whom he had imprisoned earlier, starve to death rather that run the risk of revealing their whereabouts and finding himself with a longer sentence. He returned to his activities when that sentence was shortened for "good conduct". While Sabine was held in a dungeon in his house he kidnapped Laetitia, another adolescent girl, for the same purposes. When, at his trial, the presiding judge asked him why he had also abducted her, he replied that it was Sabine's idea: "She was driving me mad, begging me to get her a friend".[5] As Sabine put it, "he lied as easily as he breathed".[6] When she was permitted by the court to put a question to the accused, she asked him why he had not murdered her. He claimed that he could not find it in himself to kill her because he had become "attached to her". This ridiculous lie of feeling affection for a human captive whom he had treated far worse than a factory-farm animal,

---

4   S. Dardenne, *I Choose to Live* (London, 2005, with Marie Thérèse Cuny) p. 72.

5   Dardenne, p. 169.

6   Dardenne, p. 123. See also the obituary of Slobodan Milosevic, the *Guardian*, 13 March 2006.

confirmed Sabine's opinion of her tormentor: "He was tiny. He was abject. He couldn't tell the truth, not even once in his life. He didn't frighten me in the least. He made me laugh." [7]

The corrosive effect of deceit was perhaps what Solzhenitsyn had in mind when he referred to the torturers in Stalin's system of injustice as filling the space that they occupied with rottenness.[8] He was a crime survivor and what he may have been driving at was the propensity of evil to reduce people. Deceit is the prerequisite. When you start that process, do you really run the risk of being taken over?

Some people might argue that this impression of the criminal as being a lesser, and less alive, personality-less kind of being simply describes a sociopathic disorder. This can be true in some cases, but it seems to me to be only a part of the picture. Just as you can destroy other people, you can destroy yourself. Those whose impression should be taken most seriously are those who have interacted with people who have chosen the abuse of life over its affirmation. The anonymous, and often voiceless, victims of sexual abuse certainly see the abuser in all his colours and moods. Much more so than the victims of violence, where the contact is fleeting and the result may be death. Repeatedly, similar descriptions to those voiced by Sabine Dardenne have emerged in statements where those who have suffered sexual abuse are given the chance to describe their tormentors: they are "pathetic", "a waste of space" and unworthy even of the emotion of anger because "they are not worth it". These impressions, when I encountered them, were not tinged with fantastic invention but were delivered in moderate terms that made them identifiable as the product of observation. They were not the kind of rhetoric thrown up by hate. I can only give my experience that this kind of remark became a near universal when the victims of all manner of criminal abuses came to describe those who had assaulted their lives. Was deceit fundamental to the way that the abuser saw himself and how he

7   Jon Henley, "Don't Pity Me", the *Guardian*, 18 April 2005.
8   A. Solzhenitsyn, *The Gulag Archipelago* (London, 1974) p. 144.

related to his victim? Was it through lies that people became able to perpetrate abuse, or were at least facilitated in their negativity?

Some have attempted to approach the problem of evil by describing it as the absence of good. In the natural world, cold is the total absence of heat and darkness is the total absence of light. You might reason that evil is merely the absence of good. The theory runs that when all goodness is suppressed then all that is left is evil. This would be to describe evil as nothing. The early Christian philosophers went so far as to describe as good all that God created; but since evil destroys good they reasoned that evil was nothing. Destruction, however, tears down what is good. Hatred poisons relations between people because those who hate have that poison in their hearts in the first place. Evil has real effect. People call evil deeds inhuman. It is probably right to call it that because for evil to run rampant the humanity of our approach to life must first be reduced. That is why there is something to be said for ideas about the absence of goodness from the servants of evil. As many who have suffered at their hands have testified, they lack something. Criminals without power are miserable creatures. Equally, criminals in the guise of divine leaders and paradise-promising ideologies are no less ridiculous; but only if you are not caught up in the myth that is their trap. When our humanity is reduced beyond a particular point, then something that exists as a force in its own right takes over and causes havoc. This is not a random occurrence. It happens in circumstances that are identifiable by their falseness and by their lack of human scale. Where there is no truthfulness, false myths begin to take over. The ground for violence is prepared by inflation of self-regard on an individual level, and group-regard and adherence to historical untruth on a social level. Humour, culture and sympathy based on a recognition of our own weakness, as part of the human package, are all diminished in those who follow aggressive impulses. These qualities are all essential components of the aliveness of our minds, of our consciousness. What marks out the people who turn to destruction is the reduction of the humanity of their personality through deceit. If there is a threshold point: then beyond that.

Consciousness is our inheritance. It is the sole means that we have to direct our actions away from compulsion and towards willed behaviour.[9] Consciousness, like all talents, is present in a greater or a lesser degree in particular people. It is, however, not just a random gift of inheritance. Consciousness can be fostered or it can be squandered. The actions of individuals can be directed to unfolding truth and sanity or to the creation of those situations that inflame contagions of mythic thinking. Each individual can only develop consciousness through a determined effort to engage with truth to the exclusion of all deceit. I do not believe that there are any exceptions to this.

Life requires us to strive to maintain the balance of sanity. Unconscious impulses can, it is true, emerge almost randomly, but perhaps most predictably in situations of personal or social crisis. These are the danger points. It is when you most need an amplification of your understanding that you are likely to grasp wildly for any solution. Events that power emotions that are too huge for our minds to deal with are like the spirits that emerge from the un-stopped bottles of folk tales. Their powers are never entirely benign. At the least, they set a test to be overcome before their help is won over. The people who love deceit, those who strive for total control over others as a substitute for self-analysis, like to let those kind of spirits loose: once they believe that they have calculated the consequences. Wrecked buildings, enemy insurrections and murdered leaders can manipulate us. In fact, any attack on the symbols of our self-definition. It is when these things happen that you most need to think. You cannot expect a sane balance to emerge from your mind if you have distorted the world by lies. We are liable to become prey to false myths when we believe falsehoods.

---

9   C.W. 8.377.

Our job is to question and to analyse. Those who accept only reality retain the facility to be guided by the unalterable world of what is visible and tangible. Consciousness is that part of the mind which sees the truth. In terms of choices there may only be two: the choice of affirming the truth, including the necessity of cleaning up the unpleasant squalor of our own lives, and the choice of living out a lie. Carl Jung had a clear view of the dangers of evoking unconscious emotions when the mind was not in control over what might emerge. His way of putting it resembles the fairytale experience of the wood-cutter's son:

> *If an archetype is not brought into reality consciously, there is no guarantee whatsoever that it will be realized in its favourable form; on the contrary, there is all the more danger of a destructive aggression. It seems as if the psyche were endowed with consciousness for the very purpose of preventing such destructive possibilities from happening.*[10]

When you live a myth you run the risk of your life being turned upside down by any encounter with reality. The point that I think that Jung was making relates to the comfort that artificial thinking brings to the human mind. If you really believe in the myth of the establishment of paradise on earth, or the myth of the divine leader, or if you believe in a false notion of your own perfection, then what are you confronted with day after day if not the stinging disappointment of how things really are?

I believe the mind that lives out a myth is continually in tension because it is affronted by the cold truth that must be shut out. If you put yourself into a conflict between infantile illusion and an intrusion of something that will shatter your myth, it is likely that you will choose to hold on to unreality. Often that can be done only by destroying reality. In many of the homicide cases that I witnessed this was a feature. How did JL feel when he managed to get into his former girlfriend's house armed with

10 C.W. 10.475.

a knife on a pretext of discussing domestic arrangements? Possibly hopeful that the relationship that held up his own false view of himself might be triumphantly affirmed. When it was not, the collapse of his fantasy provoked a rage against the individual that stood in his way. It happened to be the girl whom he claimed to love. In PL, another case, a girl who had just ended a relationship met her former boyfriend in a pub where they struck up a conversation. He insisted on returning to her flat. When he found her new boyfriend there, he took up a weapon and battered him to death. In these cases, reality confronted myth. It was not so much that a choice was made that the myth should win, but that the myth had become so much a part of the aggressor that something inside himself drove him to attack the one aspect of reality that threatened his unreal view of the world.

And when you come to bring these dreadful, but domestic, examples on to a wider stage you can usefully ask the same question. Why, for instance, were a million Tutsi murdered? Surely part of the answer must be that they were a thorn in the side of a fantasy of inflated self-righteousness that could only be removed by mass murder. Similarly, those who confront an ideology, are treated as if they have assaulted paradise. Those who adopt an ideology as fundamental to their lives shun confrontation with the truth by associating exclusively with each other. Some call outsiders heretics, or words of modern equivalence, or go so far as to describe them as physically impure. The example of those who, it seems, die on the intrusion of reality, like the death camp kommandant Franz Stangl and the abusive teacher MD, instance the lethal intrusion that truth is on the soul when it is geared to living out lies. When, as is so often the case, the lies continue beyond the commission of the crime, and into the courtroom, then self-protection can also be the spur. Even apart from keeping the possibility of acquittal alive, self-delusion keeps self-regarding respectability alive. Rudolf Höss is but one example of this.

Lies are deliberate but they create an unreal world. Like

stone or wood suddenly brought from one extreme of temperature to another, our minds shatter when reality intrudes into the opposite world of myth. What comes out is aggression against the truth.

Surely, aggression should be random and chaotic? Should destruction not be limited to lashing out at the truth rather than, like the Butare memo about "accusations in a mirror", carefully calculating how to undermine it? After all, without the resources of the human mind, you could not provoke a minority population into self-defence and then paint it as a threat that needs to be put down mercilessly? These are examples of deviousness, a function of cleverness. Certainly, it requires reason. That implies that you are using your mind. But what part of your mind: the part that works to reflect reality in consciousness or the part that takes comfort in an unreal myth? In crisis, only consciousness can help us. Unfortunately, deceit emerges as the abuse of consciousness. It is what the abuse of consciousness triggers off that is the point: the negative side of human nature has its own intelligence. People who serve evil may be two-faced. That does not mean that they cannot be clever.

Instincts strive to realise themselves. This is not to personify them. If the drives behind destruction are based on the negative side of the hidden remnants of instincts within our minds, we can expect them to realise ideas and impulses every bit as compelling as those which affirm life. We can rely on the resources of our minds to facilitate us in choosing the lies that will throw a mantle of hatred over those we wish to destroy: the right lies. False leaders will put on a show of being hero leaders. They will act as if they are men of purpose. Negative ideologies will supply all of the answers, as if they had a communication of divine will. They will supply the rituals of sacredness to those who crave the spirit but who are fractured by dishonesty.

The patterns within which these phenomena emerge will have similarities as to their fundamentals. The difference from the patterns that enhance life will be that they are a trick. I suspect that they will also be tinged with the dream-like quality of myth. As people diminish themselves through lies they will want, more and more, to run under the falsely protective mantle of the leaders whose ambition is to control everything. Their trademark will be deceit. It is they who create the false reasons for aggression. It is they who tell the people what they are to see when they look in the mirror. It is they who scheme to throw people into a panic so that they have nowhere else to look than to them and to their false vision of a shining future.

Situations of crisis must be transcended, not yielded to. Consciousness must hold its focus on reality so that truth can be allowed to co-operate with our mind. Truth is the unaltered reflection of nature. In its totality, the mind must respect nature for otherwise it loses the only fixed bearing to which it can be anchored.[11] To deny reality is not to set the mind free. Rather, the predictable result seems to be to ally it to the forces of chaos.

Lies deny creation and block out nature's gift of wisdom. The truth is positive while deceit is negative. Truth denies nothing, since it affirms reality, while deceit seeks to destroy reality. A lie may be disguised as a false interpretation or as a self-serving justification. No matter what form it takes, a lie turns the mind away from the world. Instead of looking out, we look inwards. And in looking inwards we have only the blackness of deceit. We block our view towards the solution of problems with walls made from our fear of the truth. In consequence, the machinations of those who seek to manipulate events that turn humanity towards violence are, as well as being deceitful, characteristically rigid in their thinking. Such people need to be protected by lies. Otherwise, the primitiveness of their thought will be exposed.

Our task, says Robertson Davies, is to "look at life through eyes that are as clear as one can make them".[12] I agree with this as an aspiration; though some years I have often wondered how any process other than untruth and its consequences could suc-

---

11 Aion C.W. 9II.259.
12 R. Davies, *Happy Alchemy: On the Pleasures of Music and the Theatre* (London, 1999) p. 350.

ceed. Cheating, self-regard and aggression seem to be infinitely stronger in our world, and to be growing more powerful. Is there any strength in the truth, in the sense that the truth helps people by coming to their aid? If you were a religious person, you might believe that the Divine nature requires creation to be acknowledged in truth: that those who are allied to truth work in accordance with creation and receive its benefits. In conversation with one of his friends, Saint Seraphim of Sarov said this:

> *Though the pagan philosophers also wandered in the darkness of ignorance of God, yet they sought the truth which is beloved by God. Because of this, God-pleasing seeking, they could partake of the Spirit of God. It is said, that nations who do not know God, practice by nature the demands of the law and do what is pleasing to God. The Lord so praises truth that He says of it Himself by the Holy Spirit: "Truth has sprung from the earth, and justice has looked down from heaven".*[13]

I am not equipped to say whether or not this is so. What experience has taught me is that people can affirm the truth in situations where they should have no strength. Whereas, as in the MD case or the Franz Stangl case, a realisation of the truth can destroy people, the opposite should also happen. The difference seems to be that living a lie is destructive, but affirming the truth garners strength from somewhere. At least, I trust so.

In the realm of sexual abuse, it has happened several times that an adolescent who is entrapped in a mire of abuse by an adult, suddenly takes steps to stop her tormentor. Many times I have witnessed this emerge out of consideration for another person. The reality that what has happened to her may be inflicted on her sister, or daughter, gives her the courage to overcome threats of violence and to endure the self-abnegation involved in marking oneself out as a victim of unnatural sexual urges and

---

13 Saint Seraphim of Sarov in conversation with Nicholas Motovilov, quoted in V. Zander, *Saint Seraphim of Sarov* (London, 1968) p. 286, referring to Romans 2:14 and Psalm 84:11; H. Boosalis, *The Joy of the Holy: Saint Seraphim of Sarov and Orthodox Spiritual Life* (Pennsylvania, 1993) p. 107.

extreme family dysfunction. All of a sudden, and often for no definable reason, evil is confronted and stopped. Where do people get the courage? I cannot answer that. All that can be hoped is that there might be something allied to truth that can overcome deceit; that there may also be unconscious powers at the disposal of people who affirm life. Merely from the resources of our limited minds, on our own, can we take the steps that transcend torture? Can the affirmation of truth really help us?

This question was starkly posed for me years ago by something I witnessed in a crowded Dublin courtroom. The occasion was the list for the arraignment of prisoners on all the kinds of major crime that the law requires to be tried before a jury. Those dozens of accused who might need a jury to try their cases in the months ahead were listed together to see would they plead guilty or not guilty. This process also dealt, very occasionally, with bail applications pending trial. It was all in public and with no provision for privacy. Where a person says that they are the victim of incest, they have a right to a private hearing of the charge, with only the press present as representatives of the public. Their names can never be revealed. The law however, as it then was, made no provision for a private bail hearing even in an incest case.[14]

JK, as I will call her, had been abused by her father for many years. In effect, she had been turned into his wife, but with none of the rights and dignity of a spouse. She had never led a normal life: no friends, no boyfriends, little schooling and a complete absence of love. It all was a horrible burden. I do not know what brought her eventually to make a complaint to the police. She left home, if you could call it that. Shortly afterwards she went to the police where she was taken seriously. Her father fought the resulting charge. Not just in court, by fair means if you like. He went out of his way to seek her out again in order to try to re-establish the dominion he had once exercised over her life. He found out her new address and made it his business to see her, eventually

---

14 There could have been an application to exclude uninterested persons on the basis of obscenity, but nothing sexual was to be touched on in this bail motion.

speaking to her. In tears, blandishments and requests for her to look at the misery of his life, he asked her to drop the charges: to tell the court that nothing had happened. She did not want to. Possibly, she resisted so strongly because she had younger sisters. Then he went to her, waylaid her, and threatened to "spread her blood all over the wall". She told the police. They decided that all that could be done was to try to take away his freedom pending trial through asking the court to revoke his bail bond. That application had to be made in public. JL was close to disintegrating at that point, so I was told. On the appointed day she turned up in court. Her hand was cold to the touch and she was trembling. She had bought and was wearing, you could say proudly from her appearance, an elegant new coat. She walked into the courtroom and took the stand. Her bearing was one of dignity, despite her embarrassment. The charge had to be explained to the judge. The use of the euphemism "section 2 of the 1905 Act" told every lawyer there what the issue was. It was all that could be done to maintain any pretence of privacy. Everyone knew what had happened to her; prison officers, accused persons and lawyers, especially when the charge was against a male person of the same name. In a clear voice she told her story. Her father denied intimidating her. The judge believed her. That was the end of her being one of the abused in life. At least, I hope so. The courage that she displayed was unwavering. I am not a purveyor of fairy stories. No doubt, her struggle did not end there; but which of us would have had such dignity in adversity?

Where do people who have been abused get the will to fight for truth? Carl Jung might perhaps say that this was an example of transcendence; a process whereby the unconscious mind comes to the aid of those who have lost everything except the chance to cry out for whatever help there might be out there in the universe. His expression of it is not so far from that of Saint Seraphim. Transcendence, he wrote, corresponds with the theological formula of grace.[15] He commented:

---

15 C.W. 11.822.

"psychology has no proof that it does not unfold itself at the instigation of God's will".[16] Can you get something from apparently nowhere when you do not have anywhere to turn? RH, one of Jung's patients who was suffering from alcoholism, was advised by him that all further treatment was hopeless. On Jung's advice, he went and immersed himself in a religious atmosphere and hoped for a conversion experience; his only possible hope according to the analyst. Apparently, it happened. RW's medical doctor had also advised another man, BW, that any further treatment for his condition of alcoholism was also hopeless. The advice of Jung, relayed to him through an intermediary, was all that he had left. BW later described his state as one of "ego collapse at depth". After apparently wrecking his life, completely alone and with no hope, he cried out "If there be a God, will he show Himself". In a letter to Jung, he described what happened next:

> There immediately came to me an illumination of enormous impact and dimension ... My release from alcohol obsession was immediate ... In the wake of my spiritual experience there came a vision of a society of alcoholics, each identifying with and transmitting his experience to the next ... to carry the news of the scientific hopelessness of alcoholism ... This has made conversion experiences ... available on an almost wholesale basis.[17]

According to Jung, transcendence can take over and transform the entire attitude of those who experience it. In reply to BW's letter of thanks, he wrote that a person could experience transcendence through an act of grace, by honest contact with friends or as a result of educating the mind "beyond the con-

---

16 C.W. 18.1554.
17 Bill Wilson's letter to Jung is quoted in www.bare footsworld.net/wilsonletter.html and his reply is in Letters II 624. His story is told in abridged form in Alcoholics Anonymous World Services, *Alcoholics Anonymous: The Story of How Many Thousands of Men and Women Have Recovered from Alcoholism* (New York, 2001) Chapter 1.

fines of mere rationalism".[18] That seems all to the good but a bit unrealistic in its one-dimensionality. You could ask: what about the bad side: surely it has one? If transcendence exists as a phenomenon, then it should have an opposite since the major driving forces of the mind all have a positive and a negative aspect. Jung had argued, as we have seen in Chapter 2, that every unconscious power had two sides; enhancing and destroying. Human experience seems to bear that out. If this idea as to transcendence has validity, then an opposite process must also exist. He never identified that opposite. Since the phenomenon of transcendence is based on the premise of honesty, an argument can be made that any opposite of this process is summoned up by deceit.

But why was transcendence, if it exists, not available to Franz Stangl and to the people like MD who are discovered in a horrible double life? I am suspicious of clever arguments. One such available here is that honesty was forced on them, instead of them consciously seeking it out. Whether this somehow bars the process of transcendence, I do not know. Another difference between these people and victims like Sabine Dardenne and JK is that a world of evil had been inflicted on them, not by them, and that when it collapsed it fell not on them but away from them. They are not living a myth, but instead they are the victims of those that are. Then there are the people, like the recovering alcoholic BW, who wrote after his recovery that he had done terrible harm, and the reforming criminal. I have seen a person go to prison completely embittered but emerge for a sentence review two years later as a new person. If transcendence happens in those instances through the collapse of a person's ego, as BW wrote, then the hope of life can, perhaps through something that I do not understand but which must be connected to truth, outweigh the burden of the past. This is merely a speculation. Carrying it through, it seems possible to attempt to unite all three categories of examples, but only in a metaphysical way. If

---

18 Letter to William G. Wilson, Letters II 624.

you genuinely ask to be made better, it is possible that from wherever such help may come, it may be offered not in proportion to your wrong but in generous measure.

Jung describes transcendence as the process whereby the mind is amplified so that it may be enabled to evolve from one attitude to another.[19] This function seems to be inescapably linked to truth. Jung writes that it is a process that unfolds itself at the behest of nature.[20] As such, deception can play no part since the point of lies is that they reflect nothing of the world. The reality of nature can never deny itself. Normally, we do not need either answers to big questions or exceptional fortitude. Experience, and the determined resort to habitual thought-patterns, can provide the solution to many problems. Sometimes, as in a crisis, this is not enough. We need more in terms of courage and insight than our apparent gifts have endowed us with. We need to be empowered to go beyond ourselves. Can we only become newly enabled by relying on what Jung calls the "wisdom and experience of countless centuries" that waits as a transcendent potential in the unconscious mind?[21]

Individuals who feel helpless are often confined by the inflexibility of their thinking. Every society that promotes aggression structures itself around dogmatic attitudes towards its own people and those it proclaims as the enemy. Through the conscious adoption of fixed attitudes, people can be imprisoned within a one-sided viewpoint of themselves and of the world as interpreted through a myth. A state of affairs proclaimed as a dogma, such as the heroic attributes of the leader of an ideology, requires mental support in the form of the denial of any contrary viewpoint. This is why aggressive societies tend to be enclosed systems that are fearful of any internal opposition. Truth is silenced in the determined pursuit of a self-image, or group-image, that denies the wholeness of the human mind.

---

19 C.W. 6.828.
20 C.W. 7.196.
21 C.W. 7.196.

Honesty must not be suppressed if transcendence is to occur. It seems to be through the acceptance of imperfection in the self, and in the group, that the potential for a solution becomes possible. When thinking has become petrified, then perhaps it is only ego collapse, as identified by BW, which can open up new horizons.

The unconscious can also be accessed through lies, but to disastrous effect. Those who proclaim themselves as heroes, or their group as the embodiment of a mission to establish a golden age, are beyond transcendence from one attitude to another. Falsity is one-sided. When the truth is locked out there are no opposites. Can there be any dynamic for change within an enclosed psychic system? Paradoxically, it is in apparent weakness that transcendence is enabled. The powers of the unconscious do not exist to be abused through denial, but demand to be heard as the resource through which consciousness may be increased. The unconscious yields up solutions only where the individual accepts the inadequacy of any artificial construct imposed upon the conscious mind. This is how Jung puts his point of view:

> In the end one has to admit that there are problems which one simply cannot solve on one's own resources. Such an admission has the advantage of being honest, truthful, and in accord with reality, and this prepares the ground for a compensatory reaction from the collective unconscious: you are now more inclined to give heed to a helpful idea or intuition, or to notice thoughts which had not been allowed to voice themselves before. If you have an attitude of this kind, then the helpful powers slumbering in the deeper strata of man's nature can come awake and intervene, for helplessness and weakness and the eternal experience are the eternal problem of mankind. To this problem there is also an eternal answer, otherwise it would have been all up with humanity long ago.[22]

In nurturing consciousness, Jung goes so far as to claim that the mind becomes newly created.[23]

---

22 C.W. 9I.44.
23 C.W. 12.30.

The mental attitude that accepts the burden of real self-knowledge and the limitations of experience invites the intervention of positive unconscious energy. In those circumstances, Jung claims, people are then enabled to grow away from one-sidedness and towards individuality.[24] Through the transcendent function, a person grows into being able to forego myth. This fosters the integration of conscious and unconscious thinking into a state more closely approaching wholeness.[25]

This state is the complete obverse of that which characterises the sorry remnant of our human nature when we are engaged in destruction. A function always has an opposite in the human mind. Good is in polar relation to evil, as is love to hate. It appears natural that transcendence too is balanced by an opposite effect of dis-integration. Call it what you will, it is the loss of our relation to the truth. While the transcendent function occurs only by an honest approach to life's problems and moves a person towards truth, deceptive energy draws the individual into the realm of darkness: away from consciousness. This function takes on the character of collective chaos. Actions become increasingly less conscious and more subject to the destructive impulses that are perhaps conjured up from the aeons of the violent experience of our human ancestors. These functions are not individual, but collective. Self-deception plunges the self-diminished conscious mind of the deceiver into the immense darkness that exists within our minds. Those who choose it seem to seek out each other's company and to feed off each other's lies.

Through lies, a person calls up the powers that can destroy the world. Truth is the only principle that invokes the help of nature, and of the flawed expression of nature that is our human mind.

---

24 C.W. 9I.524

25 Jung expresses this as part of the divine drama, a process whereby God took human nature as the Son and then infused the human soul by the presence of the Holy Spirit: Letter to Père Lachat – C.W. 18.1552.

Bibliography

African Rights, *Facing Genocide: The Nuba of Sudan* (London, 1995).

African Rights, *Rwanda: Death, Despair and Defiance* (London, 1995).

Alcoholics Annonymous World Services, *The Story of How Many Thousands of Men and Women Have Recovered from Alcoholism* (New York, 2001).

Alexievich, S., *Voices from Chernobyl* (London, 2005).

Al-Khalil, S., *Republic of Fear: The Politics of Modern Iraq* (London, 1991).

Aly, G. and Heim S., *Architects of Annihilation: Auschwitz and the Logic of Destruction* (London, 2002).

Andersson, T.M. (ed.), *The Sagas of Icelanders* (London, 2001).

Antonov-Ovseyenko, A., *The Time of Stalin: Portrait of a Tyranny* (New York, 1981).

Applebaum, A., *Gulag: A History of the Soviet Camps* (London, 2004).

Arendt, H., *Eichmann in Jerusalem: A Report on the Banality of Evil* (London, 1963).

Arthur, M., *Last Post: The Final Words From Our First World War Soldiers* (London, 2005).

Babuta, S. and Bragard, J.C., *Evil* (London, 1988) 112-117.

Barber, M., *The Trial of the Templars* (London, 2003).

Bardon, J., *A History of Ulster* (Belfast, 1992).

Bauer, Y., *History of the Holocaust* (London, 1982).

Bielenberg, C., *The Past is Myself* (London, 1997).

Bilton, M. and Sim, K., *Four Hours in Mai Lai: A War Crime and its Aftermath* (London, 1993).

Boyajian, D., *Armenia: The Case for a Forgotten Genocide* (New Jersey, 1972).

Browne, D.E., *Human Universals* (New York, 1991).

Brownmillar, S., *Against Our Will: Men Women and Rape* (New York, 1993).

Bryce, J. and Toynbee, A., *The Treatment of Armenians in the Ottoman Empire: Documents Presented to Viscount Grey of Culloden* (Princeton, 2000).

Bullock, A., *Hitler and Stalin: Parallel Lives* (London, 1993).

Bullock, A., *Hitler: A Study in Tyranny* (London, 1954).

Burleigh, M., *The Third Reich: A New History* (London, 2000).

Callahan, Kornely and Cohen, *Margaret Bourke White: Photographer* (London, 1998).

Chalk, F. and Jonassohn, K., *The History and Sociology of Genocide: Analyses and Case Studies* (Yale, 1990).

Chang, I., *The Rape of Nanking* (London, 1998).

Chang, J. and Halliday, J., *Mao: The Unknown Story* (London, 2005).

Chang, J., *Wild Swans* (London, 1993) 321.

Chretien, J.P., *Rwanda: Les Médias du Génocide* (Paris, 1995).

Climacus, St John (579, 649), *The Ladder of Divine Ascent*, translated by C Lubhéid and N Russell, (New Jersey, 1982).

Cohn, N., *Europe's Inner Demons: The Demonization of Christians in Medieval Europe* (London, 1993).

Cohn, N., *Warrant for Genocide: The Myth of the Jewish World Conspiracy and the Protocols of the Elders of Zion* (London, 1996).

Cornwell, J., *Powers of Darkness, Powers of Light* (London, 1991).

Crawford, J.R., *Witchcraft and Sorcery in Rhodesia* (London, 1967).

Dadrian, V., *A History of the Armenian Genocide* (Providence, 1997).

Dalrymple, W., *From the Holy Mountain: A Journey in the Shadow of Byzantium* (London, 1998).

Davies, N., *God's Playground: A History of Poland* (Oxford, 1981).

Davies, R., *Happy Alchemy: On the Pleasures of Music and the Theatre* (London, 1997, edited by J. Surridge and B. Davies).

Davies, R., *The Manticore* (London, 1972).

Dawidowicz, L., *A Holocaust Reader* (New Jersey, 1976).

Dawidowicz, L., *The War Against the Jews, 1933–1945* (London, 1977).

Dentan, R.K, *The Samai: A Nonviolent People of Malaya* (New York, 1979).

Des Forges, A., *Leave None to Tell the Story: Genocide in Rwanda* (London, 1999).

Deutcher, I., *Stalin: A Political Biography* (London, 1982).

Dillon, M., *Killer in Clowntown* (London, 1992).

Dillon, M., *Political Murder in Northern Ireland* (London, 1973).

Dillon, M., *Stone Cold: The True Story of Michael Stone* (London, 1992).

Dillon, M., *The Dirty War* (London, 1990).

Dillon, M., *The Shankill Butchers: A Case Study of Mass Murder* (London, 1989).

Dolgopol, U. and Paranjape, S., *Comfort Women: An Unfinished Ordeal* (International Commission of Jurists, Geneva, 1994).

Drechsler, H., *Let Us Die Fighting: The Struggle of the Herero and the Nama Against German Imperialism (1884–1915)*. (London, 1981).

Duus, P. (ed.), *The Cambridge History of Japan* (Cambridge, 1988).

Edwardes, M. (ed.), *Ibn Ishaq: The Life of Muhammad, Apostle of Allah* (London, 2003).

Eibl-Eibsfeldt, I., *Love and Hate: The Natural History of Behaviour Patterns* (London, 1972).

Eibl-Eibsfeldt, I., *The Biology of Peace and War: Men Animals and Aggression* (New York, 1979).

Eisenberg, A., *Witness to the Holocaust* (New York, 1981).

Eliade, M., *The Myth of the Eternal Return* (New York, 1991).

Fest, J., *Hitler* (London, 1974).

Fest, J., *The Face of the Third Reich: Portraits of the Nazi Leadership* (London, 1985).

Figes, O., *A People's Tragedy: The Russian Revolution 1891–1924* (London, 1997).

Freud, S, *Group Psychology and Analysis of the Ego* (London, 1921).

Friedlander, S., *Nazi Germany and the Jews: The Years of Persecution 1933–1939* (London, 1998).

Fromm, E., *The Anatomy of Human Destructiveness* (London, 1974, reprinted 1982).

Gambetta, D. (ed.), *Making Sense of Suicide Missions* (London, 2005).

Ganz, J., *Early Irish Myth and Sagas* (New York, 1981).

Gelhorn, M., *The Face of War* (London, 1993).

Gellateley, R., *Backing Hitler: Consent and Coercion in Nazi Germany* (London, 2001).

Gilbert, M., *The First World War* (London, 1994).

Gilbert, M., *The Holocaust: The Jewish Tragedy* (London, 1990).

Gilbert, M., *The Righteous: The Unsung Heroes of the Holocaust* (London, 2002).

Goldenhagen, D., *Hitler's Willing Executioners: Ordinary Germans and the Holocaust* (London, 1996).

Gourevitch, P., *We Wish To Inform You That Tomorrow We Will Be Killed With Our Families: Stories From Rwanda* (London, 1999).

Graber, G., *Canavans To Oblivion: The Armenian Genocide 1915* (New York, 1996).

Grandin, T., *Thinking in Pictures: And Other Reports from My Life with Autism* (New York, 1996).

Gudjonsson, G., *The Psychology of Interrogations and Confessions: A Handbook* (Chichester, 2003).

Haffner, S., *Defying Hitler: A Memoir* (London, 2002).

Hayman, R., *Hitler and Geli* (London, 1997).

Heyd, U., *Foundations of Turkish Nationalism: The Life And Teachings Of Ziya Gökalp* (London, 1950).

Hillberg, R., *The Destruction of the European Jews* (Chicago, 1961).

Hovannisian, R. (ed.), *The Armenian Genocide in Perspective.* (New Brunswick, 1988).

Hukanovic, R., *The Tenth Circle of Hell: A Memoir of Life in the Death Camps of Bosnia* (London, 1997).

Jackson, K.D., *Cambodia 1975–1978: Rendezvous With Death* (Princeton, 1989).

Jung, C.G., (edited by W. McGuire and RFC Hull) *C.G. Jung Speaking: Interviews and Encounters,* (London, 1980).

Jung, C.G., (edited by Gerhard Adler and Aniela Jaffé), *Letters* (Princeton, 1973).

Jung, C.G., *Collected Works* (London, 1994 reprint).

Jung, C.G., *Mankind and His Symbols* (London, 1978).

Kagan, D., *On the Origins of War* (London, 1997).

Kahane, D., *Lvov Ghetto Diary* (Massachusetts, 1990).

Karnow, S., *Vietnam: A History* (London, 1994).

Keegan, J., *The Face of Battle* (London, 1976).

Kershaw, I., *Hitler* (1998).

Kopelev, L., *The Education of a True Believer* (London, 1981).

Kopelev, L., *To Be Preserved Forever* (Philadelphia, 1977).

Kwitny, J., *Man of the Century: The Life and Times of Pope John Paul II* (New York, 1997).

Laing, R.D. and Esterson, A., *Sanity, Madness and the Family: Families of Schizophrenics* (London 1964, Pelican reprint 1986).

Lambley, P., *The Psychology of Apartheid* (Georgia, 1980).

Lenin, V.I., *Collected Works* (Moscow, Fifth Edition).

Lewis, J. and Steele, B., *Hell in the Pacific* (London, 2001).

Li, Z., *The Private Life of Chairman Mao* (London, 1994).

Lindaman, D. and Ward, K., *History Lessons: How Textbooks from Around the World Portray U.S. History* (New York, 2002).

Lings, M., *Muhammad* (London, 1988).

Maalouf, A., *The Crusades through Arab Eyes* (London, 1984).

Magocsi, P. (ed.), *Morality and Reality: The life and Times of Andrei Sheptyts'ki* (Edmonton, 1989).

Marrus, M.R., *The Holocaust in History* (London, 1993).

Masters, B., *Killing for Company: The Case of Dennis Nilsen* (London, 1985).

May, E. and Zelikow, P.,)eds.), *The Kennedy Tapes: Inside the White House During the Cuban Missiles Crisis* (Harvard, 1997).

McNamara, R., *In Retrospect: The Tragedy and Lessons of Vietnam* (London, 1995).

Miller, A., *The Drama of Being a Child: The Search for the True Self* (Revised edition, London 1995).

Miller, A., *Timebends: A Life* (London, 1988).

Morgenthau, H., *Ambassador Morhenthau's Story* (Ann Arbor, Michegan, 2000).

Mostert, N., *Frontiers: The epic of South Africa's Creation and the Tragedy of the Xhosa People* (London, 1992).

Murphy, G., *Saga and Myth in Ancient Ireland* (Dublin, 1955).

Nyiszli, M., *Auschwitz: A Doctor's Eye-witness Account* (London, 1973).

Ó Catháin, S. (ed.), *Scéalta Chois Cladaigh: Seán Ó hEinirí* (Dublin, 1983).

Ó Catháin, S. (ed.), *Síscéalta Ó Thír Chonaill* (Dublin, 1977).

Ó Catháin, S. (ed.), *Uair an Chloig Cois Teallaig: Pádraig Mac an Luain* (Dublin, 1985).

Overy, R., (ed.), *Interrogations: The Nazi Elite in Allied Hands* (London, 2001) .

Paskuly, S., (ed.), *Rudolf Höss Death Dealer: Memoirs of the SS Komandant of Auschwitz* (New York, 1996).

Pinker, S., *The Blank Slate: The Modern Denial of Human Nature* (London, 2002).

Pipes, R., *Russia under the Bolshevik Regime 1919–1924* (London, 1994).

Power, S., *A Problem From Hell: America and the Age of Genocide* (London, 2002).

Preston, P., *Franco: A Biography* (London, 1994).

Prunier, G., *The Rwanda Crisis: History of a Genocide* (Columbia, 1997).

Rabe, J., *The Good Man of Nanking: The Diaries of John Rabe* (London, 1998)

Rees, L., *The Nazis: A Warning From History* (London, 1997).

Riggs, H., *Days of Tragedy in Armenia: Personal Experiences in Harpoot, 1915–1917* (Ann Arbor, 1997).

Rougemont, D. de, *Talk of the Devil* (London, 1945) 50-51, originally *La Part du Diable* (Paris, 1942).

Runciman, S., *A History of the Crusades* (London, 1994).

Sack, J., *Lieutenant Calley: His Own Story* (New York, 1971).

Saunders, J., *The History of the Mongol Conquests* (London, 1979).

Sawdayee, *All Waiting To Be Hanged: Iraq Post Six-Day War Diary* (Tel Aviv, 1974).

Sereny, G., *Albert Speer: His Battle with the Truth* (London, 1995).

Sereny, G., *Into that Darkness: From Mercy Killing to Mass Murder* (London, 1974).

Service, R., *Lenin: A Biography* (London, 2000).

Sheehan, N., *A Bright Shinning Lie: John Paul Vann and America in Vietnam* (London, 1988).

Shirer, W., *Berlin Diary* (New York, 1941).

Shirer, W., *The Rise and Fall of the Third Reich* (London, 1964).

Short, P., *Mao: A Life* (London, 1999).

Shostakovich, D., related to S. Volkov, *Testimony: The Memoirs of Dimitri Shostakovich* (London, 1979).

Solzhenitsyn, A., *The First Circle* (London, 1992).

Solzhenitsyn, A., *The Gulag Archipelago* (London, 1974).

Speer, A., *Inside the Third Reich* (London, 1979).

Spence, J.D., *The Search for Modern China* (New York, 1990).

Staub, E., *The Roots of Evil: The Origins of Genocide and Other Group Violence* (Cambridge, 1989).

Stevens, A., *Archetype: A Natural History of the Self* (London, 1982).

Stoddard, L., *Into That Darkness: Nazi Germany Today* (London, 1941).

Szpilman, W., *The Pianist* (London, 2002).

Thomas, D.M., *Solzhenitsyn: A Century of His Life* (London, 1998).

Thomas, H., *The Spanish Civil War* (London, 1990).

Toynbee, A., *A Summary of Armenian History* (London, 1916).

Trachtenberg, J., *The Devil and the Jews: The Medieval Conception of the Jew and Its Relation to Modern Anti-Semitism* (Philadelphia, 1983).

Tyerman, C., (ed.), *An Eyewitness History to the Cruscades* (London, 2004).

Volkogonov, D., *Lenin: Life and Legacy* (London, 1995).

Vrijj, A., *Detecting Lies and Deceit: The Psychology of Lying and the Implications for Professional Practice* (Chester, 2000).

Walker, C., *Armenia: The Survival of a Nation* (London, 1980).

Waller, J., *Becoming Evil: How Ordinary People Commit Genocide and Mass Murder* (Oxford, 2002), 188–189, 246–247.

Walter, E. V., *Terror and Resistance: A Study of Political Violence* (1969).

Walzer, M., *Just and Unjust Wars: A Moral Argument With Historical Illustrations* (Second Edition, London, 1992).

Wickert, J. (ed.), *The Good Man of Nanking: The Diaries of John Rabe* (London, 2000).

Wood, E. and Janowski, S. (eds.), *Karski: How One Man Tried to Stop the Holocaust* (New York, 1994).

Young, L., *Japan's Total Empire: Manchuria and the Culture of Wartime Imperialism* (Berkeley, 1998).